OPPOSING EUROPE?
THE COMPARATIVE PARTY POLITICS OF
EUROSCEPTICISM

Opposing Europe?

The Comparative Party Politics of Euroscepticism

Volume 2
Comparative and Theoretical Perspectives

Edited by

ALEKS SZCZERBIAK AND PAUL TAGGART

OXFORD
UNIVERSITY PRESS

OXFORD
UNIVERSITY PRESS

Great Clarendon Street, Oxford ox2 6DP

Oxford University Press is a department of the University of Oxford.
It furthers the University's objective of excellence in research, scholarship,
and education by publishing worldwide in

Oxford New York

Auckland Cape Town Dar es Salaam Hong Kong Karachi
Kuala Lumpur Madrid Melbourne Mexico City Nairobi
New Delhi Shanghai Taipei Toronto

With offices in

Argentina Austria Brazil Chile Czech Republic France Greece
Guatemala Hungary Italy Japan Poland Portugal Singapore
South Korea Switzerland Thailand Turkey Ukraine Vietnam

Oxford is a registered trade mark of Oxford University Press
in the UK and in certain other countries

Published in the United States
by Oxford University Press Inc., New York

British Library Cataloguing in Publication Data
Data available

Library of Congress Cataloging in Publication Data
Data available

Typeset by SPI Publisher Services, Pondicherry, India
Printed in Great Britain
on acid-free paper by
Biddles Ltd., King's Lynn, Norfolk

ISBN 978-0-19-925835-2

1 3 5 7 9 10 8 6 4 2

Contents

List of Figures

List of Tables

Contributors

Dr. Agnes Batory, Central European University

Professor Nick Sitter, Norwegian School of Management

Professor Richard S. Katz, Johns Hopkins University

Karen Henderson, University of Leicester

Professor James Hughes, London School of Economics and Political Science

Dr. Gwendolyn Sasse, London School of Economics and Political Science

Dr. Claire Gordon, London School of Economics and Political Science

Dr. Giacomo Benedetto, Royal Holloway, University of London

Dr. Charles Lees, University of Sheffield

Professor Paul Taggart, University of Sussex

Professor Aleks Szczerbiak, University of Sussex

Professor Hermann Schmitt, The Mannheim Centre for European Social Research

Professor Cees van der Eijk, University of Nottingham

Professor Geoffrey Pridham, University of Bristol

1

Introduction: Researching Euroscepticism in European Party Systems: A Comparative and Theoretical Research Agenda

Aleks Szczerbiak and Paul Taggart

1.1 INTRODUCTION

In Volume 1 of this book we examined a series of country case studies of Euroscepticism in party systems across Europe. As we examined the range of data presented in that volume, clear patterns were identified on the basis of which we developed a typology of three kinds of party competition over Europe: limited, open, and constrained contestation (Taggart and Szczerbiak 2008*a*). The data in that volume were gathered as a 'mapping exercise' of Euroscepticism in party systems in order to discern and inform the broad parameters of subsequent research. In Volume 2, we build on this by shifting the focus from country case studies to a range of comparative and theoretical questions that take us beyond these preliminary findings. In this chapter, we begin by setting out a broad research agenda of comparative and theoretical issues for the study of Euroscepticism and highlight how the various chapters in this volume contribute towards answering some of the most important questions raised.

1.2 CONCEPTUALIZATION AND MEASUREMENT

1.2.1 Defining Euroscepticism in party systems

The first, and in many ways most basic issue that we would raise is one of conceptualization: how do we define Euroscepticism in party systems? In our introduction to Volume 1, we distinguished between principled

(Hard) opposition to European integration and contingent (Soft) opposition, with attitudes towards a country's membership of the European Union (EU) being viewed as the ultimate litmus test of whether one fell into the first or second camp. Consequently, we posited a definition of party-based Hard Euroscepticism as being:

[W]here there is a principled opposition to the EU and European integration and therefore can be seen in parties who think that their countries should withdraw from membership, or whose policies towards the EU are tantamount to being opposed to the whole project of European integration as it is currently conceived.

Party-based Soft Euroscepticism, on the other hand, was

[W]here there is NOT a principled objection to European integration or EU membership but where concerns on one (or a number) of policy areas leads to the expression of qualified opposition to the EU, or where there is a sense that 'national interest' is currently at odds with the EU trajectory (Taggart and Szczerbiak 2008*b*).

It is a conceptualization that has been applied extensively by scholars researching Euroscepticism but has also been the subject of critique. Indeed, as well as being designed as a (admittedly, rather crude) tool to help us conduct basic, comparative empirical research on the manifestation of Euroscepticism in European party systems, it was originally formulated with the explicit objective of stimulating further debate and alternative conceptualizations.

Katz takes up this theme in the conceptual survey at the beginning of his contribution to this volume (Chapter 7), highlighting four definitional problems related to the way that the term Euroscepticism has developed in academic and political discourse. Firstly, although the term 'Euroscepticism' has sometimes been developed as denoting opposition to the entire 'European project', Katz argues (as have we) that it should also include 'those who merely want to make haste more slowly or who express uncertainty about the wisdom of some or all of the proposed "advances"', given that the term 'scepticism' ordinarily refers to doubts or reservations rather than to outright opposition. Secondly, even if one accepts that Hard Eurosceptics oppose the entire process of EU integration, he raises the question of what it is that the Soft Eurosceptics oppose. Surveying the scholarly literature, Katz identifies several objects of scepticism including the development of any form of supranational European institutions that would or do impinge on national sovereignty and the traditional European state system; the expansion of the EU to include more members (broadening); increasing the range of responsibilities of the EU (deepening); specific institutional changes affecting the balance of authority as between the EU and the member states or among the various institutions of the EU itself; and specific EU policies, most narrowly (as the term was commonly used throughout much of the 1990s) Economic and Monetary Union (EMU). Linked to this point, Katz points argue that it has been part of the strategy of pro-integrationists to present all forms of scepticism as 'inexorably intertwined, and then to lump the Soft Eurosceptics together with the Hard', although he also acknowledges that 'the major practical proposals toward which Euroscepticism is addressed generally are package deals (encompassed in treaties) that raise possibilities for many, if not all, forms of scepticism'. Thirdly, he raises the issue of whether Euroscepticism should be operationalized in absolute or relative terms, raising the question of how opposed to (or supportive of) a particular EU policy (such as EMU) one has to be (and compared to whom) in order to be classified as Eurosceptic. For example, how far along a 10-point scale ranging from 'independent national currency' (1) to 'new common European currency' (10) would someone have to identify themselves to rank as a Eurosceptic? Fourthly, Katz raises the issue of how one assesses trends in Euroscepticism temporally, given that the EU is a dynamic concept, making the 'Europe' about which one might be 'sceptical' a moving target?

We return to these questions in the concluding chapter, where we survey the various definitional approaches and controversies and attempt to draw some tentative conclusions about how party-based Euroscepticism should be conceptualized. Here we reformulate our original Hard–Soft Euroscepticism conceptualization focusing on the importance of party attitudes towards the *EU integration project* rather than *EU membership* as key. We thereby locate the key distinction between Hard and Soft Euroscepticism as being based on either *principled* opposition to the project of European integration as embodied in the EU; in other words, based on the ceding or transfer of powers to supranational institution such as the EU (Hard); and opposition to the EU's current or future planned trajectory based on the *further* extension of competencies that the EU is planning to make (Soft).

We also consider a number of problem cases in that those who have been researching this topic have had difficulties in categorizing, and caution against definitions of party-based Euroscepticism that are over-inclusive. As Henderson points out in Chapter 5, where she surveys and evaluates several frameworks for defining and categorizing Euroscepticism specifically in relation to the post-communist (at the time she was writing, candidate) states, Soft Euroscepticism (as we originally defined it) 'has become a rather broad catch-all category that embraces some rather strange bedfellows'. In particular, we argue that commentators need to be careful to avoid the temptation of interpreting parties that *problematize* aspects of European integration, opposing whatever the EU happens to be doing at any given time (however vigorously), as Eurosceptic, which is clearly not axiomatically the case. Cases of parties being incorrectly classified as Eurosceptic (by ourselves, among others) include those who criticize the EU for failing to properly reflect their countries' national interests. As Hughes, Sasse, and Gordon point out in Chapter 8, which also focuses on the post-communist states, 'we must be wary of confusing the tough negotiating positions of parties when in government and engaged in the negotiations for EU membership with "Euroscepticism"'; which, they argue, was the case for the Hungarian Fidesz party which Batory, among others, classified as Soft Eurosceptic in her contribution (Chapter 5) to Volume 1 (Batory 2008). Other party positions and discourses that may, in our view, be wrongly categorized as party-based Euroscepticism include those that only criticize one or two EU policy areas; oppose EU enlargement; or criticize the EU for being insufficiently integrationist and/or undemocratic.

However, we also argue that any classificatory schema that attempts to be comprehensive and offer a full-blown typology of party positions must capture and reflect different degrees of enthusiasm for the European integration project as well as opposition to it, particularly the fact that just as opposition to the European integration project as embodied in the EU can be both principled and contingent, so can support for it. We, therefore, argue that the next logical step in terms of conceptualizing party-based Euroscepticism is to locate it within a broader typology of party positions on Europe that breaks down attitudes among pro-integrationist parties. However, and this—we argue—is one of the broader, generic problems of defining party positions on the European issue, including Eurosceptic ones—the more complex and fine-grained the typology is, the more difficult it is to operationalize and categorize the parties. This is the case because parties rarely elaborate their policies on the key issues of European integration in such detail that firm typological conclusions may be drawn. Put simply, these kind of typologies require a lot of data in order to categorize broad underlying party positions with the degree of precision that is required to fully operationalize them and this kind of information is often not available. As Henderson and Hughes et al.'s contributions to this volume suggest, it is particularly difficult to do this in the case of EU candidate states because often most parties have not even considered their positions on the EU future trajectory (given the abstract and hypothetical nature of this issue for them), never mind articulated them.

1.2.2 Measuring Euroscepticism in party systems

A second set of questions arise from the issue of whether or not it is possible to (and, if so, how) one 'measures' party-based Euroscepticism. In Volume 1, we used the judgements of country specialists to categorize parties as Hard and Soft Eurosceptics, based on an assessment of whether parties in the states under consideration were taking positions that accorded with our definitions. We stressed to contributors that we were concerned with official party positions where these exist rather than with the positions of party voters, activists, or parliamentarians. For measurement we suggested that key sources might be a party's public statements, the parliamentary voting on key European issues (treaties), and published party programmes and manifestos. We also emphasized that we acknowledge that what constitutes Euroscepticism in one country may not be the same as what constitutes it in another. In other words, we accepted the need for measures that were contextually sensitive. But we are aware that there are alternative conceptualizations and operationalizations of the dependent variable of party-based Euroscepticism. In his contribution to this volume (Chapter 7), for example, Katz measures Euroscepticism by examining the survey responses of individual members of the European Parliament (EP) and eleven national parliaments in 1996. On the basis of this, he develops a composite variable that encompasses opposition to increasing the range of EU responsibilities; (lack of) confidence that decisions made by the EU are in the country's interest; and support or opposition for the single European currency.

More broadly, in our concluding chapter we return to the question of measurement by considering what electoral support for Eurosceptic parties amounts to. In doing so, we evaluate critically our own earlier attempts in Volume 1 and elsewhere to 'measure' levels of party-based Euroscepticism by aggregating the vote share for Eurosceptic parties. Although we have been careful in the course of our work to avoid talking as if support levels for Eurosceptical parties are the same thing as levels of support for Euroscepticism, we have used vote share as an indication of party importance and, in the absence of an alternative, aggregated party vote share and used it to derive some sort of sense of the potential pool of voters who either vote for parties (at least in part) or who are not put off voting for parties because of their Euroscepticism. We also argued that it provides a crude indication of the potential for shifts in the level of public Euroscepticism to find expression through the party system. For example, an increase in the levels and salience of public Euroscepticism was more likely to find expression in a party system where there were already parties that are using the issue to some extent as part of their political discourse and would find it easier to sharpen their rhetoric on this or to give it a higher profile (Taggart and Szczerbiak 2002*a*: 30).

However, although we continue to argue strongly that party-based Euroscepticism is a portable concept that can be compared across, rather than just relatively within, countries, we conclude that varying (generally low) levels of salience of the European issue, which is often secondary or of an even lower priority for parties and voters, makes it tenuous at best to use voting intention as endorsement of the parties' Euroscepticism. Indeed, one of the most striking features of the issue of European integration is how little salience it has among voters in any country. It is difficult to think of any parliamentary or presidential election where European integration has played a major role in determining its outcome. This low salience of the European issue makes it impossible to 'read off' public attitudes towards European integration from the votes obtained by Eurosceptic (or pro-EU) parties as the dissonance between the vote for Hard Eurosceptic parties and the levels of opposition to EU membership that we found in our earlier research shows (Taggart and Szczerbiak 2002*a*: 22–5). In other words, it does not appear to make sense to compare aggregate vote shares across countries as a means of 'measuring' levels of party-based Euroscepticism.

1.3 CAUSES OF EUROSCEPTICISM IN PARTY SYSTEMS

1.3.1 Effects of institutional structures

While issues of conceptualization and measurement create problems for attempts to map party positions on Europe, including Eurosceptic ones, as Lees points out in Chapter 2, the fact that political parties are complicated phenomena makes it even harder to determine what drives these positions. A second cluster of theoretical and comparative issues, therefore, relates to the question of what causes parties to adopt Eurosceptic positions, and Eurosceptic or 'Eurocritical' discourses in party competition.

One important potential causal driver of the importance of Euroscepticism in party system is the impact of the institutional environment, what Kitschelt (1986) and Tarrow (1994) term 'political opportunity structures'. It seems to us, from the data presented in Volume 1 and elsewhere (Taggart and Szczerbiak 2003), that party systems may play a significant role in either the exaggeration or the minimization of the European issue in different domestic settings. Cases such as France and Finland, for example, seem to point to very different opportunity structures with different sets of incentives and costs to the expression of Euroscepticism in their respective party systems (Grunberg 2008, Raunio 2008). Aspinwall (2004) has made a similar argument for the relative importance of party-based Euroscepticism in the UK by focusing on the impact of the British electoral system. A number of comparative and theoretical questions arise from this including: What are the effects of differences in party and electoral system and how should we go about categorizing these systems in ways that adequately capture their range? This is a question that relates as much to the state of the literature on European parties and party systems, and goes to the heart of whether the changes in Europe in the last decade of the twentieth century prove the enduring vitality or insufficiency of existing concepts, frameworks, and categories. Moreover, as Henderson points out in Chapter 5, party system cause and effects are hard to unravel, and this is equally true of the impact of electoral systems.

In Chapter 2, Lees sets out to explore the impact of institutions on party-based Euroscepticism in Europe and assess whether one can posit a causal relationship at the aggregate level between certain institutions and the presence and/or relative strength of Euroscepticism in party systems. He focuses on state administrative structures and electoral and party systems hypothesizing that federations and devolved states and/or those with more proportional electoral and party systems with more 'relevant' parties should provide more benign political opportunity structures for party-based Euroscepticism. He also examines the impact of the use of referendums as a decision rule. Lees tests the impact of these variables by canvassing the opinion of country specialists engaged in research on party-based Euroscepticism in twelve countries: the Czech Republic, Finland, France, Germany, Hungary, Ireland, Italy, Norway, Poland, Slovakia, Sweden, and the UK.

However, at the aggregate level at least, Lees is unable to find a clear causal relationship between particular institutional configurations and the presence and relative strength of party-based Euroscepticism. Eurosceptic parties and/or party factions can appear to thrive or fail equally well in unitary or federal states, under majoritarian or proportional electoral systems, in unicameral or bicameral legislatures, in two-bloc or multipolar party systems, and so on. However, in the course of his analysis, Lees yields five possible new variables that he argues might have a significant bearing on the success of Eurosceptic parties: the degree of state centralization (and underlying cleavage structures); the process of European policymaking in nation states; party system 'type' and dimensions of conflict; coalition behaviour; and party funding. In addition, he suggests that the relative importance of regional and local government, which cross-cuts his state/administrative variables, might also be significant, together with the distinction between 'working' and 'adversarial' parliaments, particularly the configuration of parliamentary committees.

Lees concludes that while the idiom of 'political opportunity structures' remains an intuitive or heuristic device with some explanatory power, it resists formalization and appears to have little or no predictive power as far as party-based Euroscepticism is concerned. In other words, tapping into broader debates about structure and agency, in the absence of a more predictive model of institutional constraints, he argues that political parties can 'make the weather', adapting to institutional settings but retaining high levels of agency. In terms of party-based Euroscepticism, this, according to Lees, means that Eurosceptic discourses or agendas are not contingent on the institutional environment and are negotiable: 'Political opportunity structures matter, but in the end it is the political opportunists—the political parties—that determine the pattern of party-based Euroscepticism in each country.' Reflecting on the implications of this for methodological approaches, he argues that, 'in the absence of a more predictive model of institutional constraints, it remains the country specialists who are best able to shed light on party-based Euroscepticism on a case-by-case basis'.

1.3.2 Ideology versus strategy

Another important issue relating to causality is the question: Do ideological or strategic considerations determine whether parties are Eurosceptic? In the contributions to Volume 1, at one pole it has been argued that the European issue is useful for parties taking strategic positions (Sitter 2008). On the other hand, we have also found that ideological predispositions mean that this choice is not unlimited,[1] while some analysts argue that ideology is the sole or primary driver of party positions.[2] Clearly this directs our attention to the important comparative-theoretical question: How far can parties act strategically and how far does ideology constrain them in taking either pro- or anti-European positions? It also raises the question: Do some parties or kinds of parties find it easier to use the European issue strategically and how far different ideologies predispose parties towards support for integration or different types of Euroscepticism?

Among those who privilege strategic considerations as the key drivers of Eurosceptic party positions, two particular aspects are usually emphasized: the effects of peripherality and the impact of government participation. One of the driving questions behind our joint research has been about the issue of peripherality and how that relates to Euroscepticism. Katz gives some credence to the notion that Euroscepticism is to be found on the extremes of politics (in Chapter 7, surveying European and national parliamentarians), finding the greatest concentrations of Eurosceptics among the radical left and the far right, with most Europhiles locating themselves in the middle of the left–right spectrum. However, he also makes the important point that even the 'centrist' social democratic, Christian democratic, and liberal party families contain significant Eurosceptic currents. Although our findings in Volume 1 confirmed that Hard Eurosceptics were generally peripheral protest parties, our research has also led us to moderate our conception of Euroscepticism as *fundamentally* a peripheral phenomenon.

Turning away from the peripheries of European party systems, there are also interesting questions to be asked about when, why, and how parties of government move towards or away from Euroscepticism. Our data in Volume 1 revealed parties that have changed their positions (say moving from Hard to Softer Euroscepticism) as they came closer to involvement in government. Examples of this are the German Greens in their long move from protest party in the 1980s to a party of government. The Centre Party in Estonia also moved away from Eurosceptic to a pro-European position as it entered government (Mikkel 2008). The question arises, therefore: Does involvement in European government inevitably lead to a tempering of Euroscepticism or is it that parties must demonstrate their government potential by moderating any tendency they have towards Euroscepticism? As Henderson points out, the key problem here is clearly one of distinguishing cause from effect. In the Central and East European post-communist states on which she focuses, most notably in the case of smaller Hard Eurosceptic parties in Slovakia mentioned earlier, their attitudes to the EU appear to have *caused* their exclusion from government, because there was general elite consensus about the foreign policy imperative of attaining EU membership. However, she finds fewer indications that the development of Hard Eurosceptic stances has been the *effect* of repeated exclusion from government. Henderson argues, that it is easier to demonstrate that placement on the far left or right of the political spectrum naturally induces hostility to the EU project; although, clearly the same problems of distinguishing cause and effect apply to issue of party system peripherality.

The question of the relative importance of ideological and strategic factors in determining Eurosceptic positions is tackled in Sitter and Batory's chapter on Euroscepticism in eight agrarian parties in Western and Eastern Europe (Denmark, Finland, Hungary, Iceland, Norway, Poland, Sweden, and Switzerland). As they point out, few party families have displayed greater variation in their response to European integration. Some of these parties have their roots in the defence of agrarian and rural interests and oppose supranational European integration in principle. Some oppose particular aspects of the EU regime or plans for further integration. Others broadly welcome most aspects of the EU and its public policy regime. Whereas agrarian interest groups in the six original member states have long provided solid support for the EU and its predecessors, many of the political parties that emerged in defence of agrarian interests or identity elsewhere in Europe have proven less enthusiastic about European integration.

Sitter and Batory argue that agrarian party-based Euroscepticism is driven by causal mechanisms rooted in national party system and the strategic behaviour of the parties themselves. In other words, they argue that Euroscepticism is the product of patterns of opposition within a particular party system and how 'party strategy' develops in response to this. Party strategy, is, in turn, determined by the way parties seek to balance four core goals: long-term ones related to party management, organizational survival, and the pursuit of their core policy preferences (which, in agrarian parties, are often determined by their origins); and short-term electoral and coalition incentives that stem from the pursuit votes and access to executive office.

These 'principled' and 'strategic–tactical' goals can be mutually reinforcing or pull in different directions depending on the specific circumstances that the party finds itself. In other words, the extent to which parties' (Eurosceptic) policy preferences in orientations are translated into actual opposition to participation in European integration depends upon the quest for votes and access to executive office. Even if a party's identity or policy concerns predispose it towards Euroscepticism, electoral competition and coalition games may provide incentives for it to avoid contesting European integration. In both cases, the parties' positions relative to their competitors on the European question, and their relative position in the party system with respect to other matters, influence these incentives. Thus, according to Sitter and Batory, parties are only likely to adopt a radical Eurosceptic stance if European integration is: seen to conflict with their ideology and identity; threatens the interests of their target electorate; and, at the same time, the pressures of coalition politics do not outweigh the incentives to mobilize their supporters' discontent with, or opposition to, European integration. In the course of their analysis, Sitter and Batory make a critical distinction between what they term 'parties' assessment of

European integration' and 'patterns of Euroscepticism', and argue that it is trade-offs between long-term developments and short-term issue-appeals, together with coalition politics, that account for the lack of full congruence between the two phenomena.

Although Sitter and Batory term this a 'strategic' approach to determining the causes of party Euroscepticism, in reality 'core policy goals' are, in fact, often derived from ideological impulses. So, in reality, their approach posits a blend of ideological and strategic explanatory variables. Sitter and Batory recognize this implicitly, but nonetheless argue that 'while values and historical predispositions remain an important element in explaining and predicting agrarian parties' stance on European integration, Hard and Soft Euroscepticism is *primarily* a function of parties' strategies in vote- and office-seeking' (our emphasis). In other words, strategic–tactical considerations are the key to determining the extent to which agrarian (and, they argue, other) parties turn the European question into a contested issue.

Moreover, Sitter and Batory argue that their approach to explaining the causes of party Euroscepticism among agrarian parties provides a more general framework for analysing party shifts between moderation and radical opposition to European integration. Although their origins and association with particular interests may set the agrarians somewhat apart from other, more 'typical', families, the dynamics of their contestation of European integration is not, they claim, necessarily peculiar. On the contrary, Sitter and Batory argue that a model of party-based Euroscepticism is more robust if it can accommodate these parties rather than dismiss them as exceptions. Sitter and Batory attempt to extend their model by arguing that the way that a party pursues its strategy is determined by whether it is pursuing a sectoral electorate or is 'catch-all' or 'populist' party competing at the flanks of the party system. Agrarian party-based Euroscepticism is thus linked to a party strategy that focuses on the representation of the interests of a clearly delineated segment (agrarian or rural) of the electorate. A similar analysis might be applied to other parties that focus on single issues or interests—green, religious, or ethnic minority parties—though, of course, not necessarily with the same outcome. By extension, the Sitter–Batory model suggests that catch-all parties are likely to be less prone to Hard Euroscepticism in as much as they play down ideology and interest representation; except in cases where their economic policy jars with that of the EU or other factors, such as neutrality in the cold war, proscribed EU membership. New populist parties on the flanks of their party systems may not have the same issue concerns as agrarian parties, but their roots in protest and limited exposure to coalition politics might also make them incline towards Euroscepticism.

In the concluding chapter, we contend that the 'ideology versus strategy' debate has been misconceived by the conflation of what we argue are two distinctive phenomena: broad, underlying party positions on Europe; and the question of whether or not (and how) parties use the European issue (in this case in a contestatory way) as an element of inter-party competition. Sitter and Batory allude to a similar point when, as noted above, they distinguish between what they term 'parties' assessment of European integration' and 'patterns of Euroscepticism'. In our view, this is an important distinction and not just for the sake of conceptual and definitional clarity. We also believe that these two distinct phenomena have different causal mechanisms that explain whether or not—and, more importantly, under what circumstances—ideological–programmatic factors or strategic–tactical ones play a role in causing party-based Euroscepticism.

We argue that broad, underlying party positions on the issue of European integration (including Eurosceptic ones) are determined by a blend of the party's ideology and what it perceives to be the interests of its members. The relative importance of these two causal factors depends on whether it is a more ideological, value-based, goal-oriented party, or a more pragmatic, interest-based, office-seeking party. Whether or not (and to what extent) a party uses the European issue in party competition and how much prominence they give to it, on the other hand, depends on the party's electoral strategy and coalition-formation and government-participation tactics. Lees also alludes to this distinction between Eurosceptic party positions and the use of the Eurosceptic discourses in inter-party competition, and suggests different causal drivers, when he argues that Eurosceptic agendas can be either a key part of a party's programmatic identity (and, therefore, determined by its core ideology—what he terms 'sustained'), or parties can adopt such an agenda for short-term tactical ('heresthetic') reasons, and therefore, determined by what is considered politically feasible.

We go on to argue that the same (strategic and tactical) causal mechanisms that determine whether or not, and how, a party uses the European issue in party competition can also determine whether or not it uses what we have termed the rhetoric of 'Euro-contestation'. This refers to the *problematization* of European integration: using rhetoric that is critical of the EU, while retaining a broad, underlying position that is supportive of EU integration in principle or even of the EU's current/future integrationist trajectory.

1.3.3 The impact of transnational party cooperation

Another potentially important causal factor, which is often overlooked or neglected in accounts that focus on domestic drivers of politics, is the impact of transnational factors. In Chapter 4, Pridham examines the impact of transnational party cooperation on opportunity structures for Eurosceptic parties in five post-communist states (Bulgaria, the Czech Republic, Hungary, Romania, and Slovakia) during the period that they were candidate states. His particular focus is the question of whether this kind of cooperation excludes, constrains, or encourages Eurosceptic parties.

Pridham argues that transnational party cooperation has become more significant in recent years with the emergence of a European multiparty elite that is usually well linked with national party structures. This is as much because of its significant political networking capacity as the formal, constitutional position of European party federations, which remains relatively weak. Moreover, he argues that Central and East European party elites have tended to accord such transnational party links somewhat greater importance than party elites in longer-established EU member states, utilizing them as both an opportunity for party-political networking and international recognition, and a channel for furthering their states' accession prospects. Consequently, given that a commitment to European integration is, along with ideological affinity and support for democracy, one of the explicit conditions for parties to join the three main European party federations (conservative/Christian democrat, social democrat, and liberal), Pridham argues that transnational party cooperation should create external pressures that act to reduce, or 'soften', Euroscepticism in

Central and East European party systems. This, he argues, makes itself felt through a combination of overt conditionality and covert socialization and persuasion effects.

Pridham acknowledges that there were also factors present that limited transnational party cooperation in these states, although, he goes on to argue that these are now diminishing. Post-communist party systems have been slow to crystallize and stabilize, not least because of the impacts of multiple transformations (economic and national as well as political) on society and, hence, indirectly on party development. These fragmented and unstable party systems have made it difficult for Western European parties to identify who their 'natural' partners were.[3] Nonetheless, the cases examined by Pridham appear to demonstrate that Hard Eurosceptic parties or those with a complicated and unresolved reputation in European circles have been excluded from transnational party involvement. The fact that support for European integration is a condition of membership of the main transnational party organizations on parties interested in membership has, he argues, exerted a powerful influence. Not only has it provided a means for the integration of these elites in advance of EU membership, it also produced 'formal but also real changes in party positions and behaviour, including by Eurosceptical parties'. The direct effect of this is felt mainly on party elites: both party international officers and national leaders who did, indeed, appear to place considerable importance on European networking. The broader influence of this factor on party development is somewhat more diffuse, but can be seen through the effects of programmatic influence, policy education on EU affairs, and political assistance and training of party activists. According to Pridham, 'the combined dynamic of the European and the domestic levels acts to underpin the conformist pressures exerted by transnational party organizations'.

However, as Pridham himself points out, the role of transnational activity has ultimately to be set in the context of domestic political developments, which begs the question of how transnational factors interrelate with, and what its their relative importance compared to that of, national contextual ones. Indeed, the multifaceted nature of party-based Euroscepticism, and the numerous possible causal drivers, is illustrated clearly by Pridham's empirical case studies. In the Hungarian case, for example, it was domestic political considerations, and not just attitudes towards

European policy, which determined the way that parties sought to develop transnational party allegiances.

Moreover, Pridham also found evidence of Soft Eurosceptic parties networking through transnational channels, though usually these contacts were more successful when pursued bilaterally rather than multilaterally. The most striking example of this is the case of bilateral cooperation between Vaclav Klaus, leader of the Czech Civic Democrats, and the British Conservative Party. This is one instance where—in an attempt to export their minimalist, Soft Eurosceptic view of European integration—transnational cooperation by the British Conservatives acted to counter the general trend of transnational contacts reinforcing support for European integration and acting to reduce Euroscepticism in post-communist party system.[4]

1.4 COMPARING ACROSS EUROPE

The next theoretical–methodological question that we would raise is about the possibility and limitations of comparing member states with candidate states, and more established West European systems with the post-communist systems in Central and Eastern Europe. The question that arises from this is whether the differences over the meaning of European integration, the 'system-ness' of the party systems, the 'party-ness' of the parties, and in the meaning and understanding of left and right make pan-European comparisons fundamentally problematic for considerations of Euroscepticism; or, if not, how to deal with these issues of comparison. To put the issue more simply: should we compare Euroscepticism across the range of member and candidate states and, if so, what factors do we need to be particularly sensitive to?

Henderson tackles this question directly in Chapter 5 that considers whether Euroscepticism in Central and East European party systems is converging or diverging with that in older member states. On the one hand, she argues that, for several reasons, the debate on Europe in these countries was conducted in a radically different environment from that of previous enlargement waves and that party attitudes towards the EU in general and Euroscepticism in Central and Eastern Europe were, therefore, likely to take a rather different form than in West European states. First, these states had undergone a 'triple transition', where not only had their political systems been profoundly altered by regime change, but also the economic and social systems, and, in some cases, even the definition of the nation. Since the politics, economics, and societies of Central and Eastern Europe were in far more dynamic motion than in Western Europe, not only were their party systems in a state of relative flux compared to the more stable polities of the countries that joined the EU earlier, but party profiles on EU integration and stances on related individual policy issues would be more prone to fluctuation than was the case with previous waves of new member states. Secondly, given the magnitude of these countries post-1989 foreign policy realignment and the fact that EU membership was a much more crucial foreign policy goal, questions of European integration had a far greater consciousness than elsewhere leaving less scope for the pursuit of domestic 'national interest' until the final stages of negotiations. Thirdly, because attaining membership was considered to be vital for promoting national development, 'Europe' was viewed through the prism of domestic politics even more strongly in post-communist states than in Western Europe.

However, even if these countries had distinct characteristics both in the nature of the European agenda that they confronted and in the shape of their party systems, in our view this does not rule out comparison per se, but rather means being sensitive to the different contexts involved. Indeed, it is in this spirit that Sitter and Batory take precisely such a broad comparative perspective in Chapter 3, exploring the dynamics of change in agrarian party-based Euroscepticism in the two sets of states. Henderson also acknowledges that while post-communist states have generic strands in their prejudices against European integration (and, indeed, also in their widespread predispositions towards EU membership), which derive from their earlier communist experiences, it is nonetheless possible to construct academic propositions valid for both groups of states in the enlarging EU. She also makes a crucial distinction between two distinct periods in these countries' relations with the EU. The first, 'application' period leading up to the beginning of accession negotiations in 1998, was marked by a very general 'return to Europe' agenda, which had strong symbolic elements. In the second post-communist 'negotiation' period, from approximately 1998 until the first wave of eastern enlargement in 2004, shifts took place in both the European agenda and in these countries' party systems. In the course of the EU accession negotiations, the intricacies of the European integration agenda began to clarify, and what Czech Eurosceptics called 'Euro-realism' (Hanley 2008) dawned. As a consequence, Henderson argues, national assertiveness penetrated into the mainstream of governing parties, and has manifested itself in Euroscepticism during negotiations with the EU.

Hughes, Sasse, and Gordon make a similar point in Chapter 8 on local elite attitudes in post-communist states, arguing that by the late 1990s, Central and East European countries had switched to a much higher level of realism about the short-term costs of membership with regard to the massive legal realignment, further fiscal restraint, and economic adjustment that were required. Thus, they argue, a decade of the tri- als of transition and accession steadily eroded the idealism of the early post-communist years and raise the question of whether the early ide- alism about 'Europe' had been supplanted with more pragmatic consid- erations over the potential benefits of EU membership or even outright Euroscepticism.

In a similar vein, although, as discussed earlier, Pridham suggests that eagerness to be accepted by the major European transnational party feder- ations produced considerable conformist pressures on Eurosceptic parties in post-communist states, he also suggests some reasons why we might expect there to be *more* Euroscepticism in these states. These include growing concerns about the democratic deficit and the linkage (noted earlier) between the EU and problematic transition processes (although linkage with post-communist transformation may, of course, also produce positive evaluations of EU integration). Pridham argues that although the politicization effects of European integration were not entirely unique to these states and were also evident during previous accession waves, the degree or intensity of these effects was new, reflecting the immense administrative, economic, and political burdens facing post-communist candidate countries. Moreover, the perception in post-communist appli- cant states that they were required to meet political conditions not always observed strictly by certain member states represented a special version of this (democratic) deficit problem that could also create the conditions for disaffection. In other words, Eurosceptic parties in post-communist states could also seek to exploit dissatisfaction with the ongoing economic transformation, which could be linked to the EU or use their treatment of European policy problems, as a way of presenting themselves as populist and anti-elitist.

Finally, Henderson predicts that as the eight post-communist states that acceded to the EU in May 2004 enter a third 'membership' phase, parties in these countries are likely to develop far greater programmatic coherence and their party systems converge increasingly with those of the established EU member states. As a consequence, she argues, it is becoming far easier to classify Euroscepticism on a pan-European basis and concludes, optimistically, that 'despite the problems in analysing Euroscepticism in the candidate states, the general answer to the question whether Euroscepticism and party systems in the accession states are converging with the rest of the EU appears to be that yes, they are'.

1.5 OTHER COMPARATIVE POSSIBILITIES

While the emphasis in Volume 1 was on case studies of particular countries, this reflects the existing division of academic labour among scholars researching this topic. For future research, we would also, therefore, raise the possibility of comparisons that go beyond national case studies.

1.5.1 Euroscepticism in the European Parliament

One other comparative dimension to examine is the development of transnational party cooperation among Eurosceptic parties and party elites. Benedetto considers this in Chapter 6 on the incidence of Euroscepticism within the 1999–2004 EP. Benedetto shows that the paradox for Eurosceptic parties is that, benefiting from a 'second-order' effect (Reif and Schmitt 1980), they have achieved their greatest successes in elections to an institution that they oppose and, having taken their seats, are obliged to operate within. However, Benedetto shows they have failed to translate this into any significant impact upon the working of the EP.

Benedetto's account identifies four reasons why this has occurred, all of which stem from the fact that they were 'outsiders' in what, he argues, is a 'consensual system'. First, because their success was limited to only a few member states, the Eurosceptics were neither numerically relevant in terms of usefulness to other groups wishing to construct coalitions nor able to exercise 'blackmail' power on other parties, in the same way as anti-system forces in national parliaments have been able to. Secondly, in order to form groups and gain access to parliamentary resources, Eurosceptic parties and members of European Parliament (MEPs) have had to make alliances with those who have a different perspective on European integration at the same time as failing to build effective cross-national alliances among themselves. Thirdly, some Eurosceptics, such as the British Conservatives and Philippe de Villiers' Movement for France, viewed themselves as mainstream parties within their domestic contexts and did not, therefore, adapt themselves well to a protest-based anti-system role in the parliament. Fourthly, Benedetto argues that given that the consensus is institutionalized in the EU bodies such as the EP through a left–right grand coalition, and that most of the Parliament's activity is concerned with legislation rather than the constitutional issue of *more* or *less* Europe, the very nature of the EP as an institution makes it an unrewarding location for Eurosceptics.

Pridham makes similar points in Chapter 4 on transnational cooperation in post-communist states, arguing that this negligible alliance-building between Eurosceptic representatives in the EP and inability to construct a homogeneous political group, is compounded by a failure to establish any of the wider parallel structures common to the established party families at the European level. In part, this failure of Eurosceptic parties to find transnational partners stems from the antithesis between the nationalism that many of them espouse and the values of European integration. Moreover, the case of Eurosceptic parties in the post-communist states draws attention to the fact that, in striving for domestic and international acceptability, it is in these parties' interests to disassociate themselves as much as possible from other Eurosceptic parties that are often pariahs in their own party systems. Indeed, as noted earlier, such cooperation tends to be much more common at the bilateral level, as in the case of the British Conservative Party and the Czech Civic Democrats.

1.5.2 Comparing Euroscepticism in the European and national parliaments

Katz, in Chapter 7, illustrates another approach, that of comparing Euroscepticism among members of the EP and national parliaments, in this case the parliaments of eleven of the twelve member states that comprised the EU in 1996. Katz aims to identify the attitudinal roots of Euroscepticism and its relationship with the so-called democratic deficit by developing a composite 'Eurosceptic' variable based on survey responses that encompass: opposition to increasing the range of EU responsibilities; a lack of confidence that decisions made by the EU are in the country's interest; and opposition to the single European currency.

Katz finds that the most important sources of Euroscepticism are dissatisfaction with the democratic deficit of the EU and a lack of pride in a sense of 'European-ness', suggesting that process is more important than outcome in determining elite attitudes towards European integration. Once these two attitudinal factors are controlled for, Katz finds that both partisan and national differences continue to be significant. As noted above, he finds the greatest concentrations of Eurosceptics in the fringe party families: nationalist, far right, radical left, and green. He also finds that Sweden, Denmark, France, Britain, Greece, and (although to a lesser extent) Portugal have the most Eurosceptic European parliamentarians across all parties; while Sweden has the most Eurosceptic national parliamentarians, presumably because Britain and Denmark were not surveyed. In every case, except for that of Sweden, MEPs were slightly more pro-integration than national parliamentarians; which, in Chapter 6, Benedetto speculates is due to a strong 'second-order' success for the Left and Green parties in the Swedish elections to the EP in 1995.

1.5.3 Euroscepticism among sub-national elites

While other chapters in this volume focus on overt party-based Euroscepticism, Hughes, Sasse, and Gordon examine the attitudes of regional and local elite actors towards the EU in four Central and East European states (Estonia, Hungary, Poland, and Slovenia), and the extent to which this may reveal Euroscepticism. Only a minority of these sub-national elites identify themselves as members of political parties, and an even smaller number belong to parties that espouse Eurosceptic positions. According to these authors, it is precisely the weakness of parties as mobilizational and linkage mechanisms at the sub-national level in these states that limits the articulation of Eurosceptic views at the local level. This, they argue, warrants a focus on the degree to which these sub-national elites are connected to EU policy processes, their values have become 'Europeanized' (which they operationalize in terms of them adopting EU norms and a European identity), and whether this process reveals values that may plausibly be evaluated as Eurosceptic.

Hughes, Sasse, and Gordon find low levels of engagement with, and poor knowledge of, the EU's activities, a weak normative commitment to 'Europeanized' values; and the lack of a 'European' identity, EU accession is generally perceived as a national elite project, with most of the benefits accruing at the national rather than regional or local levels. All this, it might be argued, provides raw material for the future emergence of (Soft) Euroscepticism on the part of local elites, post-EU accession. However, Hughes, Sasse, and Gordon also find that these sub-national elites are pragmatically and positively predisposed towards the economic benefits of EU membership at the macro level. Rather, they interpret their weak connectedness to the EU as stemming from the fact that their focus has been on managing the immediate problems of transition together with their having been deliberately and structurally excluded from the accession process by both the EU and national governments. While this has not yielded Euroscepticism, it has, according to Hughes, Sasse, and Gordon, opened up a 'normative gap' in national and sub-national level elite values as well as creating local elites who are disengaged from the enlargement process and fail to see the benefits for them.

1.6 PUBLIC OPINION

Another area that provides a rich seam for researchers of Euroscepticism is the relationship between public attitudes on Europe and their expression in public institutions. Our data presented in Volume 1 and our other research suggest there is a misfit between parties and public over Europe. In particular, we found no linear relationship between levels of public opposition to European integration and electoral support for Eurosceptic parties because, as noted earlier, of the (lack of) salience of the European issue among the party's supporters or potential supporters (Taggart and Szczerbiak 2002*a*: 22–5). From a normative as well as analytical point of view it is, therefore, worth asking the question: What are the effects of the differences in the expression of Euroscepticism by the European public and its manifestation in European party systems? In one sense, this is asking the time-honoured question about when representative democracy should or should not produce institutions, policies, or elites that are not strictly representative of public opinion and what effects this has. In the more specific sense of European integration, the charges of democratic deficit or citizen apathy make these questions particularly salient as the process of European integration has appeared to rely thus far on both a permissive consensus at the mass level and an almost monolithic pro-integration propensity among political elites. The data that we presented in Volume 1 suggest that both aspects of these aspects are changing.

1.6.1 Non-voting as evidence of Euroscepticism

As Benedetto notes, due to the 'second-order' effect Eurosceptic parties have done disproportionately well in EP elections in some countries. At the same time, as Schmitt and van der Eijk point out in their contribution to this volume (Chapter 9), participation rates in EP elections are seen as a crucial indicator of political support for the EU by politicians and the media alike. The trend in participation in EP elections generally points downward, which both academics and non-academic commentators have often interpreted as indicating hostility to the European project.

Schmitt and van der Eijk examine this controversial question of whether abstentions in EP elections can be interpreted as evidence of Euroscepticism. In fact, they argue that anti-EU sentiment does not play a major role anywhere as a major factor in explaining abstention in EP elections. Social structural locations are, they argue, the single most important predictor of electoral participation followed by party support and political involvement that come in second. They conclude:

Growing levels of abstention in EP elections are not the result of a growing alienation with the EU political system or hostility towards the politics of European integration. They rather seem to result from the fact that those who used to go and vote on election day—the socially integrated and politically involved—stay home in ever greater numbers when the members of the EP are elected.

1.7 FURTHER ISSUES FOR FUTURE RESEARCH

While research on party-based Euroscepticism has expanded rapidly in recent years and this collection makes an important contribution to pushing forward theoretical and comparative debates on a number of fronts, the future research agenda on Euroscepticism in party systems is a vast one and there is clearly much that remains to be done.

1.7.1 The absence of Euroscepticism

In terms of conceptualization and measurement, as we indicated earlier and discuss in more detail in our concluding chapter, the key comparative-theoretical challenge is to locate party-based Euroscepticism within a broader typology that breaks down attitudes among pro-integrationist parties. Related to this issue of the dependent variable, we also want to raise the broader question: What does the absence of Euroscepticism in a party system mean? Part of the reason for our original interest in the study of Euroscepticism was the fact that the historical elite consensus over Europe was in favour of European integration. Trying to discern the outline of the European issue and how it has (or has not) emerged in European politics has been particularly difficult because of this consensus. Focusing on Euroscepticism allows us to have a clearer picture of the perimeters of the pro-European consensus but it still leaves us with the question of knowing how to interpret the absence of party-based Euroscepticism. We are interested, obviously, in knowing about party-based Euroscepticism for its own sake but we would like to think that this could be used more widely to illuminate the particular political dynamics of the broader European issue.

1.7.2 The impact of government involvement and peripherality

In terms of debates about causality, it may be instructive to look in particular at how the experience of government involvement has impacted upon Eurosceptic and EU-critical parties. There are a number of interesting cases here, some of which our contributors to Volume 1 identified, including the Austrian Freedom Party, the Northern League in Italy, the Left

Alliance and the Green League in Finland, the Swedish Social Democrats, the Czech Civic Democratic Party, Fidesz in Hungary, the Centre Party in Estonia, and Mečiar's Movement for a Democratic Slovakia. In particular, it would be interesting to attempt some paired comparisons of their experiences as they have moved into or out of government and on how this has affected their positions on Europe. This could work with different types of parties where similar changes have occurred, or building on work such as Sitter and Batory's chapter in this volume on agrarian parties, on parties in similar party families (such as green parties) where they have taken very different positions under different conditions. Questions of government participation aside, the linked question of when, why, and how is Euroscepticism related to peripherality in party systems, explored in some of the chapters here, remains an important one, worthy of further detailed research.

1.7.3 Comparing different enlargement waves

While this volume includes a number of comparisons that go beyond national case studies, there are still many other comparative possibilities that remain to be explored, including for example comparing paired cases of states and parties that did or will accede to the EU in different waves. Particularly interesting would be to compare the dynamics of change within party systems of some or all of the states involved in the most recent 'Mediterranean', 'Nordic', and enlargement waves. This may offer clues as to what may occur in future candidate states. The question might therefore be: What are the effects of EU accession on the European issue in party systems of acceding states?

1.7.4 Comparing sub-national party systems and local and national activists

Moreover, while Hughes, Sasse, and Gordon have, in this volume, examined sub-national (largely non-party) elites, it might also be interesting to make more explicit *comparisons of sub-national party systems*, given the potential importance of the federal dimension suggested by Lees in Chapter 2 on Germany in Volume 1 (Lees 2008—although his comparative chapter in this volume suggests that this factor is not as significant as it was originally thought to be). At the level of the party organization it might also be instructive to undertake comparisons between local party activists with national activists.

1.7.5 Diachronic comparisons

There is also scope for more diachronic comparisons that focus on the issue of change in party positions and discourses to supplement the existing synchronic comparisons. The country data presented in Volume 1 present a snapshot of country case studies and we feel strongly that the worth of the data is only fully realized if it is complemented by case studies that focus on change over time so that we can build up a particular sense of the dynamics of how the European issue works in party systems.[5] Broader comparative studies of this kind have merits but we need to address the question of how we can measure change in party positions and the way the European issue is manifested in party systems? Again, Sitter and Batory undertake this kind of exercise, to some extent, in their chapter examining how agrarian parties' positions have shifted over time.

1.7.6 Measuring the salience of Europe

Finally, we return to the crucial issue of the salience of Europe. As noted earlier, our country case studies in Volume 1 clearly indicate that European party systems differ in the relative salience of the European issue. It is clear that there may be both variation in levels of support for parties expressing Euroscepticism *and* variation in the levels of importance attached to the European issue for voters in those party systems. However, all of this begs the important and difficult question that remains: How do we measure the salience of the issue of European integration in different party and political systems, and how can we differentiate between types of salience (public salience whereby populations express Euroscepticism, the salience of Europe for party competition, and the salience of the European issue in determining election outcomes)?

Moreover, the issue of salience does not only apply to the level of party systems—different parties use the issue differently. This leads to the question: How do we measure the salience of the European issue for particular parties and their voters? As our country case studies in Volume 1 indicated, some parties, such as the French National Front, use Europe as a 'second-order' issue to bolster their standing or position on other issues (Grunberg 2008). Most parties have the issue as a very minor part of their overall identity, but others, such as the British Conservatives (Baker et al. 2008) and Danish Peoples' Party (Knudsen 2008), have made it central to their identity. Clearly, this has some relationship to the overall salience of the European issue to the party system but there is variation in how much prominence is accorded to it by parties in the same party system, and that needs to be captured in research on party-based Euroscepticism. Only when we know the overall salience of the European issue can we really interpret the importance of levels of support for parties expressing Euroscepticism.

NOTES

1. The British Conservative Party is one example (Baker et al. 2008).
2. See, for example, Marks and Wilson (2000).
3. As Pridham points out in an earlier version of his chapter, this was exacerbated by the fact that many of the leaders of the new social democratic parties were reformed communists while returning exiles with good transnational links played a less significant role in the new party systems of post-communist Central and Eastern Europe than they did in, say, the newly emerging democracies of Southern Europe in the 1980s (Pridham 2002).
4. On the Czech Civic Democrats see Hanley (2004, 2008).
5. Some contributors, however, also took an explicitly diachronic approach. See, for example, Sitter (2008).

2

The Political Opportunity Structure of Euroscepticism: Institutional Setting and Political Agency in European Polities

Charles Lees

2.1 INTRODUCTION

The purpose of this chapter is to explore the impact of institutions on party-based Euroscepticism in Europe and to assess whether one can posit a causal relationship at the aggregate level between certain institutions as independent variables and the presence and/or relative strength of party-based Euroscepticism as the dependent variable. Beyond that, it has three secondary objectives. First, to operationalize the concept of 'political opportunity structures' (or POS; Kitschelt 1986; Tarrow 1994) within a framework of institutional theory. Secondly, to apply this theoretical model to the study of party-based Euroscepticism broadly defined. Thirdly, to provide some degree of theoretically grounded but flexible comparative framework for further research. As the title suggests, the chapter focuses on institutional settings and political agency, with particular emphasis on (*a*) state and administrative structures, and (*b*) electoral and party systems. The chapter is divided into three sections. In Section 2.2 the theoretical arguments are laid out, with links drawn between the POS literature and institutional theory and a discussion of how political parties pursue Eurosceptic strategies within particular institutional settings. In Section 2.3, the institutional settings noted above are examined: first from a theoretical perspective and then—with the help of expert opinion from country specialists—empirically. In Section 2.4, the chapter concludes with a discussion of the chapter's main points, and an assessment of the viability of the POS model as a basis for further research into party-based Euroscepticism.

2.2 THEORY

2.2.1 Institutions as 'political opportunity structures'

By and large, the POS literature has focused on the opportunities for political action presented to social movements by institutions. However, one could argue that the ideas underpinning the literature can also apply to political entrepreneurs using the more conventional route of party politics. In the established literature, Tarrow (1994: 18) describes POS as 'consistent... dimensions of the political environment' and goes on to say that 'state structures create stable opportunities, but it is changing opportunities within states that provide the openings' for political action. These 'changing opportunities' come about through shifts in the configuration of institutional power, and can be grasped by social movements and political parties alike.

Tarrow's focus on institutional power begs the question: What is an institution? The word 'institution' is bandied around in political science. At one end of the scale, the rational choice literature provides a minimalist account of institutions (Laver and Schofield 1990; Tsebelis 1990; Laver and Shepsle 1995; Shepsle and Weingast 1995), in which they are the little more than a set of 'congealed tastes' (Riker 1980) or, alternatively, 'prescriptions' about the permissibility of actions in a given setting (Ostrom 1986). Moving away from rational choice approaches, Hall (1986: 19) provides us with a more developed account of institutions which, he argues, includes 'the formal rules, compliance procedures, and standard operating practices that structure the relationship between individuals in various units of the polity and economy'. Ikenberry (1988: 222–3) echoes this, arguing that institutions operate on three levels: ranging 'from specific characteristics of government institutions, to the more overarching structures of the state, to the nation's normative social order'.

Broadly speaking, the conflicting definitions and parameters of institutions found in the literature are embedded in the wider 'structure–agency' debate. This debate is germane to the study of party-based Euroscepticism, because it forces us to ask: How relevant are political parties in all of this? Can political parties 'make the weather', or do they just reflect and mobilize around deeper structural cleavages and value-orientations? In order to make the weather, parties must be able to bring about change in institutional structures and norms. Structurally inclined accounts of institutions allow for institutional change, but only of an incremental fashion. Social constructivists and other 'normative institutionalists' argue that institutions monitor the environment around them and adapt to changes in that environment. These changes may take the form of threats or opportunities for the institution. Such changes that take place conform to a 'logic of appropriateness' (March and Olsen 1984: 738), which serves to limit the range of policy alternatives and render some alternatives 'beyond the pale'. A similar model of institutional change can be found in the 'historical institutionalist' literature (Krasner 1988; Hall 1989; Skocpol 1992; King 1995). Here, institutions exist within a state of 'punctuated equilibrium' in which 'rapid bursts of change (are) followed by long periods of stasis' (Krasner 1988: 242). In other words, policy choices made at the time of institutional formation have a persistent and determinate impact over policymaking in the long run, with standard operating procedures (SOPs) routinizing activities and inhibiting anything other than incremental change.

   Although these accounts of institutional change are plausible, they both assume that values are primarily endogenous to institutions. In other words, values are embedded within institutions, and agents bring little or no individual motivations, values, or preferences from the wider environment. This raises two objections when examining party-based Euroscepticism. First, it implies that political parties are 'cultural dupes' and that their scope to make the weather is very limited, because any change that does take place within a given polity is slow and prone to high degrees of path dependence. This may be true in some instances, but not all. Second, the assumption that the changes in institutional culture and SOPs are path-dependent and site-specific in their parameters privileges comparison across time and neglects comparison across space. Regarding values as being purely endogenous to institutions makes comparison across polities highly problematic, because the logical—and easiest—way to explain any phenomena is through diachronic study, with reference to the political and normative context in which the phenomena exists, rather than looking outward to other instances. In doing so, we run the risk of generating tautological or self-referential explanations of the presence or relative strength of party-based Euroscepticism across Europe.

That said, in recent years the new institutionalist literature has seen some blurring of the utility maximizer/cultural dupe divide (Peters 1998; Weingast 1998; Checkel and Moravcsik 2001), and even the most entrenched rational choice theorist would accept that institutions do constitute significant constraints on instrumental action. In other words, institutions are more than just the passive settings for political agency. The chapter echoes these developments, arguing that institutions act as constraints upon party-based Euroscepticism and values are both exogenous and endogenous to these institutions, and also that Eurosceptic political parties operate with a normative map that is coloured both by parties' core ideology and what is considered to be politically feasible in the institutional environment within which they operate. It is to these institutions that the chapter now turns.

2.3 INSTITUTIONS

2.3.1 State and administrative structures

2.3.1.1 Arguments

The first set of institutional variables that impact upon party-based Euroscepticism are those of state and administrative structures. One such variable is the division between federal and unitary states. By and large, explicitly Eurosceptic parties operate at the margins of politics. Therefore, it can be argued that federations provide more political opportunities for Eurosceptic parties, because of the importance of sub-national party systems and the complex system of constitutionally codified checks and balances between different tiers of government which characterize such states (Lees 2002*a*). At the same time all federations are not the same and can be dichotomized between 'decentralized federalist' and 'centralized federalist' systems (Riker 1964) or, as with this chapter, arranged along a 'demos constraining–demos enabling' continuum (Stepan 2001).

Stepan's model assumes that 'all democratic federations, qua federations, are centre constraining'. He gives four reasons for this. First, the constitutional checks and balances noted above serve to protect the powers of the constituent units against the centre—leaving some issue areas beyond the centre's jurisdiction. Secondly, constitutionally protected subnational tiers of government diffuse the demos into multiple demoi, divided into multiple authority structures. Thirdly, federal constitutions require a certain level of assent from the constituent parts before amendment is possible—thus constraining the centre's room for manoeuvre. Finally, as a corollary to the previous three factors, federal constitutions are, as a rule, more complex than those of unitary states and the judiciary's status as an arbitrator of boundary disputes enhances its status as a political actor in its own right (Stepan 2001: 335–6).

Stepan argues that there are four key variables that determine the degree of constraint which can be exerted on the centre. These are: (*a*) the degree of overrepresentation in the territorial chamber; (*b*) the 'policy scope' of the territorial chamber; (*c*) the degree to which policymaking is constitutionally allocated to super majorities or to subunits of the federation; and (*d*) the degree to which the party system is polity-wide in its orientation and incentive system. Stepan applies his analysis to a number of modern federations (including the USA, Brazil, India, Austria, Belgium, and Germany) and concludes that there is a high degree of variance between federations in aggregate terms and on a dimension-to-dimension basis. Thus, all federal arrangements could provide the means for Eurosceptic parties to constrain the (generally pro-European) centre, but some provide more resources than others.

Nevertheless, federalism is not a value-neutral institutional variable and sub-national units in member states with federal systems have adopted different strategies for exploiting domestic- and EU-level opportunity structures, depending on what is regarded as appropriate to the political circumstances. Moreover, the additional transaction costs associated with federal systems may create veto players in circumstances in which there has been a broad consensus on the desirability of European integration (Scharpf 1985, 1988 on the 'joint-decision trap' in both Germany and the EU, for instance).

It follows that if the four variables noted earlier are most associated with federalism, unitary states will by and large be ranked as possessing weaker constraints on the centre. This is not to say that there no checks and balances within the unitary state: for instance, unitary states may reserve policymaking powers to subunits of the state (Stepan's third variable), and the degree to which parties are able to operate polity-wide incentive systems (the fourth variable) is not just an issue in federal states. Moreover, written constitutions, the *aquis communautaire*, and the increasing judicialization of politics constrain all states. Nevertheless, the lack of a territorially defined second chamber in unitary states implies that unitary state structures serve more as passive constraints than as active resources to be harnessed by Eurosceptic political parties. Therefore, one must assume that federalist state structures provide a better platform for party-based Euroscepticism. This is consistent with the POS literature. As Tarrow (1994: 81) observes, 'decentralised states provide a multitude of targets at the base' of the polity for agents opposed to the central polis. Moreover, they also provide constitutionally protected and independently resourced platforms from which to launch more formal and institutionalized strategies of opposition (Lees 2001). In other words, *ceteris paribus*, we would expect to see more—and more effective—instances of party-based Euroscepticism in federal states than in unitary states.

To sum up, the key variables are as follows: (*a*) the degree of overrepresentation in the territorial chamber; (*b*) the 'policy scope' of the territorial chamber; (*c*) the degree to which policymaking is constitutionally allocated to super majorities or to subunits of the federation; and (*d*) the degree to which the party system is polity-wide in its orientation and incentive systems. The first three variables all act as constraints on the centre, whilst the fourth—because it allows the centre to discipline the territory—does the opposite. It is assumed that federations tend to 'score' higher on the first three variables than unitary states, many of which are unicameral, and lower on the fourth because strong sub-national tiers of government provide alternative sources of power and resources to the centre (Lees, 2001), although this may vary according to local conditions. Thus, taken in the round we might assume that federations provide a more benign POS for party-based Euroscepticism than unitary states and, by the same token, devolved unitary states are more benign than 'strong' unitary states.

2.3.1.2 Evidence

In order to explore these assumptions further, the author canvassed the opinion of country experts[1] engaged in research into party-based Euroscepticism in order to establish if they held up. This form of expert survey-based research is an established method for plotting party positions on European integration (Laver 1994, 1995; Hix and Lord 1997; Ray 1999), but has not been utilized in the manner used in this chapter before. In addition, the N is smaller than that found in the studies noted above and the data is used in an indicative manner rather than as a means to infer statistical relationships between the variables.

The twelve countries examined were the Czech Republic, Finland, France, Germany, Hungary, Republic of Ireland, Italy, Norway, Poland, Slovakia, Sweden, and the UK. The method of data collection was a semi-structured questionnaire, which included a number of standardized questions[2] relating to Stepan's variables discussed earlier. A summary of recipients' responses is set in Table 2.1.

Before discussing these findings, three caveats must be mentioned. First, the majority of the data is judgemental opinion by party politics specialists. Therefore it might be over-subjective and may privilege the causal power of electoral and party system variables over those of state and administrative structures. Second, ten cases represents a relatively small N and any findings cannot easily be extrapolated out to the wider European polity. Third, following on from the last point, the balance between state types is skewed towards unitary states with only one federal state (Germany) being included (these caveats are discussed at greater length in the conclusion to this chapter).

Interestingly, Table 2.1 indicates that taken in the round, state structures are not considered to be strong constraints upon party-based Euroscepticism in the twelve countries under study. Six of the twelve states (the Czech Republic, Finland, Germany, Poland, Slovakia, and the UK) were deemed to exert moderate levels of constraint upon party-based Euroscepticism, three (France, Italy, and Norway) to have low levels, with another three country experts (on Hungary, Ireland, and Sweden) declining to give a judgement (this is understandable, given the complexity of the institutional variables being assessed). One cannot see a match between the type of state (federal, 'strong' unitary, or devolved unitary). Similarly,

Table 2.1. State and administrative structures as a constraint upon party-based Euroscepticism: Expert opinion on twelve countries

Level of constraint on party-based Euroscepticism	High	Medium	Low	Don't know
(I) Type of State				
(i) Federal		(G)		
(ii) 'Strong' Unitary		(FIN) (SLOV)	(F)	(H) (IR) (SWE)
(iii) Devolved Unitary		(CZ) (P) (UK)	(I) (N)	
(II) Type of Legislature				
(i) Unicameral		(FIN) (SLOV)	(N)	(H) (SWE)
(ii) Bicameral		(CZ) (G) (P) (UK)	(F) (I)	(IR)
(III) Extent of 'Territorial' Representation' in Second Chamber				
(i) High				
(ii) Moderate		(G)	(F)	
(iii) Low/None		(CZ) (P) (UK)	(I)	(IR)
(iv) N/A		(FIN)	(N)	(H)
(IV) Extent of 'Policy Powers' of Second Chamber				
(i) High			(I)	
(ii) Moderate		(CZ) (G)		
(iii) Low/None		(P) (UK)	(F) (I)	
(iv) N/A		(FIN)	(N)	(H)
(V) Extent of Policymaking Reserved for Super-Majorities/Sub-national Tiers of Government				
(i) High				
(ii) Moderate		(CZ) (G) (UK)	(I)	(SWE)
(iii) Low/None		(P) (FIN)	(F) (N)	(H) (IR)
(VI) Extent of Polity-wide Party System Incentives/Discipline				
(i) High		(CZ) (F) (P)	(I)	(H) (IR) (SWE)
(ii) Moderate		(G) (UK) (SLOV)	(F) (N)	
(iii) Low/None				
Total	0	6*	3	3

Countries: Czech Republic (CZ); Finland (FIN); France (F); Germany (G); Hungary (H); Republic of Ireland (I); Italy (I); Norway (N); Poland (P); Slovakia (SLOV), Sweden (SWE), United Kingdom (UK). II, II, and IV do not apply to unicameral legislatures.

* Partial data from Slovakia.

neither (*a*) unicameral versus bicameral legislatures, (*b*) the extent of 'policy powers' in the second chamber, nor (*c*) the extent to which policymaking is reserved for super-majorities, etc., appear in themselves to impact upon party-based Euroscepticism. This is of interest because it contradicts Stepan's assumptions about the 'demos-constraining' qualities of state structures (and federal structures in particular).

The caveats mentioned above combined with the lack of a clear pattern between types of state structure mean that it is not possible to draw conclusions at the aggregate level about the impact of state structures on party-based Euroscepticism on the strength of the ten cases. Nevertheless, at the individual-case level, country experts do point to specific structural variables which impact upon the viability of Eurosceptic parties. The three variables are: (*a*) the degree of centralization (and underlying cleavage structures); (*b*) the process of European policymaking in nation states; and (*c*) the importance of regional and local government. Of these, the first two are new whilst the third cross-cuts variables I (Type of State) and V (Extent of policymaking reserved for supermajorities and sub-national tiers of government) (as shown in Table 2.1).

- Degree of centralization: Writing about Norway, Nick Sitter argues that an historical institutionalist explanation of party-based Euroscepticism is possible—focused on the country's latent centre–periphery cleavage. Centre–periphery cleavages develop as a reaction to centralization and state-building (Lipset and Rokkan 1967*a*). Sitter argues that European integration might be seen by Norwegian Eurosceptics as analogous to efforts to centralize power in Christiania (Oslo) during the union with Sweden (1814–95), with Eurosceptics taking a similar nationalist line of resistance to 'foreign', cosmopolitan administration as their nineteenth-century forbears.

- Process of European policymaking: Mark Aspinwall, commenting on the UK, speculates that when it comes to European policymaking the UK system is effectively unicameral—thus privileging the Commons as an arena for Euroscepticism.

- The importance of regional and local government: This is the most cited single variable, and is mentioned by Sitter, Aleks Szczerbiak (Poland), and Paul Webb (the UK). However the nature of this impact is contested. On the one hand, Sitter argues that strong regional and local government in Norway has provided bases for 'counter-elites' that can use a Eurosceptic discourse to mobilize around resistance to centralization and the defence of subsidized protected sectors such as agriculture, fishing, and regional aid. This assessment of the role of sub-national government is partially supported by Szczerbiak, who argues that Poland's relatively weak regional tier of government has probably prevented the emergence of regionally based Eurosceptic factions within parties. However Szczerbiak goes on to assert that this is a secondary factor in the development of party-based Euroscepticism. Finally Webb argues that strong sub-national government can act as both a facilitator and a constraint, depending on other variables. Citing the case of the devolved institutions in Scotland and Wales, Webb points out that devolution may feed nationalist sentiment (which might manifest itself as Euroscepticism) but conversely it might encourage those nationalists who consider a 'Europe of the regions' to be the best outlet for their aspirations.

The focus on sub-national government is consistent with Stepan's arguments and those put forward in this chapter. However, the precise nature of its impact is unclear and needs further research. This is discussed at greater length in the conclusion to this chapter. What is clear is that in assessing the impact of institutions on party-based Euroscepticism, the country experts consulted attached far less importance to state structures than they did to electoral and party systems. It is to these that the chapter now turns.

2.3.2 Electoral and party systems

2.3.2.1 Arguments

Early rational choice accounts of party politics draw on Anthony Downs' (1957) analogy of party systems as markets, in which parties are regarded as analogous with firms competing with each other for voters who, in turn, are analogous with consumers. Early Downsian models conceptualized the policy dimension as a one-dimensional left–right continuum, although later models tended to supplement this with an additional dimension, often based on a authoritarian–libertarian or materialist–post-materialist dimension. What is important in relation to the chapter is that such models assume that the individual voter has an ideal policy position along the left–right continuum and that the aggregate of voters' preferences usu-ally assume a 'normal distribution': in other words, a bell curve along the left–right axis. In plurality and majoritarian electoral systems, Duverger's law decrees that the outcome over time is a party system dominated by two 'effective' parties, competing around the ideological centre of the party sys-tem for the 'median voter'. The median voter exists at the point where the aggregate of voters' preferences reaches an equilibrium, and thus effectively a consensus. The logical outcome under such systems is a centrist form of politics, in which two parties compete for the centre ground and the preferences of voters who do not share the median position are neglected in relative terms. In short, plurality and majoritarian systems can lead to a 'tyranny of the majority' (Mueller 1996: 149).

Proportional representation (PR), on the other hand, tends to produce multiparty systems in which, in most instances, no single party is able to command a majority of votes. (There are exceptions to this, of course, in which multiparty proportional systems generate a 'dominant' party, such as the Social Democrats in Sweden; or even a majority party, such as the Christian Social Union in Bavaria.) Under such conditions, it is rational for entrepreneurial parties to seek out 'niche' positions across the bell curve: representing minority ideological positions or interests. This is why such systems are more likely to sustain viable farmers' parties, green parties, communist parties, far right parties, and so forth. Thus, the general tone of politics may remain centrist, but the tyranny of the major-ity is avoided. Therefore, it is logical to assume that, under proportional systems, we are more likely to find political parties that mobilize around a Eurosceptic position. In other words, proportional systems present a more benign POS for political opportunists who wish to exploit this niche in the market.

As already noted, the two broad categories of plurality/majoritarian and proportional electoral systems produce different incentive systems for party competition—with the former tending to generate systems domi-nated by two relevant parties, competing for the median voter, and the latter leaving viable space for 'niche' parties, with the result that multiparty systems are more common. It is argued that in principle, majoritarian systems hold the danger of producing a tyranny of the majority, whilst proportional systems hold the potential to provide a more effective 'voice' for minority positions, including Eurosceptic positions. Nevertheless, this binary classification is over-simple. The two categories must be unpacked further.

An alternative classification of electoral systems is to divide them into six categories. These are: (*a*) Simple District-Level Allocation (SDLA; no threshold); (*b*) District-Level Allocation (DLA; threshold); (*c*) Additional Member Systems (AMS); (*d*) Complex PR Districting (no compensatory upper tier); (*e*) Compensatory Seats (threshold for upper-tier allocation); (*f*) Nationwide Allocation (no threshold). None of these systems are perfectly proportional, although the nationwide allocation system is closest to the ideal-type of a 'pure' proportional system advocated by public choice theorists (Mueller 1996: 132–40). (This system has been used once, in the Romanian elections of 1990, and has been described as 'the most proportional system ever used anywhere in the world' (Budge et al. 1997: 237).)

These six categories can be further differentiated. For instance, Simple District-Level systems can be further divided into plurality and PR categories, whilst more proportional systems can be further divided into Multi-Representative List versus Single Transferable Vote systems (and 'Multi-Rep' systems themselves can be divided into those that use the Hare quotient, the Droop quota, or the Imperiali quota to calculate parties' allocation of legislative seats). But, in the end, an over-deterministic focus on the mechanics of electoral rules does not bring us any further towards explaining the presence and relative strength of party-based Euroscepticism. Eurosceptic parties may be reasonably well represented (or even over-represented) within a party system, but fail to have much impact. To better explain the presence and relative strength of party-based Euroscepticism, we must also look to the institutional setting of party systems.

For the purposes of the chapter, party systems are classified by the number of 'effective' parties within them. Across Europe, there has been an increase in the degree of fractionalization of party systems over the period since 1980. As a result, the average West European parliament contains seven political parties. Nevertheless, this is a crude indicator and takes no account of the relative strength or 'effectiveness' of parties. If we count the number of 'effective' parties only, the average (West) European party system contains four parties (Lane and Ersson 1999: 142–3). Game theorists argue that, all other things being equal, the more players in a particular game, the less likely that any particular strategy or set of alternatives become dominant. This is because the potential number of winning coalitions rises exponentially as players are added.[3] This leads to the phenomenon of 'Condorcet cycling', in which any potential alternative can be beaten by another, which can be beaten by another, and so on. The larger the number of potential winning coalitions, the wider the range of issue choices available, and the more likely cycling is to occur. This is because the further away a proposed solution is to a player's ideal position, the more incentive the player has to vote it down and/or propose an alternative. The problem of cycling—and solutions to it—has been a core preoccupation of public choice theorists (Black 1948; Arrow 1951). As Kramer (1973) points out, cycling does not occur where a majority of players have identical preferences. It therefore follows that the more contentious an issue, the less likely that such a majority exists and the more likely that cycling occurs (Niemi 1969; Tullock and Campbell 1970; Koga and Nagatani 1974).

Finally, one other decision rule may potentially be part of the POS: the legal status of plebiscites and referendums within national polities. The author has argued elsewhere that the absence of such devices in the Federal Republic of Germany has served to take the heat out of the European issue. As a result, key decisions—such as the Maastricht Treaty and the introduction of the euro—have been reduced to technocratic negotiations between elites with little input from the general public (Lees 2002a). Thus, despite the fact that public opinion in Germany is not particularly pro-'Europe', the Federal Republic has remained one of the motors of European integration. In other countries—such as Denmark, France, and Ireland—the use of referendums as a decision rule has allowed Eurosceptics to raise the salience of the issue and tap into popular unease about the scope and pace of the integration process. Therefore, it follows that referendums qua referendums, are potential facilitators of party-based Euroscepticism.

To sum up, the important institutional variables are as follows: first, whether electoral systems are (*a*) plurality/majoritarian or (*b*) proportional in nature; secondly, whether they are (*a*) SDLA (no threshold), (*b*) DLA (threshold), (*c*) AMS, (*d*) Complex PR Districting (no compensatory upper tier), (*e*) Compensatory Seats (threshold for upper-tier allocation), or (*f*) Nationwide Allocation systems; third, the number of 'relevant' parties in the party system; and finally, the presence or absence of the use of referendums as a decision rule. It is assumed that the more proportional the system, and the higher the number of relevant parties, the more benign the POS for party-based Euroscepticism.

2.3.2.2 Evidence

In order to explore these assumptions, the author canvassed the country experts mentioned earlier in the chapter. Once again the author asked a number of standard questions[4] relating to Stepan's variables. A summary of recipients' responses is set out in Table 2.2, with the same caveats mentioned earlier.

Out of the twelve cases, five (France, Germany, Hungary, Sweden, and the UK) are described as exercising high levels of constraint, three (the Czech Republic, Poland, and Slovakia) have moderate levels, and three (Italy, Ireland, and Norway) have low levels. In only one case (Finland) was the respondent unwilling to categorize the electoral and party systems in this manner (and, again, this is understandable). However, with one exception (referendums) it is almost impossible to point to electoral and party system variables at the aggregate level as having a deterministic effect on party-based Euroscepticism. All the countries in question have Eurosceptic parties within the party system and reasonably high levels of 'relevant' parties, regardless of the level or pattern of institutional constraints. Moreover, there is no relationship between types of electoral system at the national level and levels of constraint upon party-based Euroscepticism. There is a small degree of skew at the sub-national level, but in as far as this is significant it seems to contradict the assumptions discussed earlier, in that it is the more 'proportional' systems (AMS and Complex PR Districting) that exercise higher levels of constraint rather than—as would be expected—DLA systems. The logic of this counter-intuitive conclusion is that either the chapter's assumptions about the impact of different electoral systems are wrong or its assumptions about the importance of sub-national government are wrong (or they are both wrong!), or that there really is no causal relationship between these institutions and levels of constraint exercised upon party-based Euroscepticism.

However, referendums do appear to have an impact. The two countries with frequent referendums (Italy and Ireland) are both classified as exercising low levels of constraint upon party-based Euroscepticism. In addition, all but three of the country experts argue that referendums act as

Table 2.2. Electoral/party systems as a constraint upon party-based Eurosceptism: Expert opinion on twelve countries

Level of constraint on party-based Euroscepticism	High	Medium	Low	Don't know
(I) Electoral System (broad terms)				
(i) Plurality	(F) (UK)		(I)	(FIN)
(ii) Proportional	(G) (SWE)	(CZ) (P) (SLOV)	(IR) (N)	
(iii) Mixed	(H)			
(II) National Electoral System (detailed)				
(i) SDLA (no threshold)	(UK)		(I) (IR)	(FIN)
(ii) DLA (threshold)		(P) (CZ)	(N)	
(iii) AMS	(F) (G)			
(iv) Complex PR Districting				
(v) Compensatory Seats	(H) (SWE)			
(vi) Nationwide Allocation		(SLOV)	(I)	
(III) Sub-national Electoral System (detailed)				
(i) SDLA (no threshold)		(SLOV)	(IR)	(FIN)
(ii) DLA (threshold)		(P)	(N)	
(iii) AMS	(F) (G) (UK)			
(iv) Complex PR Districting	(F) (SWE)			
(v) Compensatory Seats				
(vi) Nationwide Allocation			(CZ)	
(vii) N/A	(H)			
(IV) Relevant Parties (National)				
(i) 1–2				
(ii) 3–4	(G)		(CZ) (IR)	
(iii) 5–6	(H) (UK)	(P)		
(iv) 7 or more	(F) (SWE)	(SLOV)	(I) (N)	(FIN)
(V) Other Relevant Parties (Sub-national)?				
(i) Yes	(F) (G) (UK) (SWE)	(P)		
(ii) No	(H)	(SLOV)	(CZ) (I) (IR) (N)	(FIN)
(VI) Eurosceptic Parties?				
(i) Yes	(F) (G) (UK) (H) (SWE)	(P) (SLOV)	(CZ) (I) (IR) (N)	(FIN)
(ii) No				

Table 2.2. (*Continued*)

Level of constraint on party-based Euroscepticism	High	Medium	Low	Don't know
(VII) Referendums?				
(i) Frequently		(SLOV)	(I) (IR)	
(ii) Infrequently	(F) (H)	(P)		
(iii) Very infrequently	(UK) (SWE)		(N)	(FIN)
(iv) Never	(G)		(CZ)	
(VIII) Referendums as:				
(i) Constraint?	(SWE)		(I)	(FIN)
(ii) Facilitator?	(F) (H) (UK)	(P)	(IR) (N)	
(iii) N/A	(G)		(CZ)	
Total	5	2*	4	1

Countries: Czech Republic (CZ); Finland (FIN); France (F); Germany (G); Hungary (H); Republic of Ireland (I); Italy (I); Norway (N); Poland (P); Slovakia (SLOV), Sweden (SWE), United Kingdom (UK).

* Partial data from Slovakia.

a facilitator in this respect. However, it is important not to read too much into this. Writing on Italy, Lucia Quaglia argues that the high levels of pro-European sentiment within the populace means that referendums actually constrain Eurosceptic parties. Karen Henderson points out that although Slovakia has frequent referendums, the results are normally invalid because of regular low turnouts of under 50 per cent. Karin Gilland (Ireland) argues that referendums are a weapon best used by 'outsider' parties and are of little use to mainstream parties, while Nicholas Aylott (Sweden) contends that the referendum has been used once (in 1994) to 'soothe' intra-party and intra-bloc divisions over Europe (and may be used again in 2003 during the debate over Sweden joining Euroland). Thus, referendums may be a facilitator of party-based Euroscepticism, but may also act as a constraint. In short it depends on the type of party and the context in which they operate.

It is impossible to draw any conclusions about the impact of electoral and party systems on party-based Euroscepticism at the aggregate level. Nevertheless the respondents provide plenty of data on a case-by-case level. In terms of electoral systems, the key variables mentioned are: (*a*) degree of proportionality, (*b*) thresholds to representation, and (*c*) whether or not electoral systems include second round run-offs.

- The degree of proportionality: This is mentioned in five cases, although respondents come to different conclusions as to its impact. In keeping with the assumptions discussed earlier in the chapter, Sitter argues that Norway's regional system of PR encourages the development of 'niche' parties, polling around 5–15 per cent of the vote, which can capitalize on latent Euroscepticism in the electorate. This is supported by Szczerbiak, who argues that PR has given Poland a multipolar party system in which an openly Eurosceptic party (the League of Polish Families) can survive. However, Gilland argues that in Ireland the opportunities provided by proportionality is outweighed by the economic incentives of EU membership and that 'parties of government' therefore eschew Eurosceptic positions. As a result Eurosceptic parties hold less than 20 of the Dail's 166 seats. By contrast, Aylott (Sweden) argues that PR serves to defuse Euroscepticism—rather than privilege it—because parties are able to reduce intra-party conflict on the issue of Europe by balancing pro- and anti-Europeans on party lists. Finally, Aspinwall takes another approach and argues that the UK's majoritarian system serves to privilege a two-party adversarial system in which Euroscepticism inevitably comes to the fore. Like Aylott, Aspinwall sees PR as diffusing conflict over Europe rather than privileging it.

- Thresholds to representation: These are mentioned by three respondents. Kopecky argues that the Czech Republic's relatively high threshold means that Eurosceptic parties such as the Republicans (SPR-RSC) find it hard to get into parliament. This point is supported by Agnes Batory (Hungary) and to a certain extent by Webb (UK)—however, as Webb points out, although new Eurosceptic parties have been shut out of the British party system, the Conservative Party's Eurosceptic turn over the last twenty years has brought Euroscepticism to the very heart of the political system.

- Second round run-offs: Batory (Hungary) points out that 'French-style' second round run-offs produce majoritarian results, encourage cooperation between parties, and diffuse the issue of Europe.

In terms of party system variables, the three main variables mentioned by respondents are: (*a*) party system 'type' and dimensions of conflict, (*b*) coalition behaviour, and (*c*) party funding.

- Party system 'type' and dimensions of conflict: Five respondents mention this. Sitter argues that Norway's party system is characterized by Eurosceptic parties at the political centre as well as on the flanks of the more pro-European parties. This has implications for coalition-building and makes pro-European parties unusually vulnerable. Moreover, Eurosceptic parties benefit from the strong territorial (centre–periphery) dimension to inter-party conflict in Norway. As already noted, Szczerbiak argues that Poland's multipolar party system provides opportunities for Eurosceptic parties, whilst Aylott asserts that both left and right in Sweden's bipolar or two-bloc system are divided on Europe—thus providing an incentive to play down Europe as an election issue. Conti argues that, in Italy's more fluid party system, the Northern League deliberately moved to the political right in order to occupy the position left empty by the National Alliance. In doing so, it has become progressively more Eurosceptic. Kopecky, on the other hand, argues that in the Czech Republic the key dimension of party conflict remains the left–right dimension and that questions of 'national identity' (that underpin Eurosceptic discourses) are only residual to this.

- Coalition behaviour: This is mentioned by two respondents. Conti argues that the Italian electoral system forces parties to build coalitions with large ideological ranges. This means that extreme/peripheral parties are often included in governing coalitions and—in the case of coalitions of the right—the moderate or faction-based Euroscepticism of the mainstream centre-right parties is re-enforced and amplified. Sitter makes a similar point, arguing that Eurosceptic parties in Norway have raised the salience of Europe in coalition formation and maintenance (leading to the collapse of at least three centre-right coalitions to date). The underlying message from both respondents is that coalitions with wide ideological ranges are inherently unstable and vulnerable to leverage from extremist parties. This is made worse if, as is the case in Norway, Eurosceptic parties exist at the political centre and can block the formation of ideologically connected majority coalitions.[5]

- Party funding: This is mentioned by Tapio Raunio in the context of Finland. Raunio argues that state funding of parties, particularly when it is based on a party's share of seats in parliament, buttresses the Euro-orthodoxy because it is hard for new parties—including Eurosceptic parties—to break into the system. This makes a lot of sense, although, as Webb pointed out earlier, it does not stop established parties from performing a Eurosceptic turn.

2.4 DISCUSSION AND CONCLUSIONS

As noted at the beginning of the chapter, this study had four objectives. The first main objective was to explore the impact of institutions on party-based Euroscepticism in Europe and to assess whether one can posit a causal relationship at the aggregate level between certain institutions and the presence and/or relative strength of party-based Euroscepticism. The chapter has explored this relationship but has not been able to suggest a causal relationship between the independent and dependent variables at the aggregate level. Beyond this, the chapter set out three secondary objectives. The first two—to operationalize the POS concept using institutional theory and to apply this to the study of party-based Euroscepticism—have been achieved, albeit with ambiguous empirical results. Let us now assess the third objective: to provide some degree of theoretically grounded but flexible comparative framework for further research.

All but the most diehard behaviouralist would accept that, in politics, institutions matter. They form the POS for political action. In this chapter, a number of these institutions have been examined and hypotheses put forward about their impact on party-based Euroscepticism. However, at the aggregate level at least, it is hard to establish a clear causal relationship between institutions and the presence and relative strength of party-based Euroscepticism in the twelve countries examined. Eurosceptic parties and/or party factions can thrive or fail to thrive in unitary or federal states, under majoritarian or proportional electoral system, in unicameral or bicameral legislatures, in two-bloc or multipolar party systems, and so on.

So how does one move on from this? One clear response would be to increase the size of the N, and look at more European countries. There is a lot of sense in this—the larger the sample the more fine-grained the picture that emerges and, anyway, at present there is only one federal state in the sample. Therefore, it is sensible to argue for more cases to be included in future study, if only further to explore the federal–unitary variable.

A second response would be to increase the total number of variables under study. The questionnaire used in this chapter pointed to fourteen institutional variables, divided (somewhat arbitrarily, perhaps) into the two sections of state and administrative structures, and electoral and party systems. However, the unstructured part of the questionnaire has yielded five new variables: (*a*) the degree of state centralization (and underlying cleavage structures), (*b*) the process of European policymaking in nation states, (*c*) party system 'type' and dimensions of conflict, (*d*) coalition behaviour, and (*e*) party funding. In addition, the importance of regional and local government cross-cut state/administrative variables I and V (see Table 2.1). Staying within the administrative structure/party system nexus, one can think of at least one more variable—'working' versus 'adversarial' parliaments (especially the configuration of parliamentary committees)— although operationalizing it would be quite complex. Thinking further afield, one might use other variables such as geopolitics/geographical location, trade patterns/trade dependence, and—building on Sitter's analysis of Norway—cleavage structures (especially centre–periphery; urban–rural). Again, more research is suggested.

A third response would be to move away from the use of expert opinion, perhaps towards some form of global statistical analysis. This would only make sense if the number of cases and/or variables was greatly increased and the isolation and operationalization of those variables greatly refined. Even then, triangulation with expert opinion and other qualitative data would be required.

Notwithstanding the shortcomings of the data noted earlier, two conclusions can be made on the basis of the findings in this chapter. First, the idiom of POS remains an intuitive or heuristic device but resists formalization. It has some explanatory power, but little or no predictive power. Secondly, the chapter reaffirms that parties can 'make the weather'. Without revisiting the 'structure–agency' debate again, it is clear that political parties adapt to institutional settings but retain high levels of agency. In terms of party-based Euroscepticism this means that Eurosceptic discourses or agendas are not contingent on the institutional environment and are negotiable. They may be a key part of a party's programmatic identity, or

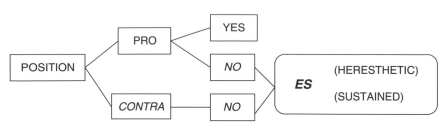

Figure 2.1. Sustained vs. heresthetic Euroscepticism (ES)

Note: This builds on concepts put forward in Lees (2002*a*). The author thanks colleagues at the ECPR Joint Sessions in Turin, especially Kris Deschouwer, for their feedback on this idea.

they may be adopted by parties for short-term tactical reasons. In other words, they may be 'sustained' or 'heresthetic' in nature. A decision tree describing the difference between the two types of Eurosceptic agenda is set out in Figure 2.1.

Heresthetic agendas are exercises in political manipulation designed to change the balance of political forces to the advantage of the heresthetician, by introducing a new dimension of issue salience into the political game (see Riker 1983). This is not to say that such agendas are always insincere or are never grounded in core beliefs, but rather that their salience at a given time and place is a means to an end rather than an end in itself. Thus, in terms of Euroscepticism, sustained agendas are those that are more or less consistently held across time and space and reflect a set of stable preferences concerning European integration, whilst heresthetic agendas are limited to particular 'issues' and reflect less stable preferences or even indifference to the issue.

However, in research terms it can be difficult to determine what a sustained Eurosceptic agenda or a heresthetic one are. In the context of the chapter, Conti's description of the Italian Northern League's shift rightwards to occupy the position left empty by the National Alliance is clearly an example of a heresthetic. On the other hand, Kopecky's description of the Czech Republic, in which the key dimension of party conflict remains the left–right dimension (and questions of 'national identity' are only residual), means that Euroscepticism is contingent on other ideological dimensions. Similarly, one can assume that the position of the True Finns—holding one seat in Europhile Finland—is a genuine one and not a heresthetic.

To conclude, political parties are complicated phenomena and although we can map their positions on Europe it is harder to determine what drives those positions, including the effect of the institutional environment. POS matter, but in the end it is the political opportunists—the political parties—that determine the pattern of party-based Euroscepticism in each country. The POS idiom remains intuitive and of heuristic use but, in the absence of a more predictive model of institutional constraints, it remains the country specialists who are best able to shed light on party-based Euroscepticism on a case-by-case basis. And in doing so such case studies must also consider the extent to which party-based Euroscepticism is *sui generis*, or if its study might also shed light on other political phenomena— such as feminist, green, or even far right politics—in which political agents have tried, with varying degrees of success, to reshape or break down a settled elite consensus.

NOTES

1. My thanks to Agnes Alexandre-Collier, Mark Aspinwall, Nicholas Aylott, Agnes Batory, Nicolo Conti, Anthony Forster, Karin Gilland, Karen Henderson, Petr Kopecky, Lucia Quaglia, Tapio Raunio, Nick Sitter, Aleks Szczerbiak, and Paul Webb for their kind help. Expert opinion on Germany is the author's. Where experts' opinion has clashed regarding a particular country, the author has mediated their opinions using the secondary literature. Therefore, responsibility for any empirical or judgemental errors is the author's alone.

2. (I) Is the country you study (i) a Federal State; (ii) a 'strong' Unitary State; or (iii) a devolved Unitary State? (II) Is the national parliament (i) Unicameral; or (ii) Bicameral? (If Unicameral, please go on to Question IV). (III) If Bicameral, would you say the level of 'territorial' representation in the second chamber is (i) High; (ii) Moderate; (ii) Low; (iii) or Don't Know? (IV) If Bicameral, would you say the level and extent of policymaking powers ascribed to the second chamber is (i) High; (ii) Moderate; (ii) Low; (iii) or Don't Know? (V) In your country specialism, would you say the degree to which policymaking is constitutionally allocated to supermajorities and/or to sub national tiers of government is (i) High; (ii) Moderate; (ii) Low; (iii) or Don't Know? (VI) In your country specialism, would you say the degree to which the party system is polity-wide in its orientation and incentive

systems is (i) High; (ii) Moderate; (ii) Low; (iii) or Don't Know? (VII) In your country specialism, would you say the degree to which state structures constrain the development and consolidation of party-based Euroscepticism to be (i) High; (ii) Moderate; (ii) Low; (iii) or Don't Know?

3. See, for example, Schubik (1967: 249) cited in Hinckley (1981: 24).

4. (I) In your country specialism, would you say the electoral system is (i) plurality/majoritarian or (ii) proportional in nature? (II) In your country specialism, which of the following classifications best describes the national electoral system? (SDLA (no threshold); DLA (threshold); AMS; Complex PR Districting (no compensatory upper tier); Compensatory Seats (threshold for upper-tier allocation); Nationwide Allocation system. (III) In your country specialism, which of the following classifications best describes the sub-national electoral systems? (as above). (IV) In your country specialism, how many 'relevant'—that is, parties that can be regarded as having an influence on the formation and maintenance of governing coalitions— parties exist in the national party system? (V) In your country specialism, are there any 'relevant' parties that exist at the sub-national level that are excluded from the national party system? (please specify) (VI) In your country specialism, are there any Eurosceptic parties at either the national *and/or* sub-national level of party system? (please specify). (VII) In your country specialism, are referendums used as a decision rule (i) Frequently (at least every five years); (ii) Infrequently (less than every five years); (iii) Very infrequently (less than every ten years); or (iv) Not at all? (please underline one). (VIII) In your country specialism, if referendums are used as a decision rule for 'European issues', do you think they are a (i) Constraint; or (ii) Facilitator or party-based Euroscepticism? (IX) In your country specialism, would you say the degree to which electoral and party systems constrain the development and consolidation of party-based Euroscepticism to be (i) High; (ii) Moderate; (iii) Low; (iv) or Don't Know?

5. Axelrod (1970) argues that members of successful coalitions will ideally be adjacent to one another along a single Downsian Left–Right ideological continuum. Such 'ideological adjacency' will serve to minimize conflicts of interest. Axelrod's 'minimal connected winning' model assumes ideological adjacency, but has no conception of the ideological distance between parties and cannot pick up the nuances of ideological conflict. De Swaan (1973), however, predicts that the winning set will comprise the minimal connected winning coalition with the smallest ideological range. The policy dimension remains a single Downsian Left–Right axis, running from progressivism to

conservatism, and all parties are assumed to have preference orderings of all potential coalitions, based upon their relative proximity to the median or 'Mparty'. De Swaan's theory is often referred to as the 'median legislator' or 'median party' model because it is based on the assumption that the party that controls the median legislator in any potential coalition is decisive because it blocks the axis along which any connected winning coalition must form.

3

Protectionism, Populism, or Participation? Agrarian Parties and the European Question in Western and East Central Europe

Nick Sitter and Agnes Batory

3.1 INTRODUCTION

European integration has raised some awkward questions for almost all national political parties in Europe, but few party families have displayed greater variation than the agrarian parties. Some of the parties that have their roots in the defence of agrarian and rural interests oppose supranational European integration in principle, others oppose particular aspects of the European Union (EU) regime or plans for further integration, and yet others broadly welcome most aspects of the EU and its public policy regime. Whereas agrarian interest groups in the six original member states have long provided solid support for the European Economic Community (EEC) and its successors, many of the political parties that emerged in defence of agrarian interests or identity elsewhere in Europe have proven less enthusiastic about European integration. Taking a broad European comparative perspective, this chapter explores the drivers behind and dynamics of change in agrarian party-based Euroscepticism. The chapter takes as a starting point the proposition that political parties seek to balance four goals—party management and organizational survival; the pursuit of core policy preferences; the quest for votes; and access to executive office—and suggests that party-based Euroscepticism is the product of party strategy and patterns of opposition in the domestic party system. It draws on both West European and post-communist cases: the

Danish, Finnish, Hungarian, Icelandic, Norwegian, Polish, Swedish, and Swiss agrarian parties.

3.2 THE AGRARIAN PARTIES: ORIGINS, STRATEGY, AND EUROSCEPTICISM

With a few significant exceptions, agrarian parties have until recently been somewhat neglected in the comparative party politics literature (Urwin 1980; Kristinsson 1991; Arter 2001*a*). But the justification for a chapter on agrarian parties builds on more than this. Both authors have argued elsewhere that Euroscepticism is not a single cleavage or dimension of political competition (Sitter 2001; Batory 2002).[1] Party-based Euroscepticism may draw on parties' identities or policy preferences and is shaped by the incentives they face in their quests for votes and office. Given that a number of agrarian parties invoke defence of a particular (national and/or rural) identity, protection of local political autonomy and rural interests, or championing farmers' economic interests, these parties provide particularly fertile ground for Euroscepticism. Yet, by no means do all of them oppose European integration, and some of the more sceptical parties have at times chosen to play down their Euroscepticism or even converted to pro-EU stances. Although their origins and association with particular interests may set the agrarians somewhat apart from other, more 'typical', families, the dynamics of their contestation of European integration is not necessarily peculiar. On the contrary, a model of party-based Euroscepticism is more robust if it can accommodate these parties, rather than dismiss them as exceptions. In the following sections it is argued that agrarian Euroscepticism is driven by causal mechanisms rooted in national party system and the strategic behaviour of the parties themselves.

3.2.1 The agrarian parties

The parties covered in this chapter share a common origin, rooted in the defence of agrarian interests of identity. Their roots are traced back to the territorial cleavages discussed by Lipset and Rokkan (1967*b*)—the centre–periphery cleavages derived from the 'national revolution' and the rural–urban cleavages that arose during the industrial revolution—rather than the Church–state or worker–owner cleavages that also grew out of the two respective 'revolutions'. Yet, whether they constitute a single 'party family' or 'ideological group' in von Beyme's (1985) terms has been disputed. Although he treats them as a separate family (von Beyme 1985: 23, 112–15), they are also discussed in the context of the liberal family (1985: 45). In their discussion of parties and Euroscepticism, Marks and Wilson (2000) subsume them under the liberal classification. Hix and Lord (1997: 33) group them under the heading 'liberals', albeit with the caveat that liberal parties with agrarian roots 'were' a separate coherent party family and have now become 'agrarian liberals' that do not share other liberal parties' views about reforms of the Common Agricultural Policy (CAP). However, the focus on the long-term development of parties adopted here justifies taking a 'genetic approach' (Mair and Mudde 1998: 225) and considering the agrarians as a party family, with common historical origins as the defining criterion of membership.

Most of the West European parties, of which the successful ones are confined to the Nordic countries and Switzerland, have roots in liberal or radical opposition to a (centralizing) conservative administration. Hence their association with the liberal parties of the nineteenth century, out of which the Scandinavian parties grew. The Norwegian and Finnish parties both grew out of nationalist movements that operated before independence (in 1905 and 1917 respectively), but like the other Nordic parties they were primarily concerned with protection of farmers' interests, in contrast to the interwar peasant populist movements in most of Eastern Europe (Urwin 1980: 236–50). The Swiss party split off from the Radicals in 1920. As the social democrats redefined the 'left', and changed the main left–right dimension of competition to the contest between themselves and the conservative right, the agrarian parties carved out a niche by developing issue- and interest-oriented appeals targeting a specific—and, at the time, considerable—section of the electorate. This generally entailed competing on a territorial dimension that cut across the primary, socio-economic left–right dimension, with the agrarians often positioned between the socialist left and conservative right in socio-economic policy. The exception is Iceland, where the Progressive Party (Framsóknarflokkurinn, FSF), formed by the merger of two young farmers' parties in 1917, came to represent the main opposition to the conservative right and, in fact, nearly merged with the social democrats in 1956 (Kristinsson 2001).

Whereas the Scandinavian, Swiss, and Czechoslovak agrarian parties in the interwar era mobilized voters across the main left–right dimension, the Polish and Hungarian peasant parties helped define the main dimension of competition, either as part of, or in opposition to, Christian national governments. When they (re-)emerged after the fall of communism in the shape of 'historical' parties, the Polish Peasant Party (Polskie Stronnictwo Ludowe, PSL) and the Hungarian Smallholder Party (Független Kisgazda, Földmunkás és Polgári Párt, FKgP) played a similar role by aligning in various government coalitions with the post-communist centre-left in Poland and the national centre-right in Hungary in the 1990s. Nevertheless, the claim to represent the countryside and the economic interests of small-scale private farming proved to be as useful for these parties in securing a niche in post-communist politics as for their earlier Scandinavian counterparts, as the most rewarding positions on the centre-left and centre-right were quickly occupied by major catch-all parties.

Yet, the genetic approach takes the analysis only so far. Cleavages are *translated* into party politics, not simply or automatically reflected in political competition. This process not only requires translators but takes place in a broader competitive context (Sartori 1968). The evolution of agrarian parties therefore depends not only on their origins, but also on their strategies for continued political competition. Most have opted for strategies that entail retaining a close link to agrarian interests, while others have expanded their appeal to broader, cross-class, rural interests (Arter 2001*b*). However, the Swiss and Danish parties have moved so far towards populist and catch-all strategies respectively that it is perhaps difficult to describe them as agrarian except in term of their origins.

3.2.2 The agrarian parties and party strategy

Borrowing from the study of the firm and paraphrasing Porter (1980/1998: xxiv), party strategy may be defined as a broad formula for how a party is going to compete, a combination of what its ends should be, and by which means these should be pursued. If (drawing on Sartori 1976) political parties are defined as organizations that seek to propel candidates to elected office in pursuit of certain policy aims, they face four main sets of goals. In addition to survival as organizations and promotion of their own policy, parties pursue the strategic and tactical goals of winning votes and securing access to government office (Müller and Strom 1999). Developing party strategy is a matter of elaborating, prioritizing, and balancing these four goals. If the common factor for the agrarian parities is their genesis, their strategies have not all evolved in the same direction. Although most of the Nordic parties have struggled with the dilemma of whether to maintain focus on their agrarian constituency or seek to appeal to a broader electorate, the Danish and Swiss parties have resolved this by opting for radically different strategies. Most of the Nordic parties at one stage or another attempted to widen their appeal. The Hungarian party's prevarication and eventual split over questions related to leadership and strategy caused its demise in 2002, and the Polish Peasant Party's decision to ally with the formerly communist Democratic Left Alliance has rendered it vulnerable to the more radical farmers' Self-Defence (Samoobrona) party.

Although broad trends in party organization, electoral competition, and policy positions are sometimes observed in Europe, this should not obscure that fact that distinct types of party strategy emerge and persist (Katz and Mair 1995, 2002; Wolinetz 2002). The extent to which parties adapt and change depends on their organization and preferences, and on how they interpret challenges. By and large, the agrarian parties have proven more immune to contagion from their competitors than other families of parties. Whereas most of the large centre-right and centre-left parties dynamically adapted to their competitors' organizational and strategic changes (Duverger 1954; Kirchheimer 1966; Epstein 1967), most agrarian parties have found the catch-all model difficult to imitate even when they tried. As the agrarian sector shrank, the Norwegian, the Swedish, and the Finnish agrarian parties all changed their name to 'Centre' between 1957 and 1965, in an effort to widen their electoral bases. But this effort met with only moderate success in Norway and Sweden (Arter 2001*b*). Having started from a much stronger position, the Finnish party came closer to the catch-all model, but ended up as what Arter (1999) has labelled 'both-and parties', that is, a party that attempts to combine an interest-based appeal to a specific group with a catch-all appeal within a given geographical area. Thus, even if a party adopts some of the organizational features or tactics of the catch-all or cartel models

(Katz and Mair 1995), involving a greater reliance on full-time party officials, public funding, and the media rather than on its membership, its
overall strategy does not necessarily change. The very survival of the agrarian parties depended on their differentiation from both social democrats
and conservatives, and thus on the representation of a distinct constituency defined in terms of identity and economic interest (Arter 1979;
Rokkan and Urwin 1982, 1983).

The main exception to this trend has been the Danish agrarian Liberal Party (Venstre) which, having gravitated towards economic liberalism through its history, eventually adopted a position on the right on
the socio-economic policy dimension and consequently also catch-all-like
features (Bille 1994; Knudsen and Rothstein 1994; Gilljam and Oscarsson
1996). Rather than making a clear-cut decision on the adoption of a
catch-all strategy, Iceland's more clientelistic Progressive Party gradually
evolved into a broader party as it expanded its pursuit of urban votes.
Kristinnson (1991, 2001) credits this to the Progressive Party's limited
institutionalization—a more elite-driven and flexible party organization
than its Norwegian and Swedish counterparts. The Swiss agrarian party
came close to a transformation from agrarian interest-based to catch-all
party, but also adopted elements of protest party strategy. Having merged
with the Democratic Party to form the Swiss People's Party (Schweizerische
Volkspartei, SVP) in 1971, it shifted towards a broader, more urban,
market-oriented appeal in response to a decline in votes, but retained its
defence of agricultural protection (Kerr 1987; Ladner 2001). This shift also
entailed strengthening its opposition to immigration and membership of
international organizations. Consequently, the party is now often considered a populist right-wing party or a party encroaching on the territory of
the extreme right (Helms 1997; Ladner 2001).

As for the agrarian parties in post-communist Hungary and Poland,
initially they were relatively successful in maintaining or reviving their
traditional electoral bases despite the fact that the social structure changed
radically during four decades of communism, late industrialization, and
urbanization. The regional patterns (if not overall levels) of the Hungarian
Smallholders' support in the early 1990s, for instance, were remarkably
similar to those of its predecessor (Körösényi 1992). Until its demise in the
wake of a series of particularly divisive internal conflicts, which caused it to
fall out of parliament in 2002, the Independent Smallholder Party claimed

the largest national organization and received a respectable share (ranging between 9 and 13 per cent) of the votes in post-communist elections. In Poland, where the country's agricultural sector had escaped the fate of collectivization and nationalization, the traditional farming constituency remained robust, with around 20 per cent of the labour force recorded as being employed in agriculture in the 1990s. For the votes of this sizable segment of the electorate the Polish Peasant Party increasingly came to face competition from Self-Defence, founded in the early 1990s as a farmers' union and later incorporated as a political party, renowned for its radicalism in supporting (and organizing) farmers' protest against the government of the day. Despite the Peasant Party's historical past, large membership and greater institutionalization (Szczerbiak 1999, 2001*b*), by the 2001 elections, Self-Defence overtook it in popularity and became the third largest force in the *Sejm*, the more powerful lower house of the Polish Parliament.

Parties face a fundamental choice whether to compete primarily along the left–right dimension, or to circumvent it. Most agrarian parties' electoral appeal entails at least a partial rejection of competition along the mainstream socio-economic dimension, although they have been obliged to align themselves along it to engage in coalition games. They are aligned to the main dimension of competition defined by the major catch-all parties through coalition-building and yet distinguished by constituency representation and their origins in territorial cleavages. It is through this prism that agrarian parties view the question of European integration, or at least the agrarian parties that pursue a 'territorial politics' strategy (Rokkan and Urwin 1983). Agrarian or rural interests provide a potential rallying point for the protection of local (and national) political power against central administration and a basis for the defence of national identity, often in a more populist form (Canovan 1981). Their origins thus provide a key to understanding the agrarians' predisposition to Euroscepticism.

3.2.3 Territorial politics, party strategy, and Euroscepticism

For most political parties, Euroscepticism—the elaboration of a platform opposed to participation in (aspects of) European integration—has been a deliberate strategic choice. For parties that seek to play down ideology, maximize votes, and compete close to the centre on the socio-economic left–right dimension, as is largely the case for the Danish Liberal party principled opposition to European integration—Hard Euroscepticism— is rarely an attractive option. This is partly because Hard Euroscepticism is associated with a considerable degree of ideological commitment, but also because parties that win government power participate in EU policymaking and therefore tend to defend the deals they negotiate on the European level (Hix and Lord 1996). Parties that prioritize interest representation (territorial politics in the case of many agrarian parties) or develop strategies for political competition based on protest against the consensus (the SVP is the agrarian case) may find it easier to contest European integration. Protest at the domestic and EU level can be mutually reinforcing (Taggart 1998). The two long-term goals related to party organization and policy preferences thus produce a tendency towards agrarian Euroscepticism under certain conditions.

However, these more principled stances on European integration may be moderated by the more immediate concerns of maximizing votes and winning office. First, agrarian parties' identity and their relationships with their domestic competitors affect their opportunities and incentives for competing on European questions. Secondly, their propensity to contest European integration depends on their attitudes to both economic (market) integration and the more value- and identity-related aspects of political integration that have implications for national identity and sovereignty (Marks and Wilson 2000: 436). Thirdly, the continuing development of vote-seeking strategy in the context of shifting public opinion influences whether any propensity towards Euroscepticism a party might harbour is translated into practical electoral appeal. Fourthly, in multiparty parliamentary systems, the parties may face short-term incentives to adopt or modify a Eurosceptic stance in terms of office-related payoffs.

The parties' present stances on European integration are set out in Table 3.1. The Danish Liberal and the Swiss People's Party have been identified as parties that have departed considerably from the agrarian territorial politics strategy. It is therefore not surprising to find that the Danish party is the most pro-EU party, in line with the suggestion that catch-all parties that often take part in governing coalitions tend not to be Eurosceptic (Sitter 2001). The Swiss People's Party's new populist strategy (opposition at the flanks of the party system) yields similarly

Table 3.1. Agrarian parties, recent election results, and stance on European integration

Name	Vote at last elections (%)	Range of vote since 1990 (%)	Stance on European integration
Denmark's Liberal Party (*Venstre*)	2001: 31.3	15.8–31.3	Pro-EU
Sweden's Centre Party (C)	2002: 6.1	5.1–8.5	Pro-EU, anti-EMU
Norway's Centre Party (Sp)	2001: 5.6	5.6–16.8	Hard Eurosceptic
Finland's Centre (KESK)	1999: 22.5	19.9–24.9	Mixed, Soft Eurosceptic
Iceland's Progressive Party (FSF)	1999: 18.4	18.4–23.3	Mixed, Soft Eurosceptic, pro-EU
The Swiss People's Party (SVP)	1999: 22.5	11.9–22.6	Hard Eurosceptic
Hungary's Independent Smallholder Party (FKGP)	2002: 0.8	0.8–13.2	Soft Eurosceptic
The Polish Peasant Party (PSL)	2001: 9.0	7.3–15.4	Soft Eurosceptic
Poland's Self-Defence (*Samoobrona*)	2001: 10.2	0.1–10.2	Hard Eurosceptic

Source: National electoral commissions; party programmes.

unsurprising Euroscepticism (Taggart 1995, 1998). The remaining parties however retained much of their original agrarian characteristics and therefore represent a different set of cases. The subsequent sections focus primarily on these. They investigate the extent to which they conform to an ideal-type strategy of representing agrarian interests, the evolution of their contestation of European integration, and the dynamics of change. There are also references to the two parties that have moved furthest from the interest-based strategy and come to bear the closest resemblance to the catch-all model.

3.3 POLICY, IDENTITY, AND EUROPEAN INTEGRATION: PROTECTIONISM, POPULISM, OR PARTICIPATION?

The starting point has been that most agrarian parties have not conformed to the main developments set out in the catch-all and cartel party models, at least not in terms of playing down partisan electoral appeal in favour of broad catch-all competition. Although several of the parties have attempted to expand their electoral bases from time to time, most have

Table 3.2. Agrarian party policy preferences and orientations by Type

Agrarian or rural interests are seen to be…	The party's origin and identity draws it towards…	
	…accepting supranational governance	…emphasizing national and participatory democracy
…compatible with EU membership	Participation in European integration acceptable	Soft Euroscepticism based on populism
…incompatible with EU membership	Soft Euroscepticism based on protectionism	Hard Euroscepticism

proven reluctant to transcend their agrarian origins. Perhaps the central development among the Scandinavian parties has been their going part of the way 'from farmyard to city square' (Arter 2001*a*), assuming something akin to a catch-all stance within a territorially defined constituency. To this extent they have become parties that represent rural interests, rather than just farmers' interests, but remain 'territorial' parties nonetheless. Most of today's agrarian parties of Western and Central Europe combine agrarian interest (protectionism) with a focus on rural or local interests, often defined in opposition to the national or European capital city and central government (populism). If these two concerns reinforce scepticism towards European integration it may well be expressed as absolute or principled (Hard) opposition, whereas if one of the two bases for questioning participation in European integration is weaker, more contingent (Soft) Euroscepticism is expected (Table 3.2).

3.3.1 The populist bases of agrarian Euroscepticism: Local politics, participatory democracy, and nationalism

Historically, politically driven territorial politics combined opposition to administrative centralization with the defence of local interest or values, defined as distinct from those of the centre. Euroscepticism therefore reflects, at least in part, the extent to which European integration is perceived as a threat to local autonomy and/or national sovereignty. Despite the European Commission's focus on regional government (which has earned it the support of most minority ethnic parties in the EU; Ray 1999), 'Brussels' is often seen as an extension of 'distant government' or the 'alien centre' even further removed from rural interests than the national central administration. Moreover, given the tendency to portray the countryside as the source of 'authentic' national identity in contrast to the cosmopolitan (and more multi-ethnic) cities, some agrarian parties are prone to define membership of the nation in ethnic (based on identity/culture) rather than civic (based on citizenship) terms (Smith 1986). As attention shifts to Brussels, any perception of a cosmopolitan threat to the nation—defined in ethnocultural terms—is likely to be multiplied if the EU is considered as a potential 'superstate'. Thus, the extent to which the politics of identity constitutes a basis for Euroscepticism in agrarian parties depends largely on how they interpret the European integration project.

Perhaps the clearest example is the Norwegian case, with Oslo associated with foreign rule during the 1814–1905 union with Sweden. This was invoked in the 1972 and 1994 referendums on EEC and EU membership, with the pro-EU camps derided as 'unionists'. Hence the 'It's far to Oslo but further to Brussels' slogan sported by Norwegian 'no' campaigners in 1972 (Madsen 2001). The Centre Party calls for 'open all-European cooperation without walls or unions' (*Senterpartiets Prinsipprogram* 1995). In this respect, the rhetoric of the Polish Peasant Party, as well as of Self-Defence, was remarkably similar to that of the Norwegian Centre Party, commonly drawing a parallel between the EU and historical forced unions as symbols of foreign domination. As the Polish Peasant Party leader put it, 'as in the past we [the PSL] did not race to be first with declarations of loyalty to Moscow, so too today and in the future, we do not intend to race against anybody with the same declarations to Brussels' (BBC International Reports, 7 November 1999). Along a similar vein the Swiss People's Party advocated bilateral relations with the EU, denouncing the 'bureaucratic and centralized' organization as a threat to Swiss 'independence and distinctiveness' (SVP *Parteiprogramm* 1999–2003).

Elsewhere in Western Europe, agrarian parties have focused less on the threats from a centralizing European bureaucracy, although this point has been invoked in more general terms. The question of ceding sovereignty to the EU looms large in the Norwegian and Swiss debates, where the agrarian parties oppose EU membership, but has come to play almost the reverse role in Iceland. The recent Icelandic debate has seen sovereignty invoked as a motive *for* EU membership, even if the Progressive Party's more Eurosceptic conservative coalition partner (Independence Party) proscribed an EU membership debate before the 2003 election. Hinting at his support for EU membership, Progressive Party leader and Foreign Minister Asgrimsson suggested that the European Economic Area constituted a greater problem for Iceland in terms of sovereignty than full EU membership would do (Asgrimsson 2002*b*).

The centrist ideology of Finland's Centre Party builds on values related to agrarianism and nationalism, including suspicion of capitalism and urban bureaucracy, that could be construed as a solid basis for opposition to European integration (Mylly 1984). However, until the end of the cold war, EU membership was considered incompatible with neutrality in both Finland and Sweden, and the question was thus less salient than in Norway. The Swedish agrarian Centre Party adopted a moderate strategy, seeking to represent the main opposition to the Social Democrats and circumventing a debate on Europe by accepting Social Democrat Prime Minister Erlander's 1961 doctrine that EU membership would be incompatible with Swedish neutrality. In the post-cold war period, the Finnish debate, in comparison with the primarily value- and identity-related debates in Norway or Sweden, focused more on economic costs and benefits, partly due to the importance of the security question related to neighbouring Russia (Svåsand and Lindström 1996; Tiilikainen 1996). The Danish (agrarian) Liberals staked out a centre-right liberal position in defence of agrarian interests associated with bourgeois values and free trade as part of the central 'cartel' of governing parties, thereby eschewing a focus on identity.

In the Central and East European cases, the Polish Peasant Party and Self-Defence as well as the Hungarian Independent Smallholder Party emphasized the countryside and farming communities as the last defence of national values, a traditional Polish/Hungarian way of life, and Christian morality, as exemplified by the Smallholders' motto 'God, Fatherland, Family' (Körösényi 1999: 44–5; Szczerbiak 1999: 1408–9). While both Polish parties used a rhetoric associating 'Brussels' with foreign domination and centralization and the Hungarian Smallholder Party warned against the risk of weakening national identity due to premature accession in the mid-1990s (FKgP *Hazánk holnap* 1995), the Polish Peasant Party and its Hungarian counterpart remained committed to the general objective of EU accession (Kopecky and Mudde 2002). Self-Defence, in contrast, qualified as a Hard Eurosceptic party (Taggart and Szczerbiak 2001*a*). Its opposition to Europe was, however, grounded primarily in economic arguments and the objective of undercutting the electoral base of the Peasant Party by the uncompromising representation of farming interests.

3.3.2 The protectionist bases of agrarian Euroscepticism: Economic interest

Economic interest is perhaps a less problematic factor with regard to the potential for Euroscepticism, although, given the prospects for reform and the uncertainties involved in negotiating both past and current enlargements (including side payments such as regional funds), a long-term cost–benefit assessment of the impact of EU membership can be difficult. In addition to the CAP—the single largest item of the community budget, with direct consequences for farmers' livelihoods—EU single market rules on competition from foreign goods (or investment) and on limiting permitted forms of subsidies and regional policy have a considerable impact on the agrarian sector. Given the salience of these questions for the agrarians' core voters, and consequently their potential value in electoral competition, there are strong incentives for the agrarian parties to claim ownership of the EU issue.

Indeed, this has been the case in the Scandinavian enlargement debates (Barnes 1996) as well as in the post-communist applicant countries. The Norwegian, Swiss, and Finnish centre parties and their electorates by and large concluded that EU membership was against their economic interests, unambiguously in the Norwegian and Swiss cases (where the parties reject even European Economic Area membership) and more controversially in the Finnish case. In Norway, opposition to the EU Common Fisheries Policy (CFP) exacerbated the problem, whereas a negotiated solution to Arctic agriculture in Finland allowed the Centre Party's leadership to advocate, and secure, a position in favour of EU membership, even if the party could not 'deliver' its followers in the referendum. Again the Danish case is the exact reverse, with Danish agrarian interest and the Liberal Party focusing more on the benefits of access to the European market than the danger of foreign competition. The conversion of the Swedish Centre Party in the 1990s was supported by the Federation of Swedish Farmers (Lantbrukarnas Riksförbund, LRF). The LRF identified the economic benefits of EU membership before the party leadership did and emerged as a driving force in the party's change of policy, which however remained a matter of debate well into the 1990s (Ryden 2000). Although Icelandic opposition to EU membership has long rested on the problems of the CFP, the country's and the Progressive Party's recent interest in EU membership likewise stems partly from reassessment of the CAP and CFP and partly the potential consequences of EU enlargement on its fisheries products' access to East European markets (Asgrimsson 2002*a*).

In East Central Europe, the question of land ownership has been added to, and at times has overshadowed, economic intervention and protection. The Polish and Hungarian agrarian parties generally advocate high levels of state intervention in the economy, with the provision of extensive social services, increasing direct subsidies to farmers and protecting local producers from international competition—objectives that EU membership clearly casts doubts upon. Unsurprisingly, the Peasant Party has been less than optimistic about the likely impact of accession on the large and uncompetitive Polish agricultural sector. It was renowned for demanding tough bargaining with Brussels during the accession negotiations (e.g. Szczerbiak 2001*a*: 10). Both, the Polish Peasants and the Hungarian National Party insisted that the transition period proposed by the Commission before agricultural producers in these countries can receive subsidies equal to those going to producers within the EU should be scrapped or significantly shortened.

This view was shared by Self-Defence. However, while the two former parties remained committed to EU membership in principle, the latter had a record of going further, not only in rhetoric but also action: the union and its leader, Andrzej Lepper, were renowned for extensive road blockades, erected in 1999 to press for government measures protecting Polish agricultural producers from European competition. In the Hungarian case, the issue of landownership (creating the legal possibility for EU citizens to buy land in Hungary following a transition period after accession) was more salient. The leadership of the divided Smallholder Party rejected 'selling out the motherland [to foreigners]' and pledged in its 2002 election manifesto to renegotiate the deal with the EU should they

Table 3.3. Agrarian party policy preferences and orientations by Case

For agrarian interests the impact of EU membership is seen as/expected to be...	The party's origin and identity draws it towards...	
	...not seeing the EU as a threat	...seeing the EU as a threat
...positive or neutral	Denmark's Liberal Party Hungary's Independent Smallholder Party Iceland's Progressive Party as of 2002 Polish Peasant Party Sweden's Centre after 1990	Sweden's Centre before 1989
...negative	Finland's Centre Iceland's Progressive Party before 2002	Norway's Centre Party Swiss People's Party Poland's Self-Defence

Source: Party documents.

be part of the new government (FKgP 2002). Altogether, the attitudes of the agrarians in Central and Eastern Europe as well as in Scandinavia were shaped by the parties' genesis in social cleavages and perceptions of the impact of EU membership/European integration on their constituencies' livelihoods (Table 3.3).

3.4 ELECTORAL COMPETITION, COALITION POLITICS, AND EUROPEAN INTEGRATION: CONTESTATION OR CONFORMITY?

The extent to which parties' policy preferences and orientations are translated into actual opposition to participation in European integration also depends on the two remaining goals—the quest for votes and access to executive office. Even if a party's identity or policy concerns predispose it towards Euroscepticism, electoral competition and collation games may provide incentives for it to avoid contesting European integration and to conform to the cross-party consensus if such a thing exists. In both cases, the parties' positions relative to their competitors on the European question and their relative position in the party system with respect to other matters influence these incentives.

As far as electoral competition is concerned, the basic strategic choice that agrarian parties face is between the logic of interest representation and catch-all competition, although the Swiss People's Party has demonstrated that agrarian parties may also opt for new populist competition at the flanks of the party system. Kirchheimer (1966: 187–8) himself suggested that transformation towards a catch-all appeal might not be an option for agrarian parties, or indeed single-issue or protest parties. Yet, although focus on a delineated section of the electorate might prompt a party to adopt its target voters' view on the EU, and therefore contest European integration if its voters are Eurosceptic, it might also face incentives to conform if there is a broader pro-EU consensus among other parties and a majority of the electorate. Electoral incentives to contest European integration therefore depend on both public opinion among the party's target electorate and the extent to which other parties have crowded out the Eurosceptic space. While some centre-left or centre-right parties use 'Soft' Eurosceptic rhetoric at times, and thereby temporarily reduce the agrarians' incentives to play on anti-EU sentiments, these parties typically remain committed to the European project (Taggart 1998). However, in certain cases an agrarian party's Euroscepticism may also be due precisely to a catch-all strategy, mirroring its main opponent's foreign policy. This was the case with the Swedish Centre Party adopting the Social Democrats' position against European integration in the 1960s (until both parties changed their stance in the early 1990s).

The second factor that may drive an agrarian party towards conformity rather than contestation is its quest to participate in governing coalitions. If the most likely and credible partners are Eurosceptic and/or the party has distanced itself from pro-EU allies (Norway) or they are prepared to ignore the question (Switzerland), Euroscepticism need not disqualify the party from office. However, faced with pro-EU partners, the logic of coalition politics is likely to provide a disincentive for Euroscepticism, as has been demonstrated most clearly by the Finnish Centre. Iceland's Progressive Party has been almost in the reverse position, unable to get the question of EU membership on the agenda due to its coalition partner's more Eurosceptic stance. Moreover, executive office not only affects parties through their efforts to gain it, but also through the tasks they are required to perform in government. Governing parties in member states participate in negotiating EU compromises, and governments in applicant

Table 3.4. Agrarian party policy electoral and coalition incentives (if the consensus/majority favours EU membership): in Principle

Incentives linked to coalition government	Incentives linked to the pursuit of votes	
	Conformity	Contestation
Conformity	Abandon Euroscepticism	Soften Euroscepticism
Contestation	Soften Euroscepticism	Harden Euroscepticism

countries continuously have to demonstrate a high level of commitment to the integration project as a whole. Moving into government therefore implies incentives to tone down or abandon Euroscepticism, while parties in opposition are freer to voice their reservations about EU membership or its terms (see Table 3.4).

3.4.1 Electoral competition and the European question

Apart from the obvious case of the Danish Liberals, who have little to gain by invoking the EU issue in electoral appeals (Aylott 1999), the Swedish Centre Party, the Icelandic Progressives, and Hungary's Smallholders face electorates that do not provide significant incentives for adopting or maintaining Eurosceptic appeals. The Swedish Centre Party moved towards a catch-all strategy in the 1960s, though this proved temporary and it was overtaken by the Moderates as the main non-socialist party in 1979 (Pierre and Widfeld 1994; Arter 1999). Moreover, as had long been the case in Norway, opposition to European integration was to some extent captured by the extreme left, with whom the centre parties did not wish to be associated. The Swedish Centre Party has focused primarily on competition with the Social Democrats, and it eventually also recommended a 'yes' vote in the 1994 referendum (Widfeld 1996). However, unlike the Social Democrat leadership, the party remains opposed to joining Economic and Monetary Union (EMU), a degree of scepticism that is reflected in the evenly divided Swedish electorate and the narrow anti-EMU majority among the party's supporters. Icelandic opinion polls indicate that the long-divided electorate is shifting from a recent plurality in favour or

EU membership towards a majority, although this has not affected party support.

The Norwegian Centre Party draws on what Rokkan (1966: 74) once described as 'the heritage of *territorial and cultural opposition* to the governing officials and the allied urban elites of academics, merchants, and industrialists'. Its opposition to European integration is among its 'heart issues', based on both the economic and non-economic dimensions of territorial politics, and echoed by both the rank-and-file members and its voters (Saglie 2000; Heidar and Saglie 2002). This reflects a comparatively high level of agrarian protection and regional policy subsidies in Norway. In a party system dominated by left–right competition between the pro-EU Conservative and Labour parties, the Centre Party has joined the Christian People's Party and the Liberals, in attempting to build a centre alternative. The electoral appeal of this centre alternative rests partly on its territorial appeal, of which Euroscepticism has become an integral part, combining the Centre Party's defence of regional policy and agriculture with the strongholds of the Liberals and the Christian People's Party in the south-western regions and among the pietist Christian counterculture (Nelsen 1993; Madeley 1994). The whaler Steinar Bastesen's new Coastal Party, which focuses on fisheries and gained one parliamentary seat in 1997 and two in 2001, has taken an even more uncompromising anti-EU stance than the Centre Party (Kystpartiet 2001).

The Centre Party of Finland decided to support EU membership in the 1994 referendum, despite strong opposition from party members and primary industry (Raunio 1999). This had much to do with its leader being prime minister at the time (see below), but also reflected the party leadership's propensity to override sector interests in favour of broader concerns, such as the prospects for enhanced security under the EU's Common Foreign and Security Policy (CFSP). Moreover, the relatively favourable outcome for the pro-EU camp had a lot to do with the EU's agricultural policy, which included derogations and a compromise that created a new structural policy objective related to sparsely populated regions (Miles 1994). Nevertheless, the party's supporters featured the lowest share of pro-EU voters in the decade up to the 1994 referendum, except for those supporting hard left parties (Tiilikainen 1996). The Centre Party has therefore faced pressure to return to a Eurosceptic stance, and has adopted a position on European integration that, with membership secured, now resists further supranational integration (KESK *Politiskt ställningstagande*, 18 June 2000).

Outside Scandinavia, the Swiss People's Party is the only agrarian party of considerable size in Western Europe. However, although its rightwards move towards a catch-all, or even populist, strategy has yielded considerable electoral gains in the 1990s, this has not provided any incentives for it to moderate its Euroscepticism. The party is comparable to the Norwegian Centre Party in its Euroscepticism, arguing that the cost of EU membership, cast in terms of both sovereignty and economic policy (including agriculture), exceed its potential benefits (SVP, *Parteiprogramm*, 1999–2003). Both parties have sought, at times with considerable success, to mobilize voters and extend their appeal based on opposition to European integration.

The allure of CAP can reasonably be expected to be stronger for the core electoral constituencies of the Central and East European agrarian parties than for the highly subsidized Norwegian farmers. However, an economic cost–benefit analysis of the expected effects of EU accession is not necessarily positive for the Peasant and Smallholder parties' countryside supporters. Public opinion data indicated that (Hard) Euroscepticism went down well with the party's supporters, most of whom intended to vote against Poland's membership of the EU in the future referendum (CBOS September 2000 in Szczerbiak 2001*a*: 13). This clearly provided compelling reasons for the Peasant Party to slow down accession or insist on (possibly unrealistic) conditions for entry. However, the party faced competition for the Eurosceptic vote from Solidarity Electoral Action (Akcja Wyborcza SolidarnoIJæ, AWS, a coalition of parties, in government in 1997–2001), especially the Christian National Union, until 2001, and, more importantly, from Self-Defence as well as several smaller parties in the *Sejm* since the 2001 elections. Moreover, while the proportion of Eurosceptics was not negligible in the Polish electorate at large in the late 1990s, the majority remained pro-EU (European Commission 2001*a*). Given the Peasant Party's attempts to broaden its electoral base beyond its core constituency, this weakened incentives for Hard Euroscepticism (Szczerbiak 2001*a*: 14). Eventually, the party opted for an uneasy combination: a Soft Eurosceptic rhetoric for the benefit of its traditional supporters while formally supporting Poland's membership of the EU so as not to alienate other potential voters (and coalition partners).

In Hungary, overall levels of public support for the EU were substantially higher than in Poland (European Commission 2001*a*). For much of the 1990s, the Smallholder Party was less vocal than its Polish counterpart about the potential risks associated with EU accession for its constituents, keeping a relatively low profile on questions of foreign policy in general. This was partly due, at least in the late 1990s, to the party's participation in the government coalition negotiating the terms of accession with the EU. However, another reason may have been the fact that its major, catch-all competitor, and between 1998 and 2002 coalition partner, the centre-right Fidesz-MPP emphasized the defence of the national interest vis-à-vis Brussels in its own 1998 election campaign, thereby pre-empting a similar move by the Smallholders. Electoral incentives to adopt a radical Eurosceptic stance in any case remained relatively weak for the Hungarian party, although its strategy for mobilizing its remaining voters for the 2002 elections included rejecting the landownership deal with the EU.

3.4.2 Coalition games and the European question

The Swedish and Danish cases are relatively straightforward. Neither party faces incentives by way of coalition politics to depart from the pro-EU agenda. Not only are the two parties now generally pro-EU in most respects, the Centre Party having settled its internal debate on this issue by 2000, but their main competitors are also pro-EU. Any tendencies towards Euroscepticism that might emerge stand to be moderated by the logic of coalition politics. This has, of course, not prevented the Centre Party from maintaining opposition to Swedish membership of EMU. Although this issue continues to divide the non-socialist parties, it has, to some extent, been removed from coalition politics by the decision to settle the issue in a referendum.

At the other end of the spectrum, the Swiss and Norwegian cases illustrate Eurosceptic parties' resistance to influence from coalition partners.

In the Norwegian case, the Centre Party's reluctance to modify its opposition to European integration has contributed to the break-up of three governments, including the two centre-right coalitions that collapsed in the run-up to the EU applications (in 1971 and in 1990), and prevented further non-socialist cooperation (Madeley 1998). More recently the party focuses its efforts on building fully-fledged Eurosceptic coalitions, although its centrist partners are more open to coalitions with the pro-EU Conservatives. Its minority coalition with two other Eurosceptic centre parties—the Christian People's Party and Liberals—collapsed after more than two-and-a-half years of struggling to push through its agenda in 2000. Under the Swiss consociational 'magic formula' that assigns the party one of seven seats in the permanent four-party coalition, the People's Party faces few incentives to modify its Euroscepticism. If anything, its recent growth in the polls has raised the issue of amending the formula (Ladner 2001).

The Finnish agrarians' case in the 1990s is more interesting in as much as the party featured a pro-EU leadership facing a Eurosceptic electorate and an almost evenly divided parliamentary party. Prime Minister and Centre Party leader Aho pushed a pro-EU membership position through a highly divided party, threatening to resign from both posts and securing a two-thirds majority in favour at the party's 1994 conference (Raunio 1999). This illustrated both the pressure on the leadership of a governing party to maintain a credible coalition, and the powers of persuasion associated with the premiership generally and Aho's personal leadership specifically (Johansson and Raunio 2001). However, the party failed to deliver its voters in the October 1994 referendum, when several senior party figures campaigned against membership with barely a third of them following the leadership's recommendation. More recently, the party has returned to a Soft Eurosceptic stance.

In other countries such as Poland, where there appears to be considerable electoral potential in agrarian Euroscepticism, the need to be acceptable to future coalition partners clearly counterbalanced these incentives (Szczerbiak 2001a: 14). Despite the conflict-ridden relationship between the agrarians and the Democratic Left Alliance during the 1993–7 government, and the Peasant Party's efforts to position itself between its former coalition partner and the (ideologically perhaps not too dissimilar)

Solidarity Electoral Action in 1997, the party again entered into a coalition with the pro-EU former communists following the 2001 elections (which it later quit, however). The case of Self-Defence also points to the importance of the moderating impact of coalition politics, except in reverse. The farmer union's populism and strongly anti-EU stance paralleled its lack of coalition potential, as its exclusion from the 2001 coalition, and initial proposition to support it externally, indicated (Radio Free Europe/ Radio Liberty Newsline, 4 October 2001). Self-Defence was, and thus continues to be, free to voice and reinforce its constituents' Eurosceptic sentiments.

The quest for office had a strong impact on the tactical behaviour of Hungary's Smallholder Party in the 1990s, especially as the issue of European integration was less salient in Hungarian electoral politics. Shifts in the Smallholders' rhetoric on Europe, detectable particularly prior to the 1998 elections, need to be seen as part of their efforts to increase the party's coalition potential by projecting a more mainstream image. It was only following a series of highly divisive internal conflicts, eventually splitting FKgP in 2001, and increasing tensions with Fidesz-MPP within the government that the moderating effects of coalition politics finally waned—hence, the 'The motherland is not for sale' slogan in the run-up to the 2002 elections. The post-communist cases as well as those in Scandinavia thus clearly attest to the modifying impact of office-seeking and policy-adaptation in coalition-building (or its absence; Table 3.5).

Table 3.5. Agrarian party policy electoral and coalition incentives (if the consensus/majority favours EU membership): in Practice

Incentives linked to coalition government	Incentives linked to the pursuit of votes	
	Conformity	Contestation
Conformity	Denmark's Liberal Party Sweden's Centre Hungary's Independent Smallholder Party until 2001	Finland's Centre Polish Peasant Party
Contestation	Iceland's Progressive Party Hungary's Independent Smallholder Party (2001–)	Norway's Centre Swiss People's Party Poland's Self-Defence

Source: Author's own estimates.

3.5 CONCLUSIONS: PROTECTIONISM, POPULISM, OR PARTICIPATION?

This analysis of agrarian parties' contestation of European integration in eight countries—some of which are EU members states, some of which are now joining the EU, and some of which have opted for weaker links with the EU—suggests that political parties are only likely to adopt a radical Eurosceptic stance if European integration is seen to conflict with their ideology and identity, threatens the interests of their target electorate, and at the same time the pressures of coalition politics do not outweigh the incentives to mobilize their supporters' discontent with, or opposition to, European integration. In other words, the expression of Euroscepticism depends on a party's identity, policy preferences, pursuit of votes and coalition games, or, in short, party strategy. It is these trade-offs between long-term developments and short-term issue appeals, together with coalition politics, that account for the lack of full congruence between parties' assessment of European integration (Table 3.3) and patterns of Euroscepticism (Table 3.5). While values and historical predispositions remain an important element in explaining and predicting agrarian parties' stance on European integration, Hard and Soft Euroscepticism is primarily a function of parties' strategies in vote- and office-seeking.

This dynamic approach to Euroscepticism provides a framework for analysis of parties' shifts between moderation and radical opposition to European integration which is applicable beyond the agrarian party family. Agrarian party-based Euroscepticism has been linked to a particular form of strategy, one that focuses on the representation of the interests of a clearly delineated segment of the electorate, whether agrarian or rural. A similar analysis might be applied to other parties that focus on single issues or interests, from green parties to pietist religious or minority ethnic parties, though of course not necessarily with the same outcome. By extension, this model suggests that catch-all parties are generally likely to be less prone to Hard Euroscepticism in as much as they play down ideology and interest representation, except in cases where their economic policy jars with that of the EU or other factors such as neutrality in the cold war proscribed EU membership. New populist parties on the flanks of their party systems may not have the same issue concerns as agrarian parties, but their roots in protest and limited exposure to coalition politics might make them incline towards Euroscepticism. The central point for the agrarian parties is that whether they feature protectionist or populist or a mixed bases for scepticism towards European integration, or have little reason to oppose it, the extent to which they turn the European question into a contested issue—or even advocate participation in European integration—depends on party strategy. And there is little reason to suspect that this is unique to agrarian parties.

NOTE

1. See also Szczerbiak and Taggart (2000) and Taggart and Szczerbiak (2001*a*).

4

European Party Cooperation and Post-Communist Politics: Euroscepticism in Transnational Perspective

Geoffrey Pridham

4.1 INTRODUCTION

Much literature on Europeanization trends has tended to focus primarily on policy redirection and to a lesser degree on institutional adaptation with some vague attention to social and cultural matters. Political aspects of this now undeniable pattern have been little explored; and, that goes also for the study of political parties and European integration with some exceptions (Gaffney 1996). But growing evidence of the politicization of European Union (EU) affairs makes this deficiency ever more serious, especially as it relates to legitimacy problems of the EU system as demonstrated in referendums held over the past decade.

Predictably, attention to these problems has concentrated on EU member states (Goetz and Hix 2000). However, it is a fair assumption that politicization effects are likely to increase in accession countries with advances in negotiations and approach to EU entry. This is because of the sharper awareness of real policy impacts, negative or positive, and because politicians make this eventuality highly visible through their competitive emphasis on accession deadlines.

Such politicization effects of European integration are not entirely new; they were also evident during previous accession waves. What is new is the degree or intensity of these effects, reflecting the greater political embrace of the EU, its widening and deepening policy concerns, the now regular question of institutional reform, and, last but not least, the immense administrative, economic, and political burdens facing candidate countries. However, radical change invariably produces countermovements and reactions. Euroscepticism has long existed in all but name, previously being typed—more accurately perhaps—as anti-Europeanism. But, it follows from the above that its potential was accordingly greater with the 2004 Eastern enlargement and that its expression was more intense. Growing concern about the EU's 'democratic deficit'—indeed, public awareness of this—created even more potential for disaffection or dissension over the 'European construction'. Furthermore, the perception in post-communist applicant states that they were required to meet political conditions not always observed strictly by certain member states represented a special version of this deficit problem that could also have create the conditions for disaffection.

These general perspectives need to be addressed when evaluating Euroscepticism in accession countries in Central and Eastern Europe (CEE) in the period of the run-up to their accession. First, they indicate that the dynamic context of Europeanization effects and reactions to them are vital in understanding this phenomenon. Secondly, it is clear that political parties offer an obvious means for expressing different conflicting attitudes to patterns of Europeanization because of their basic role as intermediary actors between state and society. And, thirdly, it is important to explore two-way effects since this allows us to assess how Europeanization effects, and broad reactions to it actually affect, the chances of Eurosceptical forces. That also allows some scope for accommodating cross-national variation.

Transnational party cooperation (TPC), involving EU-wide and sometimes international party organizations, offers a pertinent mechanism for estimating this kind of dynamic within the context of the accession process. It provides a special channel for European-level activity by, but also for European pressure on, political parties from accession countries as well as member states. As an avowedly political form of transnational networking, TPC has the further advantage of exemplifying informal or non-official integration, thereby incorporating virtually all parties from these countries whether in government or opposition. This is relevant since many Eurosceptic parties remained outside national office, hence the official handling of membership negotiations.

This chapter will, in turn examine patterns of TPC and how these generally relate to Eurosceptical forces; discuss TPC activity with reference to domestic politics in accession countries; and then explore in greater detail case studies of Eurosceptic parties and their transnational activity from five candidate countries in CEE: Hungary, the Czech Republic, Slovakia, Bulgaria, and Romania.[1] The period under examination, it should be clear, ends in 2001–2. Questions guiding this evaluation include the following:

- How far did TPC have Europeanizing effects on national member parties, and how did it respond to reactions against these? Did such effects create any significant tensions within mainstream parties?

- Are the opportunity structures presented by TPC at variance or in harmony with domestic politics in accession countries?

- Did TPC tend to exclude Eurosceptical forces, and with what consequences, or did it admit them but with constraining effects?

- In what ways does TPC reflect the ongoing dynamics of the accession process?

4.2 TRANSNATIONAL PARTY COOPERATION: CONTEXTUALIZING EUROSCEPTICISM

TPC has traditionally taken various forms in organizing national parties of the same ideological tendency. Most visible are the transnational party groups which play a dominant role in the procedural life of the European Parliament (EP). These are related as parliamentary parties to their respective European party federations, the most important three being the Party of European Socialists (PES)—successor to the previous Confederation of Socialist and Social Democratic Parties of the EC, the centre-right European People's Party (EPP), and the European Liberal, Democrat, and Reform Party (ELDR). There are similar federations for some smaller forces like the European Federation of Green Parties (EFGP), but some minor groups in the EP do not possess such extra-parliamentary structures. In addition, the party internationals (socialist, liberal, and Christian democratic) have played a parallel and sometimes overlapping role in European transnational activity, although they have memberships from across the world.

Furthermore, not to be forgotten (and often omitted from analyses of TPC), there is a great deal of bilateral TPC often between neighbouring countries and also involving local or regional party branches from different countries, sometimes modelled on, and influenced by, the developed practice in Europe (including now also CEE) of town-twinning. This is always within the ideological framework of TPC organizations; and it extended to involve CEE countries. Bilateral TPC may either express a particularly close relationship between two parties—such as between some Swedish parties and their ideological counterparts in the Baltic states, especially Estonia—or it may express a combination of joint political and social activities, notably at the local level such as between ideologically linked party branches in Vienna and Bratislava. At the same time, there were some development which paralleled official organizations of country groupings. The Socialist International (SI), for instance, formed such a grouping for socialist parties in Central Europe based on the Visegrad states.

TPC activity, existing since the inception of European integration, has over time acquired more political influence. This is essentially as a dependent variable benefiting from the EP's enhanced constitutional status as a result of successive integration treaties. At the same time, the party federations autonomously asserted themselves such as in attempting to influence policy decisions at the European Council by holding prior summits of party leaders. But there have always been problems in defining a European party system within the complex institutional structure of the EU system. The EP, albeit now more of a recognizable parliamentary institution, is still one without an organic relationship with executive power in the EU which is, in any case, fragmented. Moreover, the member parties of the TPC organizations are embedded in national politics; while declining turnout in European elections detracts from the EP's legitimacy and reflects negatively on the mobilizing capacity of the European party organizations. Nevertheless, as a form of transnational networking, TPC has intensified and acquired ever more political influence not least as senior party politicians (some of them in government leadership) became involved and there emerged a European multiparty elite which was usually well linked with national party structures.

Thus, a distinction may be drawn between this activity's relatively weak constitutional position (formal integration) and its significant political networking capacity (informal integration). This distinction is all the more relevant for political parties and their elites from the 2004 accession

countries for they, coming from states not members of the EU and therefore not participating directly in its main institutions, hoped to gain entry
to TPC organizations in advance of actual accession. Accordingly, CEE
party elites tended to give TPC a somewhat greater importance than did
party elites from EU member states. It was in the latter half of the 1990s
onwards that TPC increasingly was regarded and utilized as a channel for
furthering accession chances as well as party-political networking. For CEE
party leaders and officials, TPC activity gave them relatively easy access—
on the basis of ideological fraternity—to top politicians in EU member
states, some of them holding influential positions in government. Even
political bonds established with opposition politicians were seen as useful
in the event of their elevation to national office, hence with some possible
effect on EU enlargement decisions. This networking facility of TPC for
higher political motives was also recognized by high-level government
officials who were more constrained by official procedures and appreciated
the freedom that party contacts allowed.

From this discussion of TPC, certain problems arise with respect to
Eurosceptical parties. Transnational activity acquired its own politicization trend, particularly during the decade leading up to accession. This
creates general pressures on parties that participate in TPC, all the more
as when applying for membership they are subject to strict conditionality
demands. These concern not only democratic conditions, relating to party
outlook and structures, but also a commitment to European integration.
The first, democratic conditionality, was much developed in the 1990s,
specifically with CEE parties in mind because of concern over Communist
inheritances (Pridham 1999a: 71–2). The conditionality over European
integration is regular and has existed from the early days of TPC. In
addition, there is the question of ideological matching or determining
whether candidate parties relate to and support the basic tenets of the
party federations. The procedure here usually involves examining party
programmes, meeting and vetting leading party figures, as well as drawing
on other evidence like declarations of party leaders as well as confidential
reports.

Taken together, these three conditions represent a considerable onus on
applicant parties to prove themselves. Eurosceptical parties, certainly hard-
line ones, are thus presented with a strategic dilemma: Whether to apply

and participate and with what consequences? Furthermore, the extended accession process placed such parties under a continuing and mounting pressure, especially if negotiations for membership looked like succeeding. They faced the question of whether to opt out, true to a purist version of their Euroscepticism, or whether to either succumb to integration pressures and make the best of the situation, or, alternatively, seek to mobilize political support towards their cause? This dilemma shows an obvious link not only between parties' positions on TPC activity and their general approach to European integration, but it also points to domestic conditions, especially public support for EU accession. The discussion therefore proceeds by considering further the kinds of TPC pressures encountered by Eurosceptical parties in post-Communist countries, and then the broad relationship between TPC organizations and domestic contexts in accession countries in the light of Europeanization pressures in the run-up to accession.

4.3 TRANSNATIONAL PARTY COOPERATION, EUROSCEPTICISM, AND THE DOMESTIC POLITICS OF ENLARGEMENT IN CENTRAL AND EASTERN EUROPE

Firstly, there is the conventional left–right spectrum as operationalized by TPC. In other words, CEE parties had to conform to the standard European formations of Christian democrats and conservatives, liberals and socialists, or social democrats, not to mention greens and some smaller formations. Did this pressure to conform engender any resentment on the part of divergent political tendencies; or, how far did CEE parties become pragmatic or opportunistic for the sake of securing EU accession for their countries?

One might expect to find Eurosceptical parties relating best to the smaller European formations, given that it is mainly in these small groups, if not as independents, that Eurosceptical members of European Parliament (MEPs) are found in the EP. However, Eurosceptical parties in CEE included some major parties which have also been senior government parties like the Movement for a Democratic Slovakia (Hnutie za demokratické Slovensko, HZDS), the Civic Democratic Party (Občanská demokratická strana, ODS) in the Czech Republic, and Fidesz in Hungary. After accession the Civic Democratic Party and Fidesz did join with the European Peoples Party while the movement to a Democratic Slovdzia did not join the major party groups in the EP.

Bilateral transnational links can sometimes reveal more about the real ideological sympathies than formal TPC allegiances, even though these usually operate within the confines of the latter. Thus, certain centre-right parties in some post-communist countries demonstrated a closer link with the Bavarian Christian Social Union (Christlich-Soziale Union, CSU) rather than German Christian Democratic Union (Christlich Demokratische Union, CDU), that is, parties which are inclined to fundamental Catholicism. The CSU, somewhat more right-wing than its partner party in German politics particularly on social issues, also has a tendency to be more anti-communist and more anti-left in general. A real test would have been bilateral links between Eurosceptic parties in Western Europe and similar-minded parties in CEE countries. However, the British Conservatives, while trying to export their restrictive view of European integration, claimed to be firm about the democratic credentials of their partner parties (Normington 1996). The Conservatives' early transnational links in CEE had a distinctly neo-liberal policy orientation, exploiting the systemic shift in CEE to marketization. It was precisely this emphasis that attracted Vaclav Klaus, leader of the Czech ODS, with his economistic view of European integration. More notorious was the transnational activity of France's Jean-Marie Le Pen, who made some questionable links along the way including Russia's nationalist figure Vladimir Zhirinovsky. Also telling for CEE parties were special links with 'alternative addresses' from Brussels (as representing a pro-EU and pro-North Atlantic Treaty Organization (NATO) position). This included bilateral links with Russian parties but also with hardline, rather than reconstructed, former regime parties in post-communist Europe, a case in point being Milosevic's Socialist Party of Serbia.

Parties that did not satisfy the three conditions of parties' European policies, democratic commitment, as well as ideological compatibility could have been barred from joining or even expelled from TPC organizations, as happened respectively with the Slovak HZDS and the Hungarian Smallholders' Party in the case of the European Democrat

Union (EDU)—both on grounds of democratic conditionality. This then creates a real pressure on such parties if EU accession is proceeding and they have to clarify their transnational affiliations. There were some cases where ideological compatibility has turned out to be problematic, as in the case of Fidesz which in 2000 switched from the European Liberals to the centre-right EPP and EDU. This reflected an ideological change in that party's position in domestic politics. These cases will be discussed in Section 4.4.

Pressure over European policy might even affect mainstream parties— that is, parties which are not strictly Eurosceptical but include wings or factions that are. This can in turn create or acerbate internal tensions at a time when party development is not yet settled. Such a case is the Bulgarian Socialist Party, which, in fact, split (among other reasons) over differences on Europe and with these the question of a link with the SI (Pridham 2001: 190–1). But the most obvious category of parties in CEE which seemed likely to flout the three conditions are nationalist parties. These tended to have serious problems in the first instance in finding transnational partners on ideological grounds, although this is closely linked with the antithesis between nationalism and the values of European integration. The cases of the Slovak National Party (Slovenská národná strana, SNS) and the Greater Romania Party (Partidul România Mare, PRM) will also be discussed later. A contrast may be drawn here with parties representing ethnic minorities which placed much importance on their transnational contacts and, to that end, adapted themselves ideologically in joining TPC organizations. That is, for transnational purposes, they placed the left–right dimension above the ethnic cleavage which may be rather important in domestic politics. Such ethnic parties were willing to do this as they regarded the EU and its associated organizations, including TPC, as an international framework for the protection of minority rights.

In determining the effect of these three direct pressures at the time, it is important to relate TPC to the wider context of domestic politics for that provides an essential dynamic behind this activity. It should be noted that party systems in many CEE countries were slow to crystallize and stabilize, not least because of the impacts of the multiple transformations (economic and national as well as political) on society and, hence, indirectly on party development. These party system problems created special difficulties for, if not a limitation on, TPC in the post-communist period, although these diminished.

For instance, former regime legacies at the level of political elites were present. Interviews conducted by the author during 1993–6, both in selected CEE countries as well as in Brussels, identified a culture-boundness in East/West transnational party contacts linked to effects deriving from the imprint of four decades of communism, notably in political mentalities (such as in difficulties with open political dialogue, conceptual political language, and, indeed, initially with common languages). This might have suggested some scope for Euroscepticism in terms of anti-Western attitudes, but this problem declined somewhat with time, as evident in interviews undertaken since 1998, one factor being a generational turnover in party personnel from CEE countries involved in transnational links. As one official in the ELDR secretariat commented, there were 'now more young people: the cultural divide is disappearing' and ten years is a long time; people no longer say 'when I was in gaol; rather, last week I was in the USA' (Glasberg 2001). This was accompanied by a much wider fluency of foreign languages, above all of English, on their part. The conclusion to be drawn from these background factors is that the starting point for TPC in CEE was much more difficult than in any preceding cases of EU enlargement such as in Southern Europe.

As transnational links with CEE became more settled, a key question was whether TPC and Euroscepticism presented conflicting opportunity structures or not? On the one side, TPC represented the dominant objective of the candidate country which was the EU, but strictly speaking TPC had a direct influence mainly on party elites. They obviously included party international offices together with national leaders who, in the case of CEE parties, tended to place some importance on such European networking. Its wider influence on party development was more indirect, such as through the effects of programmatic influence, policy education on EU affairs, and political assistance and training (as of party activists by organizations such as at the Robert Schuman Institute, Budapest, which provided courses for the personnel of Christian democratic parties in CEE). On the other side, Eurosceptic parties may well have been populist such as in their treatment of European policy problems and as such may have found scope for presenting themselves as anti-elitist. They may also have sought to exploit dissatisfaction with the ongoing economic transformation which could be linked to the EU.

But it is not just a simple problem of how the three pressures from TPC impacted on national politics. Also relevant are various domestic considerations, which may have influenced TPC, such as political roles (Eurosceptical parties in government are inevitably more constrained by responsibility than opposition parties), the dynamics of party competition (including whether individual party fortunes were on the rise or falling), and, not least, the depth as well as width of public support for EU entry. In the case of Slovakia, for instance, a survey in 1998 identified a relationship between anti-Western attitudes and reservations towards the EU, while younger people were found more open than older Slovaks to trusting people from Western Europe—implying the former were less conditioned by life under the communist regime. At the same time, there was an overwhelming public preference for EU countries over Russia as partner countries. But, it was also found that party preferences cut across these patterns quite strongly and, as a later survey showed, public support for the integration of Slovakia into the EU was most influenced by political parties and their leaders (GfK Slovakia 1998; Gyarfasova and Velsic 2000). In other words, one could surmise that public opinion could be significantly influenced by the, possibly changing, position of parties on European integration; and, that TPC could have played some part in this dynamic.

In conclusion, therefore, the relationship between TPC and Eurosceptic parties has ultimately to be set in the context of domestic political—and, for that matter, also economic—developments for a full understanding of the problems that arise. But the most important thing to consider is the role and influence of TPC with respect to interactions between EU accession and domestic processes. These basic problems, together with other aspects discussed earlier, will be applied now to the case studies from five countries in CEE in the run-up to accession.

4.4 IDENTIFYING PARTY-BASED EUROSCEPTICISM: CASE STUDIES FROM EAST-CENTRAL EUROPE

In CEE, three countries with significant Eurosceptical parties have been selected. Two of these countries (Hungary and the Czech Republic) started

EU membership negotiations in 1998 (and joined NATO in 1999) and one (Slovakia) two years later in 2000 (and joined NATO in 2004). Given their differences in regime change, economic transformation, and settledness of party systems, these three cases present sufficient diversity. Public opinion tended to be more in favour of accession in both Slovakia and Hungary than in the Czech Republic.

4.4.1 Hungary

Hungary has had a multiparty system with three parties distinctly pro-integration and having straightforward TPC links in the run-up to accession (the Alliance of Free Democrats is a member of the ELDR; the Socialist Party was a member of the SI and associate member of the Party of European Socialists (PES); and, the Hungarian Democratic Forum (Magyar Demokrata Fórum, MDF) was an observer member of the EPP). The other parties presented different versions of Euroscepticism as seen through the lenses of TPC.

4.4.1.1 Fidesz

Best described as a case of national-interest (if not nationalist) Euroscepticism (Taggart and Szczerbiak 2001a: 10–11), Fidesz changed its line on Europe and this was overtly signalled through its changed transnational allegiance. Originally, it was a fully fledged European-type liberal party joining the Liberal International (LI) in 1992 (with the very young Victor Orban as its representative on the LI Bureau) and developing a close working relationship with the German Free Democratic Party (Freie Demokratische Partei, FDP) which provided much material and moral assistance in this period both directly and through its Naumann Foundation. According to its then international secretary, the involvement at this formative stage with the LI had some influence on the evolution of Fidesz's party identity and this included taking advice from LI parties on key policy issues (Ledenyi 1993). This same source said Fidesz was planning at this stage to strengthen its involvement in, and ties with, the LI including cooperation among liberal parties in East-Central Europe. At the same time, Fidesz did not entirely exclude informal links with some socialist parties in Western Europe.

The eventual shift from the European liberals to the centre-right EPP, finally decided in autumn 2000, was predicted in transnational circles for a long time. The way this occurred illustrates an ideological flexibility on Fidesz's part, one in accord with the party's own domestic shift in the same direction. The EPP first contacted Fidesz in November 1989 when trying to establish its valid partner party in Hungary. As a result of this visit, the EPP opted for the MDF because of its then organizational preparedness and its evident centre-right leanings, but Fidesz was the EPP's second choice on their list of three (Welle 1996). The EPP kept open contact with Fidesz despite its formal liberal links; and it was clear that Orban, soon to become party leader, regarded transnational links as providing a useful access to European politicians (Welle 2001). The process of changing transnational links took some time as there was a risk this ideological signal might have a divisive effect in the party and because of relations with the rival EP groups (Duhac 2000; Major 2000). Fidesz then began to benefit from this change. In summer 2001, the EPP for instance supported unreservedly Hungary's controversial Status Law allowing support for ethnic Hungarians abroad.

4.4.1.2 Smallholders' Party (FKGP)

This party comes across in transnational terms as conditionally pro-EU but in a way that caused some unease in European circles. The figure of Jozsef Torgyan, its chairman, at the time featured strongly here. It is, in fact, one case of a CEE party that joined a transnational organization early, being a refounded historical party, but was then expelled only to be readmitted some years later after having undergone changes to accommodate transnational requirements. Originally in the EDU, it was expelled in 1994 for a combination of reasons, including domestic. The FKGP's withdrawal from the Antall Government in 1992 because of disagreements over land privatization was used by the MDF (which was close to the CDU) to push for its expulsion (Beres 2000). But there was also concern over the nationalist line of the party and Torgyan's own demagogic style which disturbed the CDU in particular among EDU parties.

After 1999, the FKGP was restored to EDU membership and become also a member of the EPP, but this was only after some changes at the domestic level. First, the Socialist/Free Democrat coalition formed in 1994 caused concern in European conservative circles—illustrating an element of partisanship on the part of transnational organizations with respect to the domestic politics of member parties. The FKGP helped the right back to power by forming a coalition with Fidesz in 1998, thus pleasing these circles. Secondly, the FKGP made efforts to abandon its more extreme positions. Here the Bavarian CSU and its Seidel Foundation played an important part in pressurizing and helping to train the party in democratizing itself (Von Solemacher 2000). However, the party eventually imploded at the time of the 2002 election following severe internal tensions.

4.4.1.3 Conclusion

What is striking in the Hungarian case is the predominance of domestic factors in the country's TPC—whether ideological shifts or political roles and especially government office or political careers (as notably in Orban's case). At the same time, transnational links were taken seriously (such as by Fidesz in its caution over switching TPC affiliation) and had some real effect in conjunction with domestic factors (as with the FKGP). In short, there was an interplay between transnational and domestic opportunity structures with a predominance of the latter. The country's lead in accession negotiations, together with relatively high public support for EU membership, ensure formal consensus among the parties; but it was also evident, as expressed through TPC, that some of these parties were likely to pursue a Soft Eurosceptical line once membership was assured and Hungary filled seats in the EP.

4.4.2 The Czech Republic

The Czech party system is fairly consolidated with two main actors on the left: the Czech Social Democratic Party (Česká strana sociálni demokratická, ČSSD) and the Communist Party of Bohemia and Moravia

(Komunistická strana Čech a Moravy, KSČM). The centre-right is represented by the ODS, the Christian Democratic Union (Køeslanská a demokratická unie–Československá strana lidová, KDU-ČSL) and the Freedom Union (Unie Svobody, US). In the run-up to accession, the CSSD was a full member of the SI and an associate member of the PES, while the ODS was a member of the EDU, and both the KDU-ČSL and the US were associate members of the EPP.

4.4.2.1 Civic Democratic Party (ODS)

The ODS came across as Soft Eurosceptic and then mainly because of the selective criticisms of the EU repeated intermittently by its dominant chairman Vaclav Klaus. His particular brand of economistic Euroscepticism was supplemented by emphatic references to national sovereignty. Consistent with this approach was the pattern of ODS transnational links both multilateral and bilateral. Its membership of the conservative EDU, because it sees itself as 'liberal conservative', and not the originally Christian democratic EPP was telling. Klaus utilized EDU membership to push his own line on integration as at a conference held in Prague in December 1994 on the theme 'European Integration: Preparation for Inter-Governmental Union'.

Similarly, when looking at its bilateral links, the ODS remained distant from the CDU/CSU for two reasons: its rejection of the traditional Christian democratic (pro-federalist) concept of European integration and, previously, personal antipathy between Klaus and Kohl (Handl and Zaborowski 1999: 44–5). On the other hand, much was made of Klaus's link with the (Eurosceptical) British Conservatives. This was literally his best individual transnational link as shown by regular joint activities. In other words, the preference for the British party had both negative reasons (referring to the failed link with the German party) and positive reasons, meaning policy sympathies as over lack of enthusiasm for monetary integration and Soft Euroscepticism in general. Essentially, Klaus sees himself as a pure economic liberal and this dictated his transnational inclinations.

Altogether, there was a strong consistency in Klaus's line over time. He used transnational occasions to propagate his Eurosceptical views both while in government and later in opposition. Although Klaus, as President, took an ambiguous line during the referendum on EU membership, this addition to Eurosceptical influence did not endanger a 'yes' vote. It was not, however, difficult to imagine his party adapting to EU membership and taking up seats in the EP, as it did, for an element of pragmatism if not opportunism was never far below the surface.

4.4.2.2 Communist Party of Bohemia and Moravia (KSČM)

The KSČM fits into the category of extreme left principled opponent of European integration, seeing the EU as an instrument of capitalist monopolies. This is consistent with its sceptical view of post-1989 Czech democracy. However, in the run-up to accession it began an internal debate with some figures favouring a more open attitude to the EU in the light of its progress in areas like social policy and human rights. Its TPC links tended to reflect its traditional outlook, especially with such parties as the French and Portuguese communist parties, the hard-line Italian Rifondazione Comunista, the Socialist Party of Serbia of Milosevic, and the Russian Communist Party under Zyuganov as favoured partners; but also (semi-)reformed parties like the Spanish United Left (Izquierda Unida, IU), German Party of Democratic Socialism (Partei des Demokratischen Sozialismus, PDS), and the Bulgarian Socialist Party (Ransdorf 1995). From this it is clear it had some 'alternative addresses' to Brussels. In other words, the KSČM was largely dependent on bilateral transnational links for unreconstructed communist parties have no multilateral transnational organization; and, indeed, they suffered from a legitimacy problem at this level.

4.4.2.3 Conclusion

The Czech Republic thus presents two rather different major cases of Eurosceptic parties—one Soft and one Hard. But they differed in that Klaus's use of transnational links illustrates his preference for mobilizing support for his cause within, not without, European circles. Although one of the few most prominent single examples of a strong Eurosceptic party in CEE, the ODS's approach was very largely determined by that of its leader so that, once the Czech Republic acceded to the EU, the ODS might developed into a conventional centre-right party in transnational terms.

4.4.3 Slovakia

Despite the unsettledness of this country's party system, reflected in the emergence of new parties, the parties in government during 1998–2002 had clear transnational linkages in the run-up to accession the Party Of the Democratic Left (Strana demokratickej l'avice, SDL) was a member of the SI and observer member of the PES; the Christian Democratic Movement (Krest'anskodemokratické hnutie, KDH) was a member of the EDU and associate member of the EPP; while the Party of the Hungarian Coalition (Strana mad'arskej koalície, SMK) was an associate member of the EPP and associate member of the EDU. The Slovak Democratic and Christian Union (Slovenská demokratická a krest'anská únia, SDKÚ), founded in late 2000, became an associate member of the EPP in 2002. On the other hand, the opposition parties—HZDS and SNS—continued to have no viable transnational links, as will be discussed in the following sections.

4.4.3.1 Movement for a Democratic Slovakia (HZDS)

This party, the strongest in Slovak politics, failed to establish any meaningful transnational affiliation though not without some effort on its part. The problem was twofold: the HZDS retained its movement character (as emphasized in its name) which since its founding in 1991 expressed an ideological diversity—useful perhaps for wide electoral appeal but a barrier to TPC; and, the figure of Vladimír Mečiar who was in European circles strongly discredited but nevertheless crucial to the party's public impact. The latter problem is based on Mečiar's authoritarian practices and questionable attitude to the EU while in government before the 1998 election. Furthermore, as a governing party the HZDS showed some sympathy towards an 'alternative address' in Moscow, although this was under the guise of strengthening economic links.

Put schematically, therefore, the HZDS tested negatively in terms of the three Europeanization pressures—ideological compatibility, democratic conditionality, and pro-EU commitment. Furthermore, it did not at that time help its TPC chances by attacking the transnational links already established and valued by the then opposition parties, which came into government. In broad terms, the HZDS came across as being in the Soft Eurosceptic category although this does not do justice to its interesting complexity.

The HZDS is particularly interesting because its Eurosceptical reputation was rather more due to the past than to the position it took in the run-up to accession. Attitudes towards Mečiar in both the European Commission and TPC circles were decidedly firm and unforgiving, making perceptions of the HZDS very personalistic. This is why efforts by the party to reform itself into a proper party and to emphasize its pro-EU (and now also pro-NATO) position in opposition failed to convince international opinion. The story is the same at the transnational level.

While still a governing party, the HZDS approached various TPC organizations—reflecting indeed its own ideological diversity—but it failed to receive encouragement, also because Slovak member parties opposed its application. Equally, the HZDS had little luck with meaningful bilateral links. Among others, it cultivated some links with Milosevic's Socialist Party of Serbia—a party definitely not welcome in EU circles—and this link continued into the opposition period, in the sense of mutual attendance at party congresses and visiting delegations (Pridham 1999*b*: 1231–2). Nevertheless, at its 'transformation' congress at Trnava in March 2000 the HZDS declared itself to be a 'people's party' (*ludova strana*) —a direct import of the European nomenclature as in the EPP—and made a decisive bid for membership of the EPP and EDU, as stated at the end of the declaration. This move was dictated by a desire for 'acceptability abroad' (Keltosova 2000).

The HZDS was not, however, successful with its application to the EDU. This was rejected unanimously at the EDU's steering committee when it met in early autumn 2000, the stated reasons being the party's past and Mečiar's continuing chairmanship linked with the lack of real party reform (Agardi 2000). However, the HZDS meanwhile developed an associate link with the EDU group in the Council of Europe Assembly. In the long run, the HZDS's problems at the transnational level seemed to be tied to Mečiar's.

4.4.3.2 Slovak National Party (SNS)

The SNS was formally supportive of EU accession, but its attitudes to European integration and its marginal TPC links suggested this support did not equal strong commitment. The SNS's interpretation of European policy departed somewhat from conventional approaches to integration. While its 1998 programme referred to 'the unambiguous need of Slovakia to become a member of the European Union', it also emphasized the need to look East as well as West because of 'our undoubted relation with the Slavic nation' and denounced 'any anti-Russian or anti-Slavic manifestations as expressed by certain parts of our cosmopolitan elite' (SNS 1998: 20). According to the party chairperson, Anna Malikova, the party was against European federalism and supported EU entry 'on the understanding that the EU is a multi-nation organization' for the EU 'should remember its original principles' as an association of nation states especially concerning economic cooperation (Malikova 2000).

The SNS's TPC links were essentially bilateral as the party did not relate to any of the main formations. The former party leader, Jan Slota, famously invited Le Pen to Bratislava in September 1997, a visit that proved controversial but was in line with Slota's pleasure in shocking political gestures. Under Malikova who became leader in 1999, the party then moved away from Le Pen as being anti-EU and placed a priority on working with parties in Western Europe 'that have similar programmes, that are nationally oriented, Christian oriented', with Fini's Alleanza Nazionale in Italy as a main partner (Malikova 2000). What brought these two parties together was a common identity as 'national' parties and an emphasis on nation states in Europe (*Sme*, 6 November 2000). In short, the SNS had elements of Hard Euroscepticism (all the more when taking account of its anti-Western sentiments and hostility to NATO), but there were signs in the run-up to accession of some shift towards Soft Euroscepticism.

4.4.3.3 Christian Democratic Movement (KDH)

On the surface, the KDH appears as unproblematic given its support for EU accession and its TPC links as a Christian democratic party with the EPP and EDU in the run-up to accession. However, it does not take long to realize that it was in several respects Soft Eurosceptic. This is because of a certain cultural antipathy to Western liberalism, a Catholic fundamentalism, and a selective policy-oriented Euroscepticism (Taggart and Szczerbiak 2001*a*: 10). From the Brussels end, this caused some concern, for the KDH was seen there as 'too confessional' and somewhat out of line with the EPP's identity as a 'people's party' (Welle 2001).

In earlier times, the KDH was more positive about its TPC links and would boast that it was the Slovak party with the best international connections. Apart from belonging to the EPP and EDU, it developed bilateral links especially with Christian democratic parties in Austria, Holland, and Germany although significantly its last link was much closer with the Bavarian CSU ('as less liberal') than the CDU (Kohutiar 1995). The decline in intensity of the KDH's TPC links owed something to the fact the party chairman, Jan Carnogursky, placed much importance on them while this was less true of Pavol Hrusovsky, his successor.

Its cultural reservations about Western liberal values (which were roughly similar to such pronouncements by Pope John II) were at times expressed openly by Carnogursky, the KDH's chairman during 1990–2000, both during his leadership and after (*Sme*, 28 December 2001). These reservations were behind a KDH initiative in early 2002 for a parliamentary declaration (passed with the support of the HZDS and SNS) on the sovereignty of EU member and candidate countries in cultural–ethical issues.

4.4.3.4 Conclusion

It is clear from above-mentioned discussion that the three Slovak parties discussed bring somewhat divergent or idiosyncratic outlooks when compared with the approach of the TPC organizations. There is, in particular, a remarkable correlation between their TPC links and their positions on European integration. However, there were signs of some adaptation (especially in the period after EU negotiations began) and their versions of Soft Euroscepticism pointed to sufficient accommodation with EP requirements.

4.5 IDENTIFYING PARTY-BASED EUROSCEPTICISM: CASE STUDIES FROM SOUTH-EASTERN EUROPE

The two countries selected from South-Eastern Europe are those which gained EU membership in 2007. In both cases, there were earlier uncertainties in their democratization paths and at times a reluctance in pursuing economic reforms. Neither country had problems of state- and nation-building. These two cases, therefore, present less diversity than the three from CEE. Both countries have shown very high levels of support for EU membership at the public level.

4.5.1 Bulgaria

Bulgaria has had a reasonably settled party system, with three main actors: the Bulgarian Socialist Party (Bălgarska Socialističeska Partija, BSP), the former Communist regime party; and the United Democratic Forces, which is an alliance of centre-right forces, of which the Union of Democratic Forces (Sayuz na demokratichnite sili, SDS) is the main component; and, the Movement for Rights and Freedoms (Dvizhenie za prava i svobodi, DPS), which is a largely Turkish ethnic party. However, in the 2001 parliamentary election it was a completely new formation, the National Movement Simeon II, which won and formed a government with the DPS. Hence, a new uncertainty has entered the party system. The SDS was an associate member of the EPP; while the DPS has opted for liberal transnational links, seen as being most in accord with minority rights, and was an observer member of the LI (Ejub 2001).

4.5.1.1 Bulgarian Socialist Party (BSP)

The BSP is not a properly Eurosceptical party but its own tortuous reform process as a former communist party has affected its transnational links, especially with the SI. Furthermore, the BSP is also interesting because it is the successor to the Communist regime party in a country known for its traditional Russophilia. In other words, the problems of the BSP's adaptation may, given its importance as the major party of the left, be seen as a measure of the country's shift from East to West.

It was not until 1994 that the SI was prepared to deal openly with the BSP and even then it remained rather cautious, due to doubts about reform in the party and the opposition of some member parties of the SI. On the BSP side, there were problems in pursuing this link because of internal divisions over a range of key issues including Europe. The pro-Europe element (Alliance for Social Democracy faction), some of whom later split away to form the Euro-Left in 1997, argued strongly for the legitimacy of international recognition, but they encountered resistance from those attached to traditional communist ideals as well as from party activists (Pridham 2001: 190–1). By this time the BSP was in government (1995–7) which encouraged the BSP to pursue a new a link with the SI. However, the severe economic crisis of late 1996 plunged the government into disarray and discredited the BSP in European circles. This was magnified by signs that Prime Minister Zhan Videnov and some other BSP leaders did not fully understand political mentalities inside the EU but also, more concretely, by the government's reluctance over economic reform. In fact, internal party battles contributed to difficulties in both respects (Bokova 2001; Kanev 2001).

After 1998, relations with the SI—and with the PES—gradually resumed, helped by a new BSP leadership and some SI parties taking a more positive line. Time passed and the older activist base was, at least on European questions, more quiescent. Moreover, after 2000, Bulgaria negotiated EU membership and this certainly influenced the BSP's evolution and its clearer pursuit of transnational links. In March 2000, the BSP formed a council of European integration under Georgi Parvanov, the party chairman, to foster public discussion, liaise with NGOs, and advise the BSP on the EU chapters in the negotiations with Brussels. There was still a Eurosceptical element, contained in the Open Forum in the party, but it began to carry less weight (Stanishev 2001).

4.5.1.2 Conclusion

The case of the BSP and its transnational links reflects some features of the Bulgarian transition and how these have mixed with attitudes to European questions. There was been a remarkably close interconnection between the BSP's own evolutionary problems and its transnational links.

4.5.2 Romania

The multiparty system in Romania was been marked by various factors: the slow self-reform of the main party of the left; the fragmentation of the centre-right; the presence of a Hungarian minority party, Democratic Union of Hungarians in Romania (Uniunea Democrată Maghiară din România, UDMR); and, the existence of PRM, an ultra-nationalist party. Both the Christian Democratic National Peasants' Party (Partidul Naţional Ţărănesc Creştin şi Democrat, PNTCD) and the UDMR were associate members of the EPP (and the UDMR was also an associate member of the EDU); while the National Liberal Party (Partidul Naţional Liberal, PNL) was a member party of the ELDR.

4.5.2.1 Social Democratic Party (PSD)

The Social Democratic Party (Partidul Social Democrat, PSD), formerly the Social Democratic Party of Romania (Partidul Democraţiei Sociale din România, PDSR) until its merger with the Social Democratic Party produced this name change, has itself been somewhat influenced by transnational considerations. Originally deriving from the National Salvation Front, from which it split under another name, the PDSR represented continuity with old regime elites in national office until 1996. Some of its political practices and its reluctance over economic reform cast doubt over its European credentials, and this affected its earlier chances at the transnational level.

The PDSR originally applied for SI membership in 1993, shortly after it renamed itself as such, but there was strong opposition from some member parties on the grounds that the Romanian party was 'crypto-communist'. Nothing further developed until the PDSR lost power and went into opposition. This shock produced some changes in party thinking, including on European policy, but also on Iliescu's part for he became 'more open to Western ideas and concepts'. At its 1997 congress, the PDSR adopted a new programme oriented to social democratic values based on key documents of the SI and PES (Prisacaru 2001).

This drive to modernize the party was clearly motivated by the loss of office and desire for new electoral support, for which reason the search for a real transnational link played a legitimating role. It was strengthened once Adrian Nastase assumed the party leadership, since he devoted energy to this task but also enjoyed more credibility than Iliescu in European circles (Roll 2001). Nastase was well networked at the EU level including the EP; and became prime minister after the 2000 election.

4.5.2.2 Greater Romania Party (PRM)

As a nationalist party, whose chairman had a habit of issuing xenophobic and extremist statements, the PRM was hardly any transnational actor's favourite partner. This is quite evident for it lacked important TPC links, even bilateral ones, although contact was made with Le Pen (the last resort of right extremist parties from post-communist countries). The problem is partly that the party's ideology is diverse claiming both left-wing and centre-right orientations (Alexandrescu 2000: 267). Nevertheless, its two representatives in the Council of Europe Parliamentary Assembly were observer members of the EDU group, although denied full membership because of their extremist positions (Draghici 2001). But the real difficulty is that the party was very much associated with Corneliu Vadim Tudor, founding leader since 1991, and therefore with his pattern of outrageous statements, often hostile to the large Hungarian minority. Altogether, the PRM lacked legitimacy abroad whether at the transnational or official level.

The PRM came across, therefore, as belonging to those parties that belong to the Eurosceptical class because they were in default of European acceptability and because of its xenophobia—hence, violation of European standards. And, yet, its actual position on EU accession in the run-up—which was increasingly positive since the mid-1990s—sat uneasily with this record. In the 2000 election, the PRM used the EU star-studded logo. It is not difficult to draw the conclusion that electoral motives were behind this, given the very high public support for EU accession. As a result, there were some tension in the party between these two tendencies although they were to some degree papered over by Tudor's dominance as leader. According to a party spokesman, there was no alternative to EU membership: 'there was no possibility for any country to have a future outside the EU—if you are not in, you will die', while emphasizing the need to maintain national identity. He explained his party's security motive behind support for Euro-Atlantic integration as being anti-Russian, linked to the PRM's advocacy of unification with Moldova by peaceful means (Brudascu 2001).

4.5.2.3 Conclusion

These two Romanian parties had evidently different futures in front of them before accession. The PSD seemed headed for one of the major transnational formations after a long period of adaptation, while the PRM did not have any obvious transnational home. This did not prevent it taking its place in the EP. The country had undergone some disappointments in the past in its relations with the EU (and NATO), so was not inconceivable that another such experience might open up a political opportunity for Tudor and his populism. His European policy, while formally positive towards accession, was not deeply fixed.

4.6 CONCLUSION

The general discussion of patterns in TPC and of the five case studies from Central and Eastern and South-Eastern Europe demonstrate that Euroscepticism was a significant factor in party transnational involvement from these countries. It either produced exclusion in the case of Hard Eurosceptic parties or those with a complicated and unresolved reputation in European circles or, perhaps more importantly, it demonstrated an ability by Soft Eurosceptic parties to network within transnational channels, though usually more successfully in a bilateral rather than multilateral way. This suggests that transnational activity in the enlarged EU might well become more diverse and this could place a special strain on party group cohesion there.

Accession countries, and the parties in them, in the run-up to membership were in an asymmetric relationship with the EU, having to accommodate all the conditions it set as well as its whole legislative corpus. But that imbalance changed once these countries became member states and started asserting their national interests, as has also been apparent at times in the EP. Some statements by Hungarian and Czech elites before accession revealed an assertiveness at the European level. However, political elites in countries like Slovakia, Romania, and, to some lesser extent, Bulgaria had yet fully learnt the art of hard bargaining, pushing national interests, and exploiting the ins and outs of what used to be called the 'community method' before joining.

Our examination of TPC reveals some of these cross-national differences, but it also provides an opportunity for political learning relevant to future accession states. Parties from CEE countries, when not yet full members of the EU party federations, were nonetheless more integrated into these formations than they were at the official EU level. They already had an opportunity structure there for influencing TPC strategies and policy positions from inside. This paralleled the advance to high leadership positions in other international organizations of figures from post-communist countries: a Slovak was Organization of Security and Cooperation in Europe (OSCE) Secretary-General, its Assembly President was a Romanian, while a Lithuanian took over as chair of the Council of Europe Committee of Ministers.

An alternative, and to some degree conflicting, hypothesis to that of greater party-political diversity in the enlarged EU is one of considerable conformist pressures on Eurosceptical parties. There is much evidence of this in this chapter when studying the transnational relations developed by parties from these five countries in the run-up to accession. The party examples selected show that the three conditions placed by TPC organizations on parties interested in membership—namely, ideological compatibility, democratic conditionality, and pro-EU commitment—had a powerful influence and served to produce formal but also real changes in party positions and behaviour, including by Eurosceptical parties. It even helped to drive party reform in the case of former communist regime parties reluctant at first to embrace full-scale reconstruction as centre-left forces in these new democracies. The study of TPC has the virtue of allowing one to get behind official positions (which invariably suffer from the overwhelming desire to please Brussels) and focus on real political motives and attitudes which are often more complex. It is significant that even here the urge to pursue 'alternative addresses' to those of the EU (and NATO) was not been very strong. Transnational party links provided an important means for political elite integration in advance of EU membership and this tended to confirm the original aim to 'return to Europe'.

It is also clear from this chapter that one should not merely view Eurosceptical parties in a descriptive manner. They have, above all, to be contextualized in terms of both the dynamic of the EU accession process and also of their domestic arenas. There are repeated signs from the case studies that the onset of negotiations for EU membership, as a new reality, had a significant effect on party positions and conduct. It forced parties to adapt to specific issues and, if necessary, to adopt a less abstract approach to integration. This dynamic continued and intensified the nearer the EU membership approached. Political parties needed to find transnational partners—preferably multilateral as well as bilateral—for the purposes of networking, information access, and strengthening policy expertise, not to mention less tangible motives like political prestige and international recognition. The case studies show that in many cases this strategic choice exercised the minds of party leaders even in countries like Bulgaria which entered after the first wave of CEE accession.

Finally, the role of transnational activity has to be crucially related to domestic contexts. This is particularly so when considering the problems for this activity coming initially from party system unsettledness in the new post-communist democracies. However, as time has elapsed, some constraints like government responsibility tended to reinforce European involvement by political parties especially as accession gathered pace with membership negotiations. At first sight, it may appear strange that Eurosceptical parties, when in opposition, did not exploit the asymmetrical relationship between governments and Brussels and indeed the elitism that this encouraged in a more in populist fashion. But, then, the strong public support for EU entry in most of these countries clearly acted as a cautionary influence here. Altogether, the combined dynamic of the European and the domestic levels acted to underpin the conformist pressures exerted by transnational party organizations.

NOTE

1. Sections 4.4 and 4.5 of the chapter dealing with these case studies draw on elite interview material from the author's five-country project, 'European Union Enlargement, Democratic Conditionality and Regime Change in Post-Communist States: Slovakia in Comparative Perspective', funded by the Nuffield Foundation during 2000–1. The author wishes to thank Susannah Verney (Athens) and Vladimir Handl (Prague) for their help in updating developments in certain Greek and Czech parties.

5

Exceptionalism or Convergence? Euroscepticism and Party Systems in Central and Eastern Europe

Karen Henderson

5.1 INTRODUCTION

In the new millennium, the Central and East European countries (CEECs) have begun to emerge clearly as subjects rather than objects of the European integration process, and the importance of examining Eurosceptic forces in this region has consequently increased enormously. The shift in the focus of academic and political debate on the CEECs as European Union (EU) members has been slow but steady, and has progressed through several stages.

During the opening stage, in the mid-1990s, it was the names of West European cities that dominated most academic and political debate on EU eastward enlargement, since discussion tended to be structured around key decisions of the European Council. These included: the formulation of the 'Copenhagen criteria' in June 1993, the pre-accession strategy established by the Essen European Council in December 1994, the December 1995 Madrid decision to ask the European Commission to prepare its opinions on the initial wave of applications from post-communist states, and the decision of the December 1997 Luxembourg European Council to commence detailed accession negotiations with a first group of CEEC applicants.

However, the publication of the Commission's opinions on the candidate states in July 1997 initiated a second stage in the debate, as it greatly sharpened awareness of the internal differences between states that had often been viewed as a homogeneous post-communist mass. Detailed accession negotiations began with the Czech Republic, Estonia, Hungary, Poland, and Slovenia only (together with Cyprus). This was reinforced by the decision—unique to the eastward enlargement process—that the Commission would produce annual 'progress reports' which where effectively regularly updated opinions. Yet once the December 1999 Helsinki European Council decided to embark on negotiations with the remaining five CEECs (Bulgaria, Latvia, Lithuania, Romania, and Slovakia—together with Malta), even the importance of the European Commission as the annual judge of the candidate states rapidly declined in importance. More attention was paid to public opinion on the EU in the applicant states, and also—crucially for the analysis of party-based Euroscepticism—to the stances of political parties. Questions were more frequently raised about the influence of the domestic political situation in the applicant states on the timing and size of the first wave of eastward enlargement, and it became increasingly clear that dynamic perceptions of the advantages and drawbacks of EU membership could prove crucial in the later stages of accession negotiations (Grabbe and Hughes1998; Blazyca and Kolkiewicz 1999; Henderson 1999; Kucia 1999; Štebe 2001; Szczerbiak 2001*c*).

By the time the European Council went back to Copenhagen in December 2002 for the final decision about which post-communist states would join the EU in the first wave of eastward enlargement, it was the names of East-Central European capitals which dominated debate. 'Warsaw', 'Prague', and 'Budapest' became the key actors in the end game of arguing about accession terms. Moreover, there was a growing awareness that these were not unitary actors, but complex polities where government stances in negotiations with the EU were influenced and constrained by the exigencies of domestic political competition. Consequently, the nature of Euroscepticism in the CEECs began for the first time to be subjected to more rigorous analysis. It became accepted that the EU forms a central topic of debate and political discourse among political parties in the candidate states. The views of political actors, structured by the different party systems, are relevant not only to the success of the enlargement project, but also to the future of the EU after their accession. CEEC reactions to EU membership, in both public and elite opinion, have become more complex as general aspirations to 'return to Europe' have been superseded by the more nuanced appreciation of the advantages and disadvantages of membership that accompanied the later stages of the negotiation process.

When analysing the party politics of Euroscepticism in the early years of the third millennium, it is important to emphasize that the CEECs were at this stage not yet members of the EU—a point so obvious that it is in danger of being overlooked. The overwhelming exigency of attaining membership distorted the framework of both ideological and strategic constraints on the policy options that could be pursued. For several reasons, it can be argued that party attitudes to EU issues are likely to undergo more marked shifts in pre- and post-accession periods than has been the case in earlier enlargements.

Firstly, the foreign policy realignment that took place in the CEECs after 1989 was of a completely different magnitude to that which took place prior to the accession of the previous nine new member states. These were either non-aligned or in the same military block as the original member states, rather than having been in the enemy camp during the bitter struggle of the cold war. EU membership was therefore a much more crucial foreign policy goal, as embodied in the 'return to Europe' discourse. Particularly in the early and mid-1990s, ambiguity towards EU membership was heavily linked to residual allegiances to elements of the communist political system in the domestic sphere, even though the now non-existent Soviet Union was no longer a viable foreign policy partner, so that the alternative to EU membership appeared threatening. This gave EU membership a far greater salience in the public consciousness than elsewhere, and left far less scope for the pursuit of domestic 'national interest' until the final stages of negotiations.

Secondly, relations with the institutions of the EU differed somewhat from earlier accession waves. While a 'classical method' of enlargement already existed (Preston 1997: 18–22), the role of the European Commission was particularly heavily emphasized in CEEC candidate states, with the pronouncements of Commission officials being considered so vital for the future of candidate states that they often made headline news. Likewise, Joint Parliamentary Committee meetings with members of the European Parliament (EP) received considerable publicity. It is true that the role of the Commission in preparing not only the initial opinions on the candidate states' applications but also the regular annual progress reports gave it substantial influence over the accession process. Yet this focus of attention

often produced a false impression about the importance of the opinions
of 'Brussels bureaucrats' (Šafaříková 2001). The corollary of this was that
the decision-making powers of the European Council and member states'
governments were often underplayed, giving the impression that membership entailed a greater loss of national sovereignty than is actually the case.
As a consequence, both governments and parties in the CEECs sensed a
considerable feeling of empowerment when they finally entered the EU
and were able to promote their national interests as states.

Finally, the CEECs' own party systems were in a state of flux when
compared to the more stable polities of the countries that joined the EU
earlier. It is significant that they had undergone a 'triple transition', where
not only had their political systems been profoundly altered by regime
change, but also the economic and social systems, and in some cases even
the definition of the nation (Offe 1996). What this means is that the debate
on Europe is conducted in a radically different environment from that of
previous enlargement waves, where party systems were (even in the new
democracies of South-Eastern Europe) fairly well-established.

With this background in mind, this chapter attempts to advance the
new debate on Euroscepticism and political parties in old and new member states by examining the various theoretical frameworks for analysing
them. It focuses on largely qualitative rather than quantitative methods
of categorizing how the EU debate impacts on party politics in formerly
communist states and vice versa. While agreeing with the observation
of Taggart and Szczerbiak (2001a: 15) that definitions of Euroscepticism
based on national experiences have 'rarely travelled well', at the same time,
post-communist states can be found to have many features that are common to each other, and they are not, even as a group, entirely exceptional.
The conclusion of Hooghe, Marks, and Wilson (2002), based on current
member states, that 'European politics is domestic politics by other means',
is also crucially relevant to politics within the candidate states. EU issues
tend to be integrated into domestic political agendas to a far greater extent
in the CEECs because acquiring EU membership is far more central to
both the legislative agendas and the foreign policy aspirations of post-
communist states.

The chapter therefore begins by looking at why Euroscepticism in CEEC
candidate states was rather different from that in earlier member states.
It then surveys and evaluates several frameworks that have so far been

suggested for defining and categorizing Euroscepticism in relation to the candidate countries. Finally, it looks at how changes in the party systems in the CEECs interrelate with shifting attitudes towards 'Europe'. Since the politics, economics, and societies of Central and Eastern Europe are in far more dynamic motion than in Western Europe, party profiles within the EU and stances on individual policy issues are more prone to fluctuation than has been the case with previous waves of new member states. The question of whether or not there will eventually be a convergence in the way issues are addressed in different parts of the continent will have profound effects on how decisions are reached in the new Europe.

5.2 THE MEANING OF EUROSCEPTICISM IN 'NEW' AND 'OLD' EUROPE

When we compare opposition to European integration and the EU in member and candidate states, we cannot assume that their perceptions of what is entailed by the European integration project are identical. In the 1990s, 'Europe' was viewed through the prism of domestic politics even more strongly in post-communist states than in Western Europe because attaining membership was considered by many to be vital for promoting national development. There was a relatively neat fit between party views on the imperative of attaining membership and the placement of parties in the political system as a whole. This was because the political and economic issues involved did not form cross-cutting cleavages that divided parties internally. The political and economic Copenhagen criteria (European Commission 1994), taken together, coincided to a high degree with the political and economic package promoted by the most pro-reform parties in the CEECs. The desire to anchor democracy and the rule of law, and to assure human rights and the protection of minorities, tended to coincide with the will to create a functioning market economy.

This accorded with Kitschelt's observation in the early 1990s that East European party systems would be centred around a pro-market/libertarian versus anti-market/authoritarian axis. This meant that in CEEC candidate states, more right-wing economic views tended to be accompanied by progressive social attitudes, whereas parties that wished to preserve egalitarian, state-controlled communist-era economies tended also to oppose open, pluralist democracies that tolerated 'otherness'. In contrast, 'West European party systems in the late twentieth century tend to be oriented toward an anti-market/libertarian versus pro-market/authoritarian axis' (Kitschelt 1992: 20). This led to confusion in the application of the traditional West European labels 'right' and 'left' in the new democracies.

However, at the same time the complexion of parties in the CEECs simplified views on the EU. Euroscepticism in the West European member states has been more complex than in the CEECs because the European integration project has been built on a mix of social and political liberalism and libertarian economic principles so that the EU embraces a mix of issues that are promoted by different ends of the major axis of party competition in those states. This is no accident: the EU's agenda has been carefully constructed over successive decades to cater for a broad spectrum of political, economic, and social aspirations, which enables it to integrate the mainstream of the member states' party systems and the alternating governments that derive from them. In many West European states, therefore, the EU issue has tended to form a cross-cutting cleavage that can divide parties internally because a 'left-wing' stance favouring greater social rights, economic regulation, and political integration stands at odds with the 'right-wing' position supporting market freedoms. Milder forms of Euroscepticism arise because the balance of the EU's 'something for everyone' programme cannot please everyone all the time, and both differing national interests and shifting party electoral strategies at times create parties or factions with some critical views of the EU. More militant Euroscepticism, on the other hand, arises on the fringes of the party system since the EU's grand project cannot be infinitely elastic to the point where it is internally contradictory. It cannot, for example, easily accommodate the aspirations of communists and xenophobes who have implacable ideological objections either to its economic goals or to its goals of political and social integration.

The most strongly anti-EU forces on the left and the right in member and candidate states are generally easy to identify throughout Europe, although the CEECs, because of their party constellations, initially also produced parties with residues of the communist era thinking that combined strong state-interventionist economic policy with nationalism. However, the Copenhagen criteria clinically excluded those fringes of the party spectra whose allegiance to Soviet-style communism on the left or xenophobic nationalism on the right precluded a willingness to harmonize domestic legislation to the *acquis communautaire*. Only when such parties modified their stances (as in Romania) or were eliminated from government (as in Slovakia) were detailed negotiations on EU accession feasible. In the case of more moderate or partial opposition to the EU, comparison between parties in member and candidate states is rendered difficult by the fact that they have somewhat different understandings of what the political and economic issues of EU membership are.

This is because the political and economic dimensions of the EU project for member states differ considerably from the political and economic Copenhagen criteria, which related solely to the internal reforms necessary in candidates to make them viable members of the EU at the point when they join. This difference is less significant at the economic level of the European project, which relates to the single market and the 'four freedoms' of movement of goods, capital, services, and labour. Although this is not the same as the Copenhagen requirement that candidates establish a functioning market economy, it is very closely linked with the second part of the economic criterion that members should have 'the capacity to cope with competitive pressure and market forces within the Union'. This demand was a practical challenge for the CEECs, but it was easily comprehensible, as they had embarked on their transformation process in an era of globalization where transnational actors were a given. The necessity of integration into international markets, and gaining foreign direct investment, was self-evident for supporters of radical economic reform, and was an integral part of the transition from communism.

The post-communist democratization process, on the other hand, had been more of a domestic affair (and one that was far more problematic in some of the CEECs than in others). It had little in common with political debates at the European level, which normally relate to the supranational elements of EU decision-making. Meeting international standards of democracy internally does not necessarily entail the sharing of political decision-making on an international level. Consequently, there was considerable scope for attitudes to the EU to change markedly among parties in the candidate states once they had to participate in more complex debates about democracy in the EU. At the time they joined, however, domestic political concerns ranked far above aspirations for forging the ever-closer union of states in a united Europe.

This is perhaps ironic given the huge importance of reunifying the continent that was embodied in the 'return to Europe' slogans that were prominent in much of Central and Eastern Europe after the fall of communism. Yet this agenda embodied the desire of individual states to escape their exile in the undemocratic Soviet orbit, rather than any vision of a new federal polity with a degree of pooled sovereignty. A united Europe that guarantees the continent will never again be plunged into war—a potent symbol for the French and Germans or the Benelux countries (Gabel and Palmer 1995: 12)—is little more meaningful for Poles and Estonians than it is for the English or the Swedes. This is not because they did not suffer during the Second World War, but rather because their more recent suffering has been at the hands of the Soviet Union rather than any EU member state. If anything, the need to assure good neighbourly relations within the future EU has tended to be an irritant rather than a source of inspiration in the accession process. It has involved squabbling over emotion-laden historical disputes, with Czechoslovakia's Beneš decrees attacked by the Germans, Austrians, and Hungarians; Slovenia pressed on property rights by Italy; and Hungary criticized for passing its ethnically based 'Status Law' on Hungarian minorities abroad.

The candidate states were challenged by their membership of the Convention on the Future of Europe, which suddenly obliged them to articulate standpoints on the future decision-making procedures within the European institutions. The Convention's debates countered the widespread perception of the EU as an economic project that had tended to supersede the more idealistic 'back to Europe' image of EU membership prevailing in the early 1990s. This was a further reason why the EU had been less likely to act as a cross-cutting party cleavage in the CEECs than in existing member states: it was viewed rather one dimensionally as an economic rather than a political issue. The preoccupation with economics can be seen on two levels. First, the most controversial parts of the accession negotiations related to the sale of land and property to foreigners, free movement of labour, and agricultural subsidies. Secondly, there was a popular perception that some economic groups in society would benefit far more from membership than others. For example, the 1998 Central and Eastern Eurobarometer showed that most respondents believed that private business would gain most from membership, while low income groups, farmers, manual workers, and state enterprises would benefit least (European Commission 1998: Fig. 40). This again explains the 'neat fit' of the party political system with attitudes on the EU. The demographic groups which support EU membership most strongly, the younger and the most highly educated, are also those most closely associated with being the 'transformation winners' in post-communist change, and most likely to support pro-reform parties. Older people, rural-dwellers, women, and the less well-educated tended to be more nostalgic about the communist past, and more hostile to the adventure of joining the EU. This does not of itself make Central and Eastern Europe exceptional, since in existing member states, the better educated, professionals, and higher income groups are also more likely to support EU membership (Gabel and Palmer 1995:11; Anderson and Reichert 1996: 241). But there is a less fertile field for Euroscepticism among the professionally less successful members of stable societies because they do not feel existentially threatened by other momentous changes taking place around them.

The economic preoccupations of the CEECs do not bode well for their behaviour as future members of the EU. As Grabbe and Hughes have pointed out, states such as the UK, Sweden, and Denmark that joined the EU primarily for reasons of economic advantage have experienced greater long-term Euroscepticism than those that joined for political reasons (Grabbe and Hughes 1999: 190). The political commitment to the EU felt so strongly by the founder members has provided the strongest support base for the EU. In the medium to long term, therefore, party political stances on the EU in the new member states regarding their vision of the EU as a polity will be of utmost importance to the development of Europe.

5.3 CLASSIFYING EUROSCEPTICISM IN THE CEECs

The most exhaustive attempt to analyse Euroscepticism in Europe as a whole has been undertaken by Szczerbiak and Taggart in a series of papers presented since 2000 (Szczerbiak and Taggart 2000; Taggart and Szczerbiak 2001*a*, 2001*b*; 2002*a*). These have been valuable in synthesizing findings from case studies of individual member and candidate states, and formulating some general hypotheses about the nature of Euroscepticism. In tackling the initial problem of defining Euroscepticism, they distinguish between *Hard* and *Soft* Euroscepticism. The working definition of the former is

principled opposition to the EU and European integration [which can be seen] in parties who think that their countries should withdraw from membership, or whose policies towards the EU are tantamount to being opposed to the whole project of European integration as it is currently conceived. (Taggart and Szczerbiak 2001*b*: 4)

Soft Euroscepticism is

where there is NOT a principled objection to European integration or EU membership, but where concerns on one (or a number) of policy areas leads to the expression of qualified opposition to the EU, or where there is a sense that 'national interest' is currently at odds with the EU trajectory. (Taggart and Szczerbiak 2001*b*: 4)

The distinction is valuable because it is relatively easy to operationalize in individual case studies from both EU member and candidate states. It is also useful for generating explanations of the evolving dynamics of Euroscepticism in the CEECs, most notably the changes that take place during accession negotiations. For example, the difference between Soft and Hard Euroscepticism becomes more important as EU membership becomes less a symbolic issue and more a question of real political negotiation. Once accession negotiations commence, a government's available political options are constrained, since a decision by the EU to suspend talks would be regarded as a grave political failure. Hard Eurosceptics therefore become politically unacceptable (Henderson 2001: 21). This observation was originally based on the Slovak case, where the existence of 'Hard Euroscepticism' in some smaller parties became a relevant factor in coalition-building strategies from the late 1990s onwards. Since Hard Euroscepticism is broadly opposed to EU membership, it radically affected the coalition potential of parties once accession negotiations started. This was particularly true in 'second group' countries that began negotiations only in spring 1999. In politically significant parties, large enough to lead government coalitions, leaders such as Vladimír Mečiar of the Movement for a Democratic Slovakia (after the election defeat of 1998) and Ion Iliescu of the Party of Social Democracy of Romania (after the election defeat of 1996), distanced themselves from their more extremist mid-1990s coalition partners on the right and left, who were inclined towards 'Hard Euroscepticism' and were clearly unacceptable to both the EU and North Atlantic Treaty Organization (NATO).

This confirms Taggart and Szczerbiak's (2001*a*: 12) proposition that 'the positions of parties in their party systems is related to the expression of Euroscepticism'. Euroscepticism is 'a relatively costless stance' (Taggart and Szczerbiak 2001*a*: 12) for peripheral parties that do not participate in government, and they are thus able to profile themselves in policy terms by taking a Hard Eurosceptic stance. Hooghe, Marks, and Wilson (2002: 970–1) have also noted that 'exclusion from government leads to Euroskepticism (sic)', yet they observe further that 'the ideological positioning of parties towards the extremes of left/right dimension exerts a powerful influence on EU positioning independently of electoral performance or government participation'. The key problem is clearly one of distinguishing cause from effect. In the CEECs, most notably in the case of smaller Hard Eurosceptic parties in the Slovak Republic and Romania already mentioned, their attitudes to the EU appear to have *caused* their exclusion from government, because there is general elite consensus about the foreign policy imperative of attaining EU membership. Hard Euroscepticism excludes parties from the European integration project, whereas Soft Euroscepticism does not. However, there are, as yet, fewer indications that the development of Hard Eurosceptic stances has been the *effect* of repeated exclusion from government. It is easier to demonstrate that placement on the far left or right of the political spectrum naturally induces hostility to the EU project.

Although it can be useful to distinguish between Hard and Soft Euroscepticism in the CEECs, there have also been substantial problems in classifying the parties in the candidate states according to these categories. Unfortunately, Soft Euroscepticism has become a rather broad catch-all category that embraces both mainstream government parties which have been largely successful in pursuing their states' ambitions to join the EU, such as Viktor Orbán's Fidesz in Hungary or Václav Klaus's Civic Democratic Party in the Czech Republic, as well as more extremist parties such as the Czech Republicans, the Greater Romania Party, and the Slovak National Party (Taggart and Szczerbiak 2002*a*: 14). This is particularly questionable in the light of the fact that both the Greater Romania Party and the Slovak National Party came to be considered 'uncoalitionable' by their erstwhile larger coalition partners because of the likelihood that their inclusion in government would have negative effects on their countries' EU accession chances. The relevance of the difference between Soft and Hard Euroscepticism would be greater if the latter could be interpreted as precluding EU membership. While Mair (2000) has concluded, from an examination of current member states, that 'Europe' has had a limited impact on national party systems, this finding may well not hold for the CEECs in the current stage of development where attitudes to the EU have become a factor in coalition formation.

Furthermore, the Soft Eurosceptic category as applied by Szczerbiak and Taggart produces some rather strange bedfellows. Klaus's Civic Democratic Party, which public opinion surveys have shown to have the most pro-EU voters in the Czech Republic (*Integrace* 2000; STEM 2000: 9), ends up together with Mečiar's Movement for a Democratic Slovakia, which did so much to take Slovakia on a divergent integration trajectory after the division of Czechoslovakia, and which has some of the most Eurosceptic voters in Slovakia (Henderson 2001: 8). While it has been noted that popular support for EU membership does not always tally with the extent of party-based Euroscepticism (Taggart and Szczerbiak 2001*b*: 23–4), it nonetheless appears likely that either the categories, or their application, need some modification.

It is not unusual for pioneering attempts to impose order on apparent chaos to have teething problems with definitions. Their advantage is that they create a structure for generating further analysis. The first major critique of the Soft/Hard Euroscepticism framework was produced by Kopecký and Mudde in an analysis of party attitudes towards Europe in the Visegrad Four states (Czech Republic, Hungary, Poland, and Slovakia). They questioned the broad definition of Soft Euroscepticism and the somewhat blurred distinction between Soft and Hard Euroscepticism for reasons similar to those given earlier. They also noted the failure to distinguish between 'the ideas of European integration, on the one hand, and the European Union as the current embodiment of these ideas, on the other hand'. In their view, this had led to the term 'Euroscepticism' being wrongly ascribed to 'parties and ideologies that are in essence pro-European as well as to those that are outright anti-European' (Kopecký and Mudde 2002: 300). Instead, Kopecký and Mudde prefer to distinguish between 'diffuse' and 'specific' support for European integration. The former is understood as 'support for the general *ideas* of European integration that underlie the EU', while the latter denotes 'support for the general *practice* of European integration, that is, the EU as it is and as it is developing' (Kopecký and Mudde 2002: 300). They, therefore, created a four-field matrix, where an axis of 'Support for European integration' differentiates 'Europhiles', who believe in the key ideas of European integration, and 'Europhobes', who do not. A second axis of 'Support for the EU' differentiates EU-optimists, who believe in the EU in its current form or that which is developing, and EU-pessimists, who do not support its current form or direction of development. This produces more categories of parties, since EU-optimists may have critical views on individual EU policies; and EU-pessimists are not necessarily opposed to EU membership in principle, as they may 'simply consider the current EU to be a serious deviation from their interpretation of the founding ideas of European integration' (Kopecký and Mudde 2002: 302).

On the basis of these distinctions, Kopecký and Mudde have constructed four ideal types of party positions in Europe, into which they placed the political parties of the four Visegrad states (see Table 5.1). This categorization has a marked advantage over attempts to divide the same parties into Soft and Hard Eurosceptics as it produces clustering of parties that look intuitively more rational than those produced by Szczerbiak and Taggart. In part, this results not from the theoretical models, but rather from subjective judgements about where individual parties stand in ideological and policy terms. For example, the group of 'Euroenthusiast' parties, who are both Europhile on European integration and EU-optimist in their attitude to the EU, comprises parties gaining in total half or more of the vote in the Visegrad states. This accords with the generally positive opinion that the general public hold about EU membership in the Visegrad Four. In the diametrically opposite camp, the Slovak National Party and the Czech Republicans, who are classified as Soft Eurosceptic by Szczerbiak and Taggart, are assigned by Kopecký and Mudde to the company of the 'Hard' Eurosceptic Czech Communists and the Hungarian Justice and Life Party in a 'Euroreject' group which is both Europhobe and EU-pessimist.

Most significantly, however, the four-category matrix introduces two further diametrically opposite groups of parties, most of which are categorized as Soft Eurosceptic by Szczerbiak and Taggart. These are the 'Europragmatists' who are Europhobe on integration as a whole but

Table 5.1. Classification of parties in Visegrad Four states according to position on Europe

	SUPPORT FOR EUROPEAN INTEGRATION	
	Europhile	*Europhobe*
EU-optimist SUPPORT FOR EU	EUROENTHUSIASTS Civic Platform Democratic Left Alliance Freedom Union **Polish Peasant Party (S)** Hungarian Democratic Forum Hungarian Socialist Party Alliance of Free Democrats **Fidesz (S)** Czech Social Democratic Party Christian Democratic Union Freedom Union Democratic Union Slovak Democratic Coalition Party of the Democratic Left Party of the Hungarian Coalition	EUROPRAGMATISTS **Independent Smallholders Party (S)** **Movement for a Democratic Slovakia* (S)**
EU-pessimist	EUROSCEPTICS **Solidarity Electoral Action* (S—Christian National Union)** **Law and Justice Party (S)** Christian Democratic People's Party* **Civil Democratic Party (S)** **Christian Democratic Movement (S)**	EUROREJECTS *League of Polish Families (H)* *Self-Defence (H)* *Justice and Life* (H)* **Republicans (S)** *Communist Party of Bohemia & Moravia* (H)* **Slovak National Party (S)**

* Kopecky and Mudde note that the party is difficult to classify, as it hovers between two types.
(S) Classified as Soft Eurosceptic by Szczerbiak and Taggart (printed in bold).
(H) Classified as Hard Eurosceptic by Szczerbiak and Taggart (printed in bold italics).
Source: Adapted from Kopecký and Mudde (2002: 316) and Taggart and Szczerbiak (2002a).

EU-optimist and supporters of EU membership; and 'Eurosceptics', who are Europhile on European integration in general, yet EU-pessimist in support for the EU. The greater complexity of this model has the advantage of separating 'Eurosceptic' centre-right parties such as the Klaus's Civic

Democratic Party in the Czech Republic and the Christian Democratic Movement in Slovakia from the 'Europragmatists'. In the case of the Visegrad Four this is a small group encompassing only the deeply divided and chaotic Hungarian Smallholders, and, crucially, Mečiar's Movement for a Democratic Slovakia, which was for a decade the largest single party in Slovakia. The distinction is that Kopecký and Mudde's Euroscepticism—diverging somewhat from popular usage of the term—assumes a basic Europhilia, since without a feeling of belonging to a European community there is no basis for scepticism about how this project is being pursued. Europragmatists, however, may embrace the EU for strategic domestic political reasons, such as existing in a society where failure in the European integration stakes is viewed as an electoral liability, without having any allegiance to broader goals of pan-European integration. For example, for a nationalist in a small and newly independent state, EU membership may be necessary to raise its international status: recognition as a sovereign equal is imperative for self-legitimation. Likewise, for an agriculturally based party, EU subsidies may appear too good an offer to refuse. Such considerations can explain the Euro-pragmatism of the Movement for a Democratic Slovakia and the Hungarian Smallholders respectively.

Ironically, the difference between Eurosceptics and Europragmatists is most marked in their attitudes not to Europe, but to the USA. Eurosceptics—most notably Klaus in the Czech Republic—have reservations about the European project because, as Tiersky (2001: 2) described in a West European context, they question 'whether a "Europe" independent of the United States, a "European Europe" pursuing its own new continentwide interests, is not a historic folly'. This is certainly not the case for Euro-pragmatists, who are more likely to display a cultural reticence and foreign policy hostility towards the USA with roots in a more Eastern, or communist, sense of exceptionalism.

This distinction between Eurosceptics and Euro-pragmatists is also of considerable import for the development of party *systems*. It allows a better fit between 'party families' and views on Europe. Eurosceptic parties tend to belong to centre-right transnational European party organizations—most notably the European Democratic Union or, within the EP, the European People's Party. Mečiar's party, on the other hand, has notoriously courted many but joined none. Its pragmatism is such that it has proved enormously difficult to position (Williams 2000).

Nevertheless, Kopecký and Mudde's four ideal types divided according to support for European integration and support for the EU are not entirely unproblematic. They posit that the key question is one of 'strategy or ideology'. Their argument is that whereas strategy on EU issues may have some affect on stances adopted, it is ideology which plays the main role. This view is underpinned by their observation that parties in the Visegrad Four may move from being 'Euroenthusiast' to Eurosceptic or vice versa, but 'they do not move across the horizontal lines into either the Europragmatic or Euroreject category' (Kopecký and Mudde 2002: 319). In other words, strategy determines whether a party changes its level of support for the EU, linked either to a party's position in the party system, or to its stance on individual points of EU policy. However, a deeper-rooted ideology determines attitudes to the European integration project as a whole.

Kopecký and Mudde argue further that 'party families' tend to be consistent in whether they belong to the Europhile or Europhobe stream, but vary for strategic reasons on their attitudes to the EU. Social democrats and left liberals are Europhile and support the EU, whereas conservative liberals and Christian democrats support European integration, and are thus Europhile, but are sometimes also Eurosceptics who question aspects of EU policy. The extreme right and communists, on the other hand, are always Europhobes on issues of European integration. Euro-pragmatists, however, pose a problem, since pragmatism is incompatible with ideological rigidity, and a party flexible enough to embrace EU membership for strategic reasons may well also prove flexible enough to make the transition from Europhobia to Europhilia. The major weakness in the argument is one of imprecise definitions. What their analysis lacks is a systematic statement of the substantive attitudes towards European integration which divide Europhobia from Europhilia. The dividing line which parties do not cross is not explicitly defined.

This is particularly important when searching for a model of Euroscepticism applicable to both members and candidates since, as discussed in Section 5.2, perceptions of the economic and political issues involved in EU membership differ in the two sets of states. It is notable that Kopecký and Mudde define Europhiles as believing 'in the key ideas of European integration underlying the EU: institutionalized co-operation on the basis of pooled sovereignty (the political element) and an integrated liberal market economy (the economic element)' (Kopecký and Mudde 2002: 301). This is the very essence of the 'member state' EU agenda. It is thus possible that the 'Europhobes' of Central and Eastern European differ not because of resolute ideology, but because they are laggards who (together with their voters) have yet to adapt to the realities of living in a post-communist society, and are still working to a completely different agenda.

It therefore remains to be demonstrated conclusively that Kopecký and Mudde's four-field matrix of 'Euroenthusiasts, Eurosceptics, Europragmatists, and Eurorejects' is superior to Szczerbiak and Taggart's three-field linear model of pro-EU parties, Soft Eurosceptics, and Hard Eurosceptics at a pan-European level. In their analyses of the Visegrad Four, the major disharmony between the analyses of the two sets of authors relates to their assessment of individual parties' policies, which in the fluid political situation of the CEECs is likely to be subject to updating and revision, rather than to the logic of their models, which are intended to have a longer-lasting and more universal explanatory potential and are hence of far greater import. 'Euroenthusiasts', in Kopecký and Mudde's terminology, and Szczerbiak and Taggart's pro-EU parties (those not classified as either Soft or Hard Eurosceptics) are easily recognizable as representing more or less the same group of parties. Kopecký and Mudde's Eurosceptics are, broadly speaking, Szczerbiak and Taggart's Soft Eurosceptics, and the 'Eurorejects' are Hard Eurosceptics. It is essentially only the category of Europhobic 'Europragmatists' that is distinct to Kopecký and Mudde's matrix. However, the sole large party in this group, Mečiar's Movement for a Democratic Slovakia, a specifically Slovak phenomenon, which is described as 'phoney Europhile' elsewhere in this volume (Henderson 2008), and which also showed strong signs of disintegrating under the weight of its own internal contradictions as EU accession neared in early 2003. In these circumstances, a single party scarcely merits its own category of Euroscepticism at a pan-European level, and should perhaps rather be regarded as a transitory phenomenon linked to the specific temporary conditions existing during the exit from communism and transition to EU membership. Similarly, discrepancies in identifying individual Visegrad parties' Soft or Hard Euroscepticism may also be regarded as a temporary phenomenon of the post-communist transition. In some cases, this arises because parties still demonstrate the communist-era tendency of saying one thing and doing another (Henderson 2000). While this is most notable in the case of the 'Europragmatic' Movement for a Democratic Slovakia, it also causes problems with nationalist and communist parties, whose programmes and election manifestos not infrequently show an acceptance of EU membership lacking in the verbal utterances of the parties' leading politicians.

What is crucial, however, for creating common pan-European definitions of Euroscepticism is the fact that ideology—considered key by Kopecký and Mudde in their definitions of Europhobes in the Visegrad states—is also one of the major indicators for identifying Hard Euroscepticism in current member states, with the importance of ideology for underpinning Euroscepticism recognized already in Taggart's earlier writing (1998: 382). The proposition may therefore be advanced that, while post-communist states have generic strands in their prejudices against European integration (and indeed also in their widespread predisposition to EU membership) which derive specifically from their earlier communist experiences, it is nonetheless possible to construct academic propositions valid for both groups of parties in the enlarging EU.

5.4 PARTY SYSTEMS AND EUROPEAN INTEGRATION

The next question to be asked is whether the party systems in the CEECs have influenced the nature of Euroscepticism there, or whether, in fact, the European integration issue has affected the way party systems have developed? If the former proposition is true, we would expect exceptionalism in the nature of Euroscepticism in the new member states, whereas the latter would demonstrate that convergence was taking place. It is hard to give a clear answer since the last decade has witnessed simultaneous changes both in the party systems of Central and Eastern Europe, and in local political and popular perceptions of what the European project actually involves. The two have, at least to an extent, been interrelated, which means that cause and effect are often hard to unravel.

However, a better understanding of the dynamics of change can be reached by dividing the post-communist era into two distinct periods. The first, 'application' period leads up until accession negotiations begin in 1998, and the second, 'negotiation' period lasts until the first wave of eastern enlargement in 2004, when it is probable that a third, distinct, 'membership' period will begin. Both periods that will be examined show distinct characteristics both in the nature of the European agenda that confronted the CEECs, and in the shape of their party systems.

The first period was marked by a very general 'return to Europe' agenda, which had strong symbolic elements. Joining the EU was viewed as a way of definitively exiting from the Soviet orbit, but also as a means of returning as quickly as possible to where the states would have been if the communist takeovers of the 1940s had never happened. 'Return to Europe' was a Czechoslovak 1990 election slogan, and it was among the Czechs— the most prosperous and politically advanced society ever to be subjected to communism and one that was, from 1993, surrounded on three sides by EU member states—that the drive to return was most frantic, and that EU membership was most clearly conceived as natural destiny. In Bulgaria and Romania, however, striving to belong to Europe was a preoccupation that went back to the time of the Turkish occupation, and which continued into the new millennium since they were excluded from the first wave of eastern enlargement.

The party systems of this first period can be divided into four main sections, whose profiles can all in some measure be linked to attitudes to EU membership. The mainstays of the 'return to Europe' camp were parties with links to the forces who had overthrown communism. Although they rearranged themselves many times over the 1990s, they belonged to the pro-market/libertarian end of what Kitschelt considered the main axis of party competition in East Central Europe. Both their economic reform agendas and political and social value orientations were compatible with the criteria the EU established for aspiring member states. They were frequently in government, and contained the core of the parties that Kopecký and Mudde later described as 'Euroenthusiasts'. The next most prominent group of parties, who also led governments in the 1990s, can be described as 'residual communists', who clustered around the opposite, anti-market/authoritarian end of Kitschelt's axis of party competition. They were frequently tainted by nationalism, hesitant about economic reform, and cautious of the West: they did not easily obtain membership in international party organizations. Nevertheless, in 1995 three of them— the Bulgarian Socialist Party, the Party of Social Democracy in Romania, and the Movement for a Democratic Slovakia—submitted applications for their countries to join the EU. It was this camp, therefore, that can be considered the forerunner of what Kopecký and Mudde labelled 'Europragmatists'. Ideologically, they did not belong to the European mainstream, but strategically, they wanted EU membership.

The last two camps in the party system were smaller. The first group comprised largely Catholics, such as the Slovak and Hungarian Christian Democrats and the Polish Christian National Union, who were anti-communist and therefore naturally went into coalition with the 'return to Europe' parties. However, whereas the latter had no doubt that, without the unfortunate communist interlude, they would have been in the EU already, the former had alternative images of what their countries might have become if left to their own devices, and had reservations about the secular, consumerist West. They later, therefore, naturally formed part of Kopecký and Mudde's 'Eurosceptic' bloc.

The final camp comprises the extremists of left and right who became Kopecký and Mudde's 'Eurorejects'. On the left, they were communist diehards who split off from communist successor parties that became social democratic (and gravitated to the Socialist International and the 'return to Europe' camp), and they were too ideologically pure to join more populist 'residual communist' parties that garnered enough support to lead governments. On the right, they represented the naked face of nationalism.

In the second post-communist period, from approximately 1998 onwards, shifts took place both in the European agenda and in the party systems. In the course of EU accession negotiations, the intricacies of the European integration agenda began to clarify, and what Czech Eurosceptics called 'Eurorealism' (ODS 2001) dawned. Financial interests, most notably relating to the sale of real estate, agricultural and regional subsidies, and the free movement of labour, came to the fore, as did arguments about sovereignty and Catholic values, and 'future of Europe' debates about the institutional representation of small (and larger) states. Shifts in the party systems in the CEECs also gave more scope for such issues to be articulated in party programmes, and exploited in government/opposition contestation (Sitter 2002).

In terms of the party systems, the most significant shift was in the main axis of party competition. Kitschelt's original hypothesis that competition in East European party systems would be centred around a pro-market/libertarian versus anti-market/authoritarian axis has, over a decade, gradually diminished in validity. Major parties are realigning themselves along the axis more familiar in Western democracies. Parties on the economic right, most notably Fidesz in Hungary, the Civic Democratic Party in the Czech Republic, and Solidarity Electoral Action in Poland, have increasingly absorbed elements of right-wing value orientation such as social conservatism and nationalism. As a consequence of this, national assertiveness has penetrated into the mainstream of governing parties, and has manifested itself in Euroscepticism during negotiations with the EU. The economic right is joining the Catholics such as the Christian Democratic Movement in Slovakia in the Eurosceptic field. At the same time, convention arguments, such as the place of God in the European Constitution, allow the Catholics to articulate their views more strongly, freed from earlier constraints of needing to project a common front with the liberals against the residues of communism.

At the same time, parties on the economic left have been forced, in part by the exigencies of fulfilling the EU's economic criteria, to abandon the economic illusions of the communist period as they gradually make their way rightwards to somewhere left of centre, and their voters slowly come to terms with modern capitalism. Part of this process is that the 'residual communist' parties and voters are being brought over from the Europhobe to the Europhile part of the party system. Just as in member states, Europe 'imposes severe constraints on the policy manoeuvrability of governments and on the parties that make up those governments', and constrains their freedom (Mair 2000). In some respects, West European social democrats have undergone a similar experience to the communist successor parties of their Eastern neighbours: they have realized that certain national economic policies are simply not feasible in a heavily interdependent and internationalized world economy. As in the case of established EU members states, social democrats in the CEECs came 'to recognize that the European Union was the "only game in town", and adjusted their policies accordingly' (Marks and Wilson 1999: 118). It is also notable that the centre-left in Central and Eastern Europe is less susceptible to Euroscepticism than the centre-right, and in this its behaviour is consistent with that observed in member states. Marks and Wilson (2000: 443) noted in the West European context that 'if social democracy at the national level is weak or difficult to sustain, then European integration is likely to be viewed positively as a means to establish social democratic regulations within the EU as a whole'. The CEECs, as economically weak states, can only have their welfare regime improved by West European standards, and should therefore have social democratic parties that are pro-integration. Once communist residues, with promises of well-being that could not be delivered, are overcome, the left of the political spectrum has much to gain from EU membership. The fact that EU membership is commonly perceived in candidate states to be an economic project benefiting 'transition winners' had earlier tended to obscure this fact.

The net result of the issue realignment within parties is that, as has been observed elsewhere, opposition to Europe in its various forms becomes more prevalent on the right of the political system (Taggart and Szczerbiak 2001*b*: 21). It is particularly relevant, however, that a recent expert survey of party positions in EU member states showed that the most powerful predictor of a party's attitudes to European integration issues is the extent to which it was traditional/authoritarian/nationalist rather than Green/alternative/liberal (Hooghe, Marks, and Wilson 2002). The fact that economically right-wing parties in the accession countries are increasingly adopting right-wing value orientations means that they fit into the Eurosceptic profile fairly neatly. It is also notable that the Central and East European parties originally belonging to the 'back to Europe' camp who retained their liberalism in both economic and social issues remained strongly pro-EU. It appears likely, therefore, that the new member states will confirm that a left–right dimension relating to value orientation rather than economic issues fits better with the measure of Euroscepticism.

The final shift in party systems has been that 'Euroreject' parties, which are either unreformed communist or so nationalist and rural–conservative that they cannot come to terms with the demands of a market economy, are pushed to the periphery of the political system and become uncoalitionable in an age of EU accession. It is striking that of seven parties originally classified as 'Euroreject' by Kopecký and Mudde in their article published in 2002, only three—two Polish and one Czech—were actually in parliament at the end of that year. Colourful extremist maverick parties of the left and right had ceased to be the ubiquitous phenomenon of the early post-communist years, when they had flourished thanks to confused voters and an un-institutionalized party system where newcomers did not have to compete against the sophisticated campaigning machines of long-established parties. Instead, they became the occasional marginal players on a more West European pattern.

The consequence of all these shifts in the party systems of Central and Eastern Europe is that they now have a far greater programmatic coherence, and more similarity to the systems of the established EU member states. As a consequence, it is becoming far easier to classify Euroscepticism on a pan-European basis.

5.5 CONCLUSION

There have so far been two major problems in mapping Euroscepticism in Central and Eastern Europe. The first was that initial attempts were made in the early stages of the 'negotiation' period, when their party systems were still to some extent influenced by the original cleavage between 'return to Europe' reformers and residual communists that had been predominant in the earlier 'application' period. This led to a continued volatility in the party system, where successive elections often produced parliamentary parties with new names, but leading members and programmes that overlapped with earlier parties. This left considerable scope for political scientists to make different judgements about whether any party was, or was not, Eurosceptic. Also, confusion was sown by the continued existence of Euro-pragmatists, who were a manifestation of East European exceptionalism, and a phenomenon produced by a specific set of historical circumstances.

The second problem is that the issues addressed by candidate states are not the same as those faced by member states. Many of the questions about party stances to individual EU policies, such as environmental, asylum, and fiscal policies (Hooghe, Marks, and Wilson 2002), that are asked in surveys on member states are still impossible to answer in the case of candidate states. As the policy stances of Central and East European parties become clearer, more systematic classification of the level and nature of their Euroscepticism will also become possible.

However, despite the problems in analysing Euroscepticism in the candidate states, the general answer to the question whether Euroscepticism and party systems in the accession states are converging with the rest of the EU appears to be that yes, they are. This does not mean that there are no differences in attitudes to Europe, and some of them are likely to remain. For example, Christian democracy—a main promoter of European integration in the original European Community—is more Eurosceptic in the East. The likelihood of a Christian-based catch-all party developing is reduced by forty years of communist secularization, and, historically, Catholicism in the East of Europe had often become the defender of national interest rather than an internationalizing force. The EU may also be challenged by the nationalist preoccupations and complexes of small states which, even if nominally long in existence, have only recently gained full sovereignty in decision-making after liberation from Soviet domination. Furthermore, there may well be an upsurge in Soft Euroscepticism when the new members are no longer constrained by the straightjacket of long, arduous, and prescriptive accession negotiations. Since non-accession was not an electorally viable option, parties with an aspiration to govern had become locked into the EU's framework of expectations. They had to address the concerns of Eurosceptic parts of the population while treading a thin dividing line to avoid stalling negotiations, while opposition parties were in a position to demand that they achieve the impossible in negotiations. The opposition/government dynamic is likely to converge more clearly with that in the rest of the EU after accession.

The EU may well find that its new members are awkward partners, particularly because they still have a reduced pool of politicians with long years of experience in the art of democratic negotiation. It is not likely, however, that they will produce patterns of Euroscepticism radically different from those in current members. The extremes of the left–right spectrum will produce ideological Europhobes, who are best labelled 'Hard Eurosceptics' since, for better or worse, the journalistic term Euroscepticism has become established in political science usage as shorthand for the views of dissenters whose objections are nearer to phobia than scepticism. 'Soft Eurosceptics' will embrace a broad range of resistance to aspects of EU policy engendered both by parties' programmatic orientations and their manoeuvring for electoral advantage. Rather than exceptionalism, what is likely to be observed among the new members is the diversity celebrated in the EU's new motto.

6

Explaining the Failure of Euroscepticism in the European Parliament

Giacomo Benedetto

6.1 INTRODUCTION

Eurosceptics have failed to transform success in the European elections of certain member states into legislative and campaigning achievements within the European Parliament. This is at a time when the Parliament has developed a substantial role within the European Union (EU) legislative system that Eurosceptics oppose. Negligible alliance-building between Eurosceptic representatives is compounded by the failure to construct a homogeneous political group or any of the wider parallel structures common to the established party families at the European level. This chapter shows that unless other issues are also pursued, as is the case for the Soft Eurosceptics who have other policy interests, the European Parliament is an unrewarding location for Eurosceptics. Most of the Parliament's activity is concerned with legislation, rather than the constitutional issue of *more* or *less* Europe. The meagre representation and internal divisions of Eurosceptics mean that they are unable to exercise 'blackmail' power on other parties, in the same way as anti-system forces in national parliaments.

In 1994, single-issue Eurosceptic movements in Denmark and France were successful in the European elections, allowing them to form a Eurosceptic political group that had no connection with the extreme right. This achievement was reinforced in 1999 when the Eurosceptic list of Charles Pasqua and Philippe de Villiers received 13.5 per cent of the vote, coming second only to the Socialists. In Denmark, the June Movement, People's Movement against the EU, and Danish People's Party received

16.1, 7.3, and 5.8 per cent of the votes respectively (see Table 6.2). This is significantly higher than the 12 per cent gained by the Danish People's Party and 2.4 per cent gained by the Unity List Red-Greens in the Danish national elections of 2001, indicating that the Hard Eurosceptics *borrow* a significant amount of their votes at European elections from other parties, mainly the Social Democrats. The results of 1999 allowed for the formation of one avowedly Eurosceptic group, the Europe of Democracies and Diversities (EDD), and one which is an alliance of Eurosceptics and nationalists, the Union for a Europe of Nations (UEN). Only limited alliance-building has occurred between these two groups and the more long-standing Eurosceptics of the Green and Radical Left groups.

This chapter maps the incidence of Euroscepticism within the European Parliament. It analyses the behaviour of Eurosceptics members of European Parliament (MEPs) elected in 1999 that are not drawn from the extreme right. It compares the challenges of movement-based, often single-issue Euroscepticism on the right, with that on the left which is more concerned with social and economic issues. The paradox for Eurosceptic nationalist parties is that their greatest electoral successes have occurred in elections to an institution that they oppose and, having taken their seats, they are obliged to operate within it. Section 6.2 assesses the nature of Euroscepticism in the European Parliament. Sections 6.3–6.6 address the characteristics of Eurosceptic political groups, as well as the groups that contain Eurosceptic minorities. Section 6.7 looks forward to the arrival of Eurosceptic MEPs from Central and Eastern Europe as a consequence of enlargement.

6.2 GROUP FORMATION AND THE NATURE OF EUROSCEPTICISM IN THE EUROPEAN PARLIAMENT

Rule 29 of the Parliament's Rules of Procedure states the conditions for the formation of political groups. In 1999 apart from 'political affinity', these include a minimum number of members: twenty-three if they come from at least two member states, eighteen from three member states, or fourteen from four or more member states. A high level of compromise has been necessary for single-issue parties and Hard Eurosceptics to reach the minimum thresholds for group formation, given their heterogeneous

Table 6.1. State of the political groups in the European Parliament, 1999–2001

Group	MEPs
United Left (GUE)	42
Greens	48
Socialists (PES)	180
Liberals (ELDR)	51
European People's Party (EPP)	233
Europe of Democracies and Diversities (EDD)	16
Union for a Europe of Nations (UEN)	30
Non-attached (NA)	26
Total	626

origins. Group membership provides MEPs with extra staffing and office expenses, as well as representation on the Conference of Presidents, which decides the parliamentary agenda. It also offers access to office within the parliamentary hierarchy, to positions like committee president and rapporteur.

The most important groups correspond to the transnational federations, defined by Hix and Lord (1997: 167) as 'nascent Euro parties'. They are institutionalized in the sense of providing continuity, being well organized, and (usually) corresponding to a significant party in each member state. The Socialists (Party of European Socialists, PES), Christian Democrats and Conservatives (European People's Party, EPP), and Liberals (European Liberal, Democrat and Reform Party, ELDR) fit this classification, although the Greens have taken on many of its characteristics. The Radical Left (European United Left also known as Gauche Unitaire Européen, GUE) Group is also reasonably institutionalized, offering continuity for its members drawn from the communist and far left family. Table 6.1 shows that, following the 1999 elections, the previously dominant Socialists were reduced to 180 members, while 233 MEPs joined the EPP Group. Together these two groups continued to control two-thirds of the seats in the Parliament. With 51, 48, and 42 seats respectively, the Liberals, Greens, and Radical Left have been in a better position to make themselves relevant for the purpose of coalition formation than some of the hardest Eurosceptics. In July 1999, the EPP and Liberal Groups concluded a pact for the duration of the Parliament that applied to the election of the Parliament's President, the Parliament's internal reform process, and mutual consultation in policy formation.

There is a degree of Euroscepticism present, as a minority, within the EPP, Green, and Radical Left Groups. Previously the EPP was a group and party federation of federalist Christian Democratic parties. Its enlargement to other, smaller groups of the centre-right, some of which were Eurosceptic led to changes. While the Spanish People's Party, Nordic Conservatives, Portuguese Social Democrats, and Forza Italia are pro-integration, this is less the case for the British Conservatives, French Gaullists, and Nordic Christian parties. The greatest disparity within the Group is that of the British Conservatives, who vote against the rest of the Group in up to one-third of occasions.[1] The Radical Left Group is the heir of the communist group but has extended to the extreme left,[2] to ex-communists from Greece, Spain, Sweden, Finland, and Germany, and two left socialist parties.[3] The Greens have extended to the regionalist European Free Alliance[4] which is supportive of integration. Whether the Greens and Radical Left are sceptic or not, their main interests are focused on other policy issues.

Despite an inherent compromise with the system, some Eurosceptics are interested in playing a full role in the life of the Parliament because they want to influence outcomes on issues not connected purely with the pro- and anti-integration dimension. Some may wish to act *responsibly* as potential parties of government, while others are less concerned with these prospects. However, the harder Eurosceptics of the UEN Group with thirty MEPs and EDD Group with sixteen MEPs are numerically irrelevant in terms of usefulness to other groups wishing to construct coalitions.

The nascent Euro parties are the dominant players within the party system of the EU. Their members are represented within the national governments, on the European Commission, and dominate the European Parliament. For Eurosceptics, membership of the more institutionalized groups like the Greens, Radical Left, and the right-wing UEN[5] entail some compromise with non-Eurosceptics. Membership of the purist EDD Group[6] involves less compromise, yet provides less opportunity for influence or access to the kind of resources offered by the groups of the established party families. Following the typology of Taggart and Szczerbiak (2002*a*),

Euroscepticism within the European Parliament can be viewed as either Hard or Soft. The Hard Eurosceptics are those who believe their member state should withdraw from the EU or whose attitude to integration is very hostile. These include most of the EDD Group, the Swedish Greens, and the Swedish and Finnish left (ex-communist) parties. However, the only single-issue *exit* parties are the UK Independence Party and People's Movement from Denmark. The Swedish and Finnish parties belong to institutionalized party families that have other policy priorities. Some members of the Rally and Movement for France and British Conservatives can be regarded as Hard Eurosceptics, even if they do not explicitly favour abandoning engagement with the EU, their support for membership is so conditional that it amounts to leaving the EU.

The rest of this chapter looks at how, despite good performances in European Parliament elections, Eurosceptics have not had a significant effect on the functioning of the Parliament. In essence, there are four reasons for this, all concerned with being outsiders in a consensual system:

1. Eurosceptics, particularly the harder type, constitute a small minority in the Parliament.

2. They are heterogeneous and are divided between left and right.

3. Consensus is institutionalized in the EU, with a left–right grand coalition occurring within the Parliament, Council of Ministers, and European Commission, and pre-dating the arrival of harder Eurosceptics in the Parliament. In short, the grand coalition in Parliament predates any need in the future for the larger groups to work together so as to avoid compromise with Eurosceptics.

4. Some of the right-wing Hard Eurosceptics, such as the some of the British Conservatives and Philippe de Villiers' Movement for France, within their domestic contexts, do not see themselves as anti-system parties and do not adapt themselves well to a protest-based anti-system role in the Parliament.

However, these conditions do not apply to those whose Euroscepticism can be defined as Soft. The Soft Eurosceptics are those who are critical of further integration, perhaps wishing to reverse it, although they do not favour withdrawal. Soft Eurosceptics draw on an underlying opposition to aspects of integration, particularly if this is part of an anti-system approach that also applies to policy areas not connected to integration. The scepticism of institutionalized protest parties like those of the Green or Communist and ex-Communist families is conditioned by long-term policy suspicions of '*Brussels*', a response to significant Euroscepticism within domestic public opinion and the need to distinguish themselves from the cartel of government and pro-system opposition parties (Taggart 1998: 372).

One of the challenges for Eurosceptics elected to the European Parliament is that many of the parliamentary groups divide on the pro- and anti-integration dimension. In order to form groups and gain access to resources, parties have to make alliances, sometimes not always with those who share a similar perspective on integration. This is the case for the Greens, the Radical Left, the UEN, and British Conservative membership of the EPP. Meanwhile, the EDD is united on the pro- and anti-integration dimension, but divided between forces of left and right. One factor that binds Eurosceptic MEPs is that they are necessarily anti-system with regard to the EU and located on the periphery of the political group system of the European Parliament (see Table 6.2).

Aside from the Danish case, Table 6.2 shows that both Hard and Soft Eurosceptic parties were rewarded through a second-order (Reif and Schmitt 1980) effect in the 1999 elections, compared to their usual scores in national elections. In 1999, the Austrian Freedom Party was still growing, before suffering a significant fall in popularity by 2002. The Flemish Bloc, Finnish Left Alliance and Christian League, Communist Refoundation from Italy, and the far-left Socialists from the Netherlands were all in periods of growth during 1999, improving their proportion of the vote in subsequent national elections. France has multiple anti-system and Eurosceptic parties on both left and right, which gain votes from each other as well as from the French centre-left and centre-right. The National Front had just faced an internal leadership crisis in 1999 and gained a poor 5.7 per cent compared to its previous standards. However, the personality of Jean-Marie Le Pen was rewarded for the third consecutive time in the presidential elections of 2002. The extreme-left Workers' Struggle and Revolutionary Communist League together broke the 5 per cent barrier in 1999 and increased their share of the votes in the personalized contest of the presidential elections of 2002, before shrinking

Table 6.2. MEPs, self-perception of Euroscepticism, and percentage vote for Eurosceptic parties, 1999 and most recent national elections

Member State	Party	Scep*	Group	Vote in EP election of 1999	MEPs	Total surveys† returned	Sceptics	Vote in National Election	Year of National Election
Austria	Freedom	Soft	NA	23.5	5	1	0	10.0	2002
Belgium	Flemish Bloc	Hard	NA	9.2	2	0	—	11.6	2003
Denmark	June Movement‡	Hard	EDD	16.1	3	1	1	—	
	People's Movement	Hard	EDD	7.3	1	0	—	—	
	Unity List Red-Greens	Hard	—	—	0	—	—	2.4	2001
	Socialist People's	Soft	GUE	7.1	1	1	1	6.4	2001
	People's Party	Hard	UEN	5.8	1	1	1	12.0	2001
Finland	Left Alliance	Hard	GUE	9.1	1	0	—	9.9	2003
	Christian League	Soft	EPP	2.4	1	0	—	5.3	2003
France	Movement for France	Hard	UEN	13.5§	6	0	—	0.8	Legislative 2002
	Rally for France	Hard	UEN		6	0	—	0.4	Legislative 2002
	Communist	Soft	GUE	6.8	6	0	—	3.4	Presidential 2002
								4.8	Legislative 2002
	Workers' Struggle	Soft	GUE	5.2**	3	0	—	5.7	Presidential 2002
								1.2	Legislative 2002
	Revolutionary Communist	Hard	GUE		2	1	1	4.2	Presidential 2002
	Citizens' Movement††	Hard	PES		2	0	—	1.3	Legislative 2002
								5.3	Presidential 2002
	Hunting, Fishing, Nature, Traditions	Hard	EDD	6.8	6	2	1	1.1	Legislative 2002
								4.3	Presidential 2002
								1.7	Legislative 2002

(cont.)

Table 6.2. (*Continued*)

Member State	Party	Scep*	Group	Vote in EP election of 1999	MEPs	Total surveys† returned	Sceptics	Vote in National Election	Year of National Election
	National Front	Hard	NA	5.7	5	1	1	16.9	Presidential 2002
								11.3	Legislative 2002
Germany	Democratic Socialist	Soft	GUE	5.8	6	0		4.3	2002
Great Britain	Conservative	Soft	EPP	35.8	36	18	8	32.7	2001
	UK Independence	Hard	EDD	7.0	3	0	—	1.5	2001
	Greens	Soft	Greens	6.2	2	0	—	0.6	2001
Northern Ireland	Ulster Unionist	Soft	EPP	17.6	1	0	—	26.8	2001
	Democratic Unionist	Hard	NA	28.4	1	0	—	22.5	2001
	Sinn Fein	Soft	—	17.3	0	0	—	21.7	2001
Greece	Communist	Hard	GUE	8.7	3	1	1	5.5	2000
	Democratic Social	Soft	GUE	6.9	2	0	—	2.7	2000
Ireland	Greens	Soft	Greens	6.7	2	0	—	3.8	2002
	Sinn Fein	Soft	—	6.3	0	—	—	6.5	2002
Italy	Northern League	Soft	NA	4.5	4	1	1	3.9	2001
	Communist Refoundation	Soft	GUE	4.3	4	0	—	5.0	2001
	Flame Tricolour	Soft	NA	1.6	1	0	—	0.4	2001
Luxembourg	None								
The Netherlands	Christian Union	Hard	EDD	8.7‡‡	2	1	1	2.1	2003
	Political Reform	Hard	EDD		1	1	1	1.6	2003
	Socialist	Hard	GUE	5	1	0	—	6.3	2003
	Pim Fortuyn§§	Soft	—	—	0	—	—	5.7	2003

Portugal	People's	Soft	UEN	8.2	2	1	1	8.8	2002
	Communist	Hard	GUE	10.3	2	1	1	7.0	2002
Spain	Batasuna	Soft	NA	1.5	1	0	—	0.4	2000
Sweden	Left	Hard	GUE	15.8	3	0	—	8.3	2002
	Greens	Hard	Greens	9.4	2	0	—	4.6	2002

* Scep is the measurement of whether a party's Euroscepticism is 'Hard' or 'Soft' according to the typology of Taggart and Sczcerbiak (2002).

† As part of the 'How MEPs Vote' project of the Economic and Social Research Council's 'One Europe or Several' series, code L213 25 2019, all 626 MEPs were sent detailed surveys, of which 200 replied. This column shows the total number of MEPs from each respective Eurosceptic party that replied, 32 out of 130. The adjacent column shows how many of the respondents from each Eurosceptic party categorize themselves as Eurosceptics. One of the questions asked respondents to place themselves on a scale from 1 to 10, where those choosing 1 believe that 'European integration has gone too far' and those choosing 10 believe that 'the EU should become a federal state immediately'. I have classified as Eurosceptic those respondents who place themselves between 1 and 4 on this scale.

‡ June and People's Movements only contest European elections, and have an alliance with the Unity List Red–Greens which does not present candidates at European elections.

§ The Movement and Rally for France were allied in 1999 as the Rally for France-Independence of Europe list, achieving 13.5 percent of the vote.

** In the 1999 European elections, Workers' Struggle and the Revolutionary Communist League presented a joint list which received 5.2 percent of the vote.

†† Due to an electoral alliance at the European elections, two members of the Citizens' Movement were elected on the French Socialist list which received 22 percent of the vote. However, the French Socialist Party was in no sense Eurosceptic.

‡‡ Christian Union and Political Reform present a joint list at European elections.

§§ The Pim Fortuyn List is a new party, founded since the 1999 European elections.

back to just over 1 per cent each in the legislative elections one month later. The French Communists, as well as the Hunting, Fishing, Nature, Traditions movement performed significantly better in 1999 than in 2002. The most notable case of this was that of the Rally and Movement for France, achieving 13.5 per cent, before falling back to below 1 per cent of the votes in the legislative elections of 2002, having failed to field candidates in the presidential contest. The East German-based Democratic Socialists achieved their highest national score ever in 1999 of 5.8 per cent of the votes. The British Conservatives, UK Independence Party, English Greens, Greek Communists, Irish Greens, Dutch Calvinists, Portuguese Communists, and Swedish Left and Green parties all performed significantly better in 1999 than was the case in subsequent national elections.

As a part of the 'How MEPs Vote' project,[7] all 626 MEPs were sent detailed surveys in 2000, of which 200 replied. Of these, 32 out of 130 MEPs from Eurosceptic parties replied. Those respondents identifying themselves Eurosceptics are also shown in Table 6.2. Response rates were highly variable according to party, but eight out of eighteen British Conservative respondents identified themselves as Eurosceptic, as did all those who replied from every party, except the Austrian Freedom Party and the French Hunters. Although not listed by me as Eurosceptic parties, two out of three of the Bavarian Social Christians to reply identified themselves as Eurosceptics, as did one out of the eleven German Christian Democrats, two out of three Swedish Social Democrats, and one of two Finnish Centre Party MEPs, the only member of the Liberal Group to do so. The only comparable survey on pro- and anti-integration attitudes of parliamentarians (discussed in Katz's chapter in this volume) was the 1996 'Political Representation in Europe' study, which involved face-to-face interviews with MEPs and a postal survey to the members of eleven national parliaments (Schmitt and Thomassen 1999). The most pro-integration parliamentarians from across all parties were found to be those from Italy, Luxembourg, Spain, and Belgium. British and Danish national parliamentarians were not surveyed, so the most sceptical were identified as those from Sweden. In every case, except for that of Sweden, MEPs were slightly more pro-integration than national parliamentarians, presumably due to a strong second-order success for the Left and Green parties in the Swedish elections to the European Parliament in 1995.

6.3 THE EUROSCEPTIC POLITICAL GROUPS: THE GROUP OF THE UNION FOR A EUROPE OF NATIONS AND THE GROUP FOR A EUROPE OF DEMOCRACIES AND DIVERSITIES

Following the 1999 elections, Fianna Fail, the Portuguese People's Party, the Danish June and People's Movements, and the Dutch Calvinists of Political Reform and the Christian Union were left looking for new partners that were not of the extreme right. The UEN was formed out of a partial merger between the Union for Europe[8] and Europe of Nations groups. It consisted of Fianna Fail, the Portuguese party, Charles Pasqua's Eurosceptic Gaullists of the Rally for France, and their Movement for France allies led by Philippe de Villiers, who had been elected on a joint list. Their smaller partner was the Danish People's Party, a new 'new populist' party (Taggart 1995), espousing a right-wing, Eurosceptic, low-tax agenda, inherited from its Progress Party predecessor. The Group was joined a few weeks later by the former extreme-right party from Italy, National Alliance. Although the French and Danish components of the Group are new parties whose fortunes fluctuate from one election to another, the Irish, Italian, and Portuguese parties are institutionalized, electorally stable, and hold or have held national government office. They are not parties that have split in protest from larger parties. Fianna Fail is the main party of government in Ireland, while the Italian and Portuguese parties have, since 2001 and 2002 respectively, been the main coalition partners of larger centre-right parties. This was one of the attractions in forming the Group for Charles Pasqua.[9] The key for the UEN was not to be a Group whose primary goal was Euroscepticism, so much as a respectable, right-wing, and non-federalist alternative to the EPP. For Pasqua, it was more important to have allies in government or with good prospects of government in the future. An alliance with the 'left-wing' Danish Eurosceptics, Dutch Calvinists, or UK Independence Party was therefore ruled out.

Following the signing of the Treaty of Athens in April 2003, parliamentary observers from the Accession States were permitted to attend sessions of the European Parliament. The failure of the Czech Civic Democrats to join the UEN was a disappointment for the Group, which had carefully courted the Czech party. Having unsuccessfully applied to split their observer delegation to the Parliament between the UEN and the Liberal

Group, the Civic Democrats, as the main opposition party of the Czech Republic, calculated that their interests were better served by joining the EPP.[10]

While right of centre national parties like Fianna Fail may be compatible with new populism to a certain degree, the Movement and Rally for France are based on the charisma of their founders, with weak yet centralized structures. The more movement-based Movement for France, as a result of disagreements with the Rally for France and a funding scandal, left the UEN Group in January 2001. Its departure reduced the Group's size, but made it more consistent as an alliance of right-wing, potential parties of government.

The wording of the Political Charter of the UEN Group avoids language that is overtly Eurosceptic. It is clearly influenced by the Gaullist origins of the Rally and pro-integration views of the Group's Italian and Irish members in supporting 'a strong Europe which would not allow itself to be submitted to any foreign political, economic, or cultural domination and which develops its own security and foreign policy'.[11]

The Charter of Fundamental Rights, drafted alongside the Treaty of Nice, was approved by the Irish government. The Fianna Fail MEPs voted in favour of it, alongside those from National Alliance. National Alliance MEPs were ideologically consistent in emphasizing duties as well as rights within the Charter. Regarding the right to marry, they wanted to protect the 'natural family, composed of man and woman', otherwise the rights of the family would be threatened by 'alternative patterns'.[12] National Alliance suggests the way to a Europe of Nations, with a common foreign and defence policy, is through enhanced cooperation. As government parties, both Fianna Fail and National Alliance voted in favour of Parliament's opinion on the Treaty of Nice which urged ratification, unlike the rest of the Group.

In January 2001, following the conclusion of the Intergovernmental Conference at Nice, Romano Prodi announced that the Commission was looking at tabling proposals for European transnational parties to receive public funding. National Alliance was among the most keen to endorse the launch of the Alliance for a Europe of Nations to serve as a right-wing alternative to the EPP. Following the signing of the Charter of the Alliance for a Europe of Nations, Cristiana Muscardini, the delegation leader of National Alliance and vice-president of the Group issued an enthusiastic statement that emphasized the compatibility of Eurosceptics and nationalist pro-integrationists within the same Group:

Our project is based on a European confederation which respects national identities, economic culture, and the European culture of safe, nutritious food, for a Europe free of hegemonies, ready to support democracy against any form of oligarchy, be it political, economic, national or transnational.[13]

The language of the Rally for France is grounded in Gaullism, with reference to a Europe of nation states 'stretching from the Atlantic to the Urals' (Benoît 1997: 50). Pasqua's Gaullist version of Euroscepticism, dating from his campaign against the Maastricht Treaty in 1992, was state focused. Pasqua founded the Rally in 1998, when he decided to break from the Rally for the Republic, which he viewed as having betrayed Gaullism. The need to protect France from incursions in sovereignty featured in Pasqua's rejection of the Treaty of Nice:

Apart from the re-weighting of votes in the Council of Ministers and protection of the Cultural Exception, they [Jospin and Chirac] have ceded on everything: on the number of French deputies at the European Parliament, from now on far fewer than the German deputies; on the removal of one of our two Commissioners in Brussels, which brings France down to the same level as Luxembourg; and our right of veto on dozens of vital subjects.

The only clear result is that France is becoming a second class province of a federal state dominated by Germany and whose strategic and military objectives are those desired by Washington.[14]

Although the parties of the UEN are right-wing, they are in no sense free market. They support a statist right-wing tradition of protectionism and welfare provision. Georges Berthu, leader of the Movement for France delegation in the Parliament, suggests a 'network model' for Europe (Berthu 2000: 13). Under this, there would be a contract between citizens and the people they elect. This is compatible with the 'variable geometry' model for a multi-speed Europe, so that all will be free to choose on integration. He argues that a return to the Luxembourg Compromise of the 1960s is more necessary than ever (Berthu 2000: 45). This would mean returning to the need for unanimity in all votes on the Council of Ministers. Berthu differs from his former colleagues of the UEN, including the Danish People's Party, in opposing the Single European Act, arguing that the Luxembourg

Compromise meant that 'de Gaulle had neutralized not one, but several supranational viruses at once, which the Single Act liberated in 1987' (Berthu 2000: 58). His support for EU membership is therefore so conditional that it conforms to the typology of Taggart and Szczerbiak (2002*a*) for Hard Euroscepticism.

The Movement for France and Danish People's Party were the most anti-integrationist of the parties in the UEN. However, the Danish party differs from the Movement in supporting free trade and the Single Market. It is opposed to pooling foreign, defence, or monetary policy, but is supportive of enhanced cooperation for those member states that choose to take part.[15] Its ideal view of the EU is intergovernmental and does not raise objections to the Council of Ministers, unlike its fellow June and People's Movements from Denmark. Its Euroscepticism is Hard in its opposition to the existence of the European Parliament:

The Danish People's Party would like decisions in the EU, to be made by the Council of Ministers in order that the European Parliament's own powers are reduced. The Danish People's Party would preferably like to see the European Parliament closed down.[16]

The harder Eurosceptic group is the EDD, composed of the Danes from the June and People's Movements, the Dutch Calvinists from Political Reform and Christian Union, and two newly represented forces, the UK Independence Party and the French Hunting, Fishing, Nature, and Traditions movement. Only the Danish and British components of this group are single-issue Eurosceptic parties. Hunting, Fishing, Nature, and Traditions is a single-issue party dedicated to agriculture, rural development, and the environment. Its belief that 'these questions should be decided in France and not in Brussels'[17] is compatible with membership of the Group.

The views of the Danish EDD members are similar to those of the Movement for France on the question of integration. They believe the EU can never be democratic because it is too distant and citizens only identify with the national level. Unlike the People's Movement, the June Movement does not want Denmark to leave the EU, but opposes all further integration. Relations with other members of the Group are not perfect on account of the EDD's heterogeneity. The Dutch Calvinists have 'rather antiquated' views on the rights of women. Meanwhile the 'right-wing attitudes' of the UK Independence Party are minimized by its high levels of absenteeism. The factor that holds the Group together is its common Eurosceptic attitude and the material advantages of group formation.[18]

Total defections between the members of the Hard Eurosceptic groups have been much greater than those affecting the major pro-system groups. Following the departure of the six MEPs of the Movement for France from the UEN, continuing disagreements within the Rally for France led to three of Pasqua's six MEPs defecting from the Group in March 2001, joining the EDD. The EDD has also lost one of its UK Independence Party members and two of its Danish members on account of internal disagreements within their delegations. These disagreements often arise from differences as to how best to oppose the EU system from within, as well as difficulties in building consensus between parties with heterogeneous preferences.

6.4 EUROSCEPTICISM WITHIN POLITICAL GROUPS: THE GREENS AND THE RADICAL LEFT

Although the Greens and Radical Left may agree with some of the right-wing Eurosceptics on issues concerning lack of democracy, as well as sovereignty, the main critique is that European integration has ignored the needs of ordinary working people and subjects like the environment. Within the Green Group, there has been a recent tendency to move away from Euroscepticism towards constructive criticism of integration. The co-presidents of the Group elected in December 2001, Daniel Cohn-Bendit and Monica Frassoni, are both federalists. The only MEPs in the Green Group that maintain Eurosceptic policies are the English, Irish, and Swedish, who accounted for only six of its forty-eight members in 1999.

The Swedish Greens display the hardest Euroscepticism in the Group. One of the party's slogans is 'Yes to the World but NO to the European Union'. The party believes a referendum should be held on withdrawal from the EU, since environmental standards are threatened and economic independence has been lost.[19] The scepticism of Irish Greens, like that of the Swedes, is determined by what they view as implications for Irish and Swedish neutrality and opposition to military and economic integration. They believe that important policies should not be decided in far away institutions and that while the Treaties of Amsterdam and Maastricht transferred powers to the EU institutions, no powers were devolved back to the nation states or regions (McKenna 1997; Gahrton 1998).

The scepticism of the Irish Greens is softer in so far as they do not believe that Ireland should leave the EU. In the view of one of the Irish Green MEPs, EU legislation has had a modernizing effect on Ireland, providing it with an environmental policy and enhanced rights for women, although lack of accountability is a problem. Green issues are much more important than the constitutional question of Irish membership so 'we are more interested in pursuing policy with the Group than in being sceptical'. In any case, she does not view intergovernmentalism as the solution, since the Council is the least accountable of all the institutions and 'this is not the way to adequately deal with globalization'.[20]

The Radical Left is also divided on constitutional issues, with Hard Eurosceptics and federalists in the Group. Like the Greens, the Group unites around issues that are not directly concerned with EU membership. Since the success of the centre-right in the 1999 European elections, there is a limited convergence between the left-wing groups, particularly on environmental issues 'where we are happy to follow the lead of the Greens'.[21]

The Group is most divided on constitutional issues. This was exemplified by the vote on granting Parliament's assent to the Charter of Fundamental Rights in November 2000. The Group's Hard Eurosceptics are found within the Swedish and Finnish Left parties, who believe their countries should leave the EU, the extreme-left Socialist Party of the Netherlands and Revolutionary Communist League from France, and the Greek and Portuguese Communist parties.

The views of the Swedish Left Party are almost identical to those of the Swedish Greens. Its criticism is based on the EU being 'capitalist and undemocratic' and the risk of monetary union undermining social achievements.[22] A Swedish official of the Group suggested that his party shares the same perspective as the Danish June Movement on European integration, although his is a 'real party', interested in pursuing policies of its party family. The party takes the view that, although opposed to EU membership, it should represent its voters in the Parliament and participate in committees of policies relevant to them. One of its MEPs, Jonas Sjöstedt, had previously been a member of the Constitutional Affairs Committee, which interested him as a Eurosceptic. However, it has no legislative power and is 'full of federalists', so he decided to divert his energies to the Environment Committee, which is a powerful committee and an important policy area for the party. The other two MEPs of the party are members of the Employment and Social Affairs Committee, traditionally a policy area of interest to the Left, and the Women's and Equal Rights Committee. The latter is not a powerful committee but women's rights are a policy issue valued by the party.[23]

Esko Seppänen, the single MEP of the Finnish Left Alliance, is perhaps the hardest sceptic in the Group. He is actively involved in SOS Democracy, with right-wing Eurosceptics. He is highly critical of any defence identity for the EU, arguing that it would be controlled by NATO and the USA and would threaten peaceful countries.[24] Seppänen's criticisms are more pronounced than those of other left-wing Eurosceptics, although his objections to military and economic integration are shared by them. His statement on the Parliament website is grounded in the same language as that used by the French, Greek, and Portuguese Communists during the cold war.

The Radical Left plays what it sees as a constructive role in the Parliament. In 1999, the Group withdrew its candidate for the presidency of the Parliament in favour of the Socialist, Mario Soares, in the cause of left unity. The Group's Leader, Francis Wurtz announced that he wanted to work with the Greens and the Socialists on the 'big issues', specified as: relations with the South, lack of confidence from the people in democracy, greater involvement for the Parliament in the Intergovernmental Conference leading to Nice, more democratic control over the European Central Bank, combating the 'neo-liberal culture' of the European institutions, and greater emphasis on food safety and tax harmonization.[25] However, Wurtz stood as his Group's candidate for the presidency of the Parliament in January 2002. On this occasion the Group wished to maintain its identity rather than simply support the Socialist candidate. The Green Group also fielded its own candidate.

The judgement of Wurtz on the Treaty of Nice was highly critical. He asked if it is necessary to 'dissolve the essence of our societies in a mercantile logic', a familiar return to the economic critique of integration. He called for common policies on economic, social, cultural, and environmental matters and lamented the 'minimization' of the Charter of Fundamental Rights[26] and concluded with an attack on intergovernmentalism, symbolizing a break from the previous Euroscepticism of the communist family.

Although there is a significant Eurosceptic presence within the Radical Left Group, it constitutes a minority. The approach of the Group can be more accurately defined as anti-system without necessarily being Eurosceptic.

6.5 THE EUROSCEPTIC ALLIANCE: SOS DEMOCRACY

SOS Democracy is a cross-party, Hard Eurosceptic organization, open to MEPs from left and right. It was established in 1998 by members of the former Europe of Nations Group, as well as the Swedish and Finnish Left parties and the Swedish Greens. It has support from the more Eurosceptic contingent of British Conservatives, as well as single-issue Eurosceptics of the UEN and EDD Groups. It proposes working with Eurosceptic groups in civil society across Europe to foster a pan-European debate on alternatives to integration[27] and is linked to The European Alliance of EU-Critical Movements (TEAM). The latter was established at a *counter-summit* held parallel to the European Council at Edinburgh in 1992. According to a Swedish official of the Radical Left Group, the effect of SOS Democracy is limited, because there are too many disagreements on other issues and it has come to be dominated by the right.[28]

The declaration of SOS Democracy is critical of the EU's 'rigid institutional framework', as well as centralization and the Brussels bureaucracy. It makes reference to nation states, identity, and freedom, which are curtailed by European integration. The subordination of national constitutions is one its main concerns, as well as the dangers of the Central Bank and the dangers of the co-decision procedure in giving the European Parliament the right to overrule the member states.[29] The British Conservative MEPs within SOS Democracy wish to 'renegotiate' EU membership rather than withdraw. This amounts to Hard Euroscepticism, as defined by Taggart and Szczerbiak (2002*a*) since 'renegotiation' is an unrealistic demand. This ideal is similar to the views of James Goldsmith (1994: 67–9) in supporting an intergovernmental free trade area, with very limited supranational institutions. Conservatives who oppose membership of the EPP Group point out that there is 'no difference' between continental Christian

Democracy and Tony Blair's Labour Party. One Eurosceptic Conservative believes the thirty-five members of SOS Democracy are the only 'real sceptics' in the Parliament. The only way to have an effect on 'defeating federalism' is to vote with hard-line federalists against measures that they consider 'not federalist enough'. This is the only way in which 'blackmail potential' (Sartori 1976) can be exercised by Eurosceptics in the Parliament. Otherwise it is not possible to have much effect except through using the media. The fact that 'more than twice as many people vote . . . in Big Brother [television reality show in United Kingdom] than vote in European elections' indicates that the system is without legitimacy.[30]

In January 2002, Jens-Peter Bonde, leader of the EDD Group, SOS Democracy, and the Danish June Movement, stood as President of the Parliament against the candidates of the major groups. This was the first time that an anti-system or Eurosceptic candidature for the presidency occurred since the 1980s, when Jean-Marie Le Pen had stood on various occasions. However, in terms of votes gained, Bonde was more successful than previous outsiders. Bonde made an appeal beyond his core constituency of Hard Eurosceptics to those MEPs who supported greater reform and openness within the Parliament. In the second round of voting, he gained 77 votes, compared to 277 for Patrick Cox of the Liberal and EPP Groups and 226 for David Martin of the Socialist Group, indicating the success of his appeal beyond the Hard Eurosceptics of SOS Democracy.

6.6 ENLARGEMENT, THE 2004 EUROPEAN PARLIAMENT ELECTIONS, AND BEYOND

In May 2003, 162 parliamentary observers were appointed to the European Parliament from the accession states (Table 6.3). The observers can be treated effectively as precursors to the MEPs elected in 2004 and so are worthy of comment here.[31] Of these, 15 observers came from Hard Eurosceptic parties, while 41 came from Soft Eurosceptic parties. This compares with 51 MEPs from Hard Eurosceptic parties and 79 from Soft Eurosceptic parties in the Parliament of 626 members elected in 1999. The observers have been appointed in proportion to their representation in their domestic parliaments.

Table 6.3. Parties of observers to the European Parliament from the accession states and their percentage vote in the most recent national elections

Accession State	Party	Scep	Group	Observers	Vote in National Election	Year of National Election
Czech Republic	Civic Democrats	Soft	EPP	8	24.5	2002
	Communist	Hard	GUE	3	18.5	2002
Cyprus	Progressive Workers	Soft	GUE	2	34.7	2001
Estonia	People's Union	Soft	UEN	1	13.0	2003
Hungary	Fidesz	Soft	EPP	9	41.1*	2002
	Democrats	Soft	EPP	3		
Latvia	Fatherland and Freedom	Soft	UEN	1	5.4	2002
Lithuania	None					
Malta	Labour	Hard	PES	2	47.5	2003
Poland	People's Party	Soft	EPP	4	9.0	2001
	Law and Justice	Soft	UEN	4	9.5	2001
	Self-Defence	Hard	NA	4	10.2	2001
	League of Polish Families	Hard	NA	3	7.9	2001
	Senate Bloc[†]	Soft	EPP	3		
	Conservative People's	Soft	EPP	1		
	Polish Peasant Bloc	Hard	NA	1		
	Catholic National	Hard	NA	1		
Slovakia	Democratic Slovakia	Soft	NA	2	19.5	2002
	People's Union[‡]	Soft	UEN	1		
	Christian Democrats	Soft	EPP	2	8.3	2002
	Communist	Hard	GUE	1	6.3	2002
Slovenia	None					

*Fidesz and the Hungarian Democrats concluded an electoral alliance in the most recent elections, gaining 41.1 per cent of the vote.

[†] The Senate Bloc, Conservative People's Party, Polish Peasant Bloc, and Catholic National Movement are parties that have parliamentary representation but have arisen through splits from other parties since the most recent elections in Poland.

[‡] The Slovak People's Union has parliamentary representation and has arisen through a split with the Movement for a Democratic Slovakia since the most recent elections.

The prevalence of Soft Euroscepticism in the accession states has already been noted by Taggart and Szczerbiak (2002*a*). Much of this Soft Euroscepticism will be found in an enlarged and increasingly heterogeneous EPP Group after the entry of the Czech Civic Democrats, Hungarian Fidesz, Slovak Christian Democrats, and a polarized centre-right opposition in Poland. The Polish delegation to the EPP contains five parties, of which four can be described as Soft Eurosceptic.

The UEN Group acquired seven observers: the People's Union from Estonia, which is a largely agrarian party displaying Soft Euroscepticism; Latvian Fatherland and Freedom, which are right-wing nationalists; a splinter from the Movement for a Democratic Slovakia called the Slovak People's Union;[32] and from Poland, an anti-corruption party, Justice and Law, with four members. The hopes of the UEN in attracting the Czech Civic Democrats were not realized.

Ten of Poland's fifty-four observers have failed to join a Group, either through self-exclusion or inability to find allies. They comprise Self-Defence, the League of Polish Families, the Polish Peasant Bloc, and the National Catholic Movement, and can all be considered Hard Eurosceptics. The Movement for a Democratic Slovakia, anxious to distance itself from a Hard Eurosceptic discourse of the past, has been unable to find allies in the European Parliament.

The Hard Eurosceptic communist parties of the Czech and Slovak Republics have joined the Radical Left Group, together with the softer Progressive Workers (AKEL) from Cyprus and pro-integration Socialists from Latvia. This shows that the growth potential of the Radical Left following enlargement may be limited. The Green Group has gained one new member from Latvia alone, which is not a Eurosceptic party, while the Socialist Eurosceptics feature only the Maltese Labour Party. The Hard Eurosceptics of the EDD Group have not gained any members from the Accession States.

6.7 CONCLUSION

The success of single-issue Eurosceptic parties in European elections has not had a significant effect on the European Parliament, because this success has been limited to only a few member states. However, it has allowed the formation of new political groups that are Eurosceptic, in the case of the EDD (and its successor group, Independence and Democracy which attracted 37 MEPs at the start of the 2004 Parliament), or significantly Eurosceptic, in the case of the UEN. Efforts at building consensus between Eurosceptics are undermined by the heterogeneity of their parties and the greater salience of left–right divisions. Even Hard Eurosceptic parties within the left-wing groups have other interests beyond the constitutional question of EU membership that they wish to pursue within their party families.

The levels of institutionalization of different parties determines their coherence at the European level. Many of the right-wing Eurosceptic parties have weak structures focused around the personalities of their leaders, and peak at European elections, which mean that they often lack a strong base at national or local levels. The extent of *compromise* with the European Parliament system, in terms of taking up reports or forming alliances with non-sceptics, is a significant challenge for Eurosceptic MEPs, as seen by the relative fluidity in the membership of the UEN and EDD Groups. Despite the efforts of some individuals, including the founders of SOS Democracy, Eurosceptics remain divided in the European Parliament on account of the demands made by differing nationalist constituencies. This division is evident not only from the dispersal of Eurosceptics between different groups, but also within the groups that they have formed.

NOTES

1. Data collected as part of the 'How MEPs Vote' project, funded by the Economic and Social Research Council, code L213 25 2019.
2. The extreme-left Workers' Struggle and Revolutionary Communist League from France and the Socialist Party from the Netherlands.
3. The Socialist People's Party from Denmark and Democratic Social Movement from Greece.
4. This consists of left-wing regionalist parties from Scotland, Wales, Flanders, and Spain.
5. The UEN consists of the relatively pro-integration National Alliance from Italy, Fianna Fail from Ireland and the more Eurosceptic Rally for France

of Charles Pasqua, the Portuguese People's Party, and the Danish People's Party.

6. The EDD includes the UK Independence Party, the June Movement and People's Movement against the EU from Denmark, Hunting, Fishing, Nature, and Traditions from France, and three Dutch Calvinists from Political Reform and the Christian Union.

7. Economic and Social Research Council 'One Europe or Several' series, code L213 25 2019.

8. The principal members of this group had been Fianna Fail, the French Gaullists, and the Portuguese People's Party.

9. Interview, Pierre Monzani, Deputy Secretary-General, UEN Group, Brussels, January 2001.

10. Correspondence with Sean Hanley, May 2003, citing Czech Press Agency (CTK).

11. Political Charter of the Group of the Union for a Europe of Nations, Brussels, July 1999.

12. Documento della Delegazione di Alleanza Nazionale al Parlamento Europeo relativo alla Carta dei diritti fondamentali, alla riforma istituzionale ed all'allargamento dell'Unione Europea (undated).

13. National Alliance press release, Rome, 30 March 2001.

14. Statement of Charles Pasqua on the Summit of Nice, Rally for France press release, Paris, 12 December 2000.

15. Programme of the Danish People's Party, Copenhagen (undated).

16. Programme of the Danish People's Party, Copenhagen (undated).

17. Interview, Ulla Sandbæk MEP, Brussels, January 2001.

18. Interview, Ulla Sandbæk MEP, Brussels, January 2001.

19. Green Party of Sweden Programme, Stockholm (undated).

20. Interview, Nuala Ahern MEP, Brussels, January 2001.

21. Interview, Jan Johansson, Radical Left Group, Brussels, January 2001.

22. Swedish Left Party (2000) 'A socialist offensive'.

23. Interview, Jan Johansson, Brussels, January 2001.

24. Esko Seppänen MEP at the Radical Left Group Seminar in Tallinn, 24 August 2000.

25. *L'Humanité*, 21 July 1999.

26. Francis Wurtz in press release, Radical Left Group, Strasbourg, 12 December 2000.

27. Interview, Daniel Hannan MEP, Brussels, January 2001.

28. Interview, Jan Johansson, Brussels, January 2001.

29. 'SOS Democracy' appeal, Strasbourg, 10 March 1998.
30. Interview, Daniel Hannan MEP, Brussels, January 2001.
31. Eurosceptic parties performed well in the 2004 elections to the European Parliament, making gains in Poland, Latvia, Great Britain, and Sweden, but falling back in Estonia, Slovakia, Denmark, and France.
32. Correspondence with Karen Henderson, May 2003.

7

Euroscepticism in Parliament: A Comparative Analysis of the European and National Parliaments

Richard S. Katz

7.1 INTRODUCTION

'Euroscepticism' is a relatively new term, although the general attitudes to which it refers—opposition to, or doubts about, the progress of the 'European project' are as old as the project itself.[1] Certainly, one could say that it was 'Euroscepticism' that led Britain not to join the European Coal and Steel Community and that informed domestic opposition to entry into the European Economic Community (EEC)/European Communities (EC)/European Union (EU) within each of the states that has joined since then—and, of course, in countries such as Norway, where referenda have rejected accession to the EU. The failure of scholars to examine the phenomenon of Euroscepticism has been the result of the conjunction of three factors. First, the EEC seemed to many to be relatively unimportant; into the 1980s, the EC's budget was less than 1 per cent of aggregate GDP—and indeed even in 1999 was only 1.11 per cent of GNP and about 2.5 per cent of total public expenditures (Nugent 1999: 390); the range of policy areas in which the EC was involved was small; with decisions made by unanimous accord, the EC appeared unthreatening to the primacy of the national states. Secondly, and no doubt in part because of this perception of marginality, the EC was studied almost exclusively by Europhiles. There were debates about how European integration would or should proceed (e.g. Haas 1958; Lindberg 1963; Hoffmann 1966), but opponents of the European project were understood by most of those studying European integration simply to be on the wrong side of history, and therefore of little importance as objects of study. Thirdly, at the elite level there appeared to be a substantive consensus, at least among the major parties, in favour of further integration, and at the mass level there appeared to be what was later identified as a 'permissive consensus' to allow integration to proceed unchallenged (Lindberg and Scheingold 1970).

With the Single European Act and then with the Maastricht Treaty, this situation underwent substantial change. The range of policy areas in which the EU was a significant player expanded dramatically, as did the range of questions that might be decided by qualified majority vote. This growth in importance invited study by those who were not committed to the 'European ideal'. Economic and Monetary Union (EMU) become a highly visible bone of contention, both between and within parties in some countries, and even more among countries, with Britain, Sweden, and Denmark choosing not to enter the Eurozone. Referenda in Denmark, France, and Ireland suggested that the era of a permissive consensus might be over. Euroscepticism was recognized as a significant phenomenon.

To date, most work on Euroscepticism has focused on individual countries and/or on the positions taken by national parties. In this chapter, the unit of analysis is individuals rather than parties, and the geographic scope encompasses the entire EU as it was in 1996. In particular, the chapter examines Euroscepticism among members of the European Parliament (EP) and members of the national parliaments of eleven member states. The objectives are first, to identify the attitudinal roots of Euroscepticism, and second, to consider what the relationship between Euroscepticism and the so-called democratic deficit.

7.2 DATA AND SETTING

The data analysed in this chapter come from the 1996 'Political Representation in Europe' study. This study involved face-to-face interviews with 314 members of the EP, as well as postal surveys of members of 11 of the national parliaments. Full information regarding sampling and response rates are available in Schmitt and Thomassen (1999) and Katz and Wessels (1999). For this analysis, data within each of the two (members of European Parliament (MEP) and members of national parliament

Table 7.1. Raw and weighted *N*s, 'Political Representation in Europe' study

	MEPs		MNPs	
	Raw	Weighted	Raw	Weighted
Austria	10	7.0		
Belgium	18	8.4	132	48.2
Denmark	8	4.9		
Finland	11	4.0		
France	36	48.7	146	277.9
Germany	46	69.8	317	390.9
Greece	11	8.1	60	49.9
Ireland	9	3.6	71	17.1
Italy	46	51.7	94	274.8
Luxembourg	4	0.3	28	1.8
The Netherlands	21	12.4	65	73.7
Portugal	16	8.3	54	47.6
Spain	36	31.0	130	188.1
Sweden	14	7.4	315	42.0
UK	28	48.4		
Total	314	314.0	1,412	1,412.0

(MNP)) samples were weighted to reflect each country's proportion of the European population, and then within country to reflect the relative size of party groups in the corresponding parliament. Table 7.1 reports the raw and weighted *N*s.

At the time of these surveys, Sweden, Austria, and Finland had just joined the EU; the first European election in Finland took place in September 1995, while the first European election in the other two countries was not held until October 1996. While the process that would ultimately lead to expansion of the EU into the former Soviet bloc had begun, both the timing and the extent of expansion still were open questions. Certainly few would have foreseen that ten new members, including Malta and Cyprus, would be joining en masse in 2004, or that by 2007 all the former east European Soviet satellites except the Balkans and including three former Soviet republics would be EU members.

Along with expansion, other continuing issues were the balance of power both between national and European levels, and between the EP and the other institutions of EU governance. With respect to the first of these issues, MEPs had a clear personal interest in increasing the authority of the EU, and hence of their own institution. While it is questionable, at least in some cases, whether Europeanization means a loss of influence for the national parliaments (it is, after all, impossible to lose to Europe influence that one has already lost to the national cabinet), MNPs may at least have an indirect self-interest in maintaining the influence of national political institutions as a whole.

With respect to the second issue, it is significant that, notwithstanding increases in its powers under the Single European Act and the Maastricht Treaty, the EP was (and still is) clearly in a weak position vis-à-vis the Commission and the Council. Although the EP has been organized by party group or family (rather than by nationality), the common interest of MEPs to increase the status of the EP as an institution has led to a preference for large majorities able to present a united front to the other EU institutions, and hence for the building of consensus among the three major party groups.

7.3 DEFINING EUROSCEPTICISM

Analysing Euroscepticism forces one to address several questions. First, what is the 'scepticism' of Euroscepticism? As the term has developed in political discourse, Euroscepticism denotes opposition to 'the European project' (itself a rather loosely defined concept), notwithstanding that 'scepticism' ordinarily refers to doubts or reservations rather than to outright opposition. But should the label 'Eurosceptic' be reserved for those who reject the entire idea of European integration and would like to see the EU disbanded or at least to see their countries withdraw, or does it include those who merely want to make the integration process happen a little more slowly or who express uncertainty about the wisdom of some or all the proposed 'advances'. Adapting to the vocabulary suggested by Taggart and Szczerbiak (2008*b*), I understand there to be a continuum of support or opposition to European integration, with the total rejectionists, or 'Hard Eurosceptics', at one end, 'Europhiles' at the other end, and those who manifest qualified opposition, 'Soft Eurosceptics', occupying a range of positions towards, but not at, the Hard Eurosceptic end.

Secondly, even if one accepts that Hard Eurosceptics oppose the entire process of Europeanization, what is it that the Soft Eurosceptics oppose? One can distinguish several objects of scepticism in the scholarly literature and in popular political discourse. Euroscepticism most generally refers to opposition to the development of any form of supranational European institutions that would or do impinge on national sovereignty and the traditional European state system. More specifically, this could mean: opposition to the expansion of the EU to include more members (broadening); opposition to increasing the range of responsibilities of the EU (deepening); or opposition to specific institutional changes affecting the balance of authority as between the EU and the member states or among the various institutions of the EU itself. Euroscepticism may also refer to doubts about the efficacy of specific policies of the EU. Most narrowly, but also perhaps most commonly in the late 1990s, Euroscepticism could mean opposition to EMU in particular.

This unpacking of the idea of Euroscepticism requires two comments. On the one hand, while these possible forms of scepticism are in principle separable, it has clearly been part of the strategy of Europhiles to present them as inexorably intertwined, and then to lump the Soft Eurosceptics together with the Hard. By emphasizing the purported necessity of maintaining an integrationist momentum, they have attempted to cast scepticism about any particular part of their proposals as potentially unraveling the entire project and threatening the undoubted economic benefits that EU members already enjoy.[2] Thus, for example, while an element of general scepticism about the European project undoubtedly underlies specific scepticism about EMU, the converse process of generalizing from scepticism concerning EMU to scepticism about Europe in general is strengthened when those who oppose a common monetary system, and even those who merely express doubts about the particular way in which EMU has been structured, are accused of being anti-EU tout court. And moreover, the self-serving alarmism of those who claim that any slowing of the pace of integration may lead to the disintegration of the EU can only feed the scepticism of those who are afraid of being sold a bill of goods.

On the other hand, while these forms of scepticism are in principle separable, the major practical proposals towards which Euroscepticism is addressed generally are package deals that raise possibilities for many, if not all, forms of scepticism. The Nice Treaty, for example, laid the institutional groundwork for geographic expansion (broadening), restricted the national veto in some thirty areas (deepening), and altered the balance of voting power among the member states but had to be accepted or rejected as a package by the Irish electorate, who in rejecting the Treaty were interpreted as being Eurosceptic in general.[3]

The third question (closely related to the first) is whether Euroscepticism is to be operationalized in absolute or relative terms. For example, consider the following question (to which I will return in the analysis later) taken from the 1996 study of MEPs and MNPs:

Q12_1: Should <COUNTRY> keep its <NATIONAL CURRENCY> and make it more independent from other European currencies, or should the aim be a new common European currency?

Respondents were asked to identify their own position on a scale running from 'independent national currency' (1) to 'new common European currency' (10). Who are the Eurosceptics? Those scoring themselves at 1 or 2, that is, expressing strong opposition to a common currency? Those scoring themselves at 5 or below, that is, in the less integrationist half of the scale? Those scoring themselves below 7, that is, at positions that might reasonably be interpreted as indicating some doubts about a European currency? Those scoring themselves below the sample median or mean, that is, among the less integrationist half of the respondents (as is implicitly the case when correlations are reported)?

This ambiguity then interacts with a fourth question or problem, rhow to assess trends in Euroscepticism over time, given that the Europe about which one might be sceptical is in effect a moving target. At the time of Maastricht, expansion meant the accession of Austria, Finland, and Sweden (and perhaps Norway and Switzerland), all firmly in Western Europe in both economic and political/historical terms; in 1996, expansion meant the gradual and eventual accession of the some of the relatively more prosperous countries of Central and Eastern Europe; six years later, it meant the accession in 2004 of virtually all of them (plus Malta and Cyprus), notwithstanding their radically different economic positions and recent political histories, with Romania and Bulgaria scheduled to join in 2007. Is scepticism about broadening in 1990 equivalent to scepticism about broadening in 2002? The powers of the EP were vastly greater in

1996 than they were in 1984. Does comparison of responses to questions asked about increasing the powers of the EP at the two times say anything about changing Euroscepticism? To what extent are such Eurobarometer questions as 'In general, are you for or against efforts being made to unify [Western] Europe?' comparable over time when the status quo against which those ongoing efforts might be judged is constantly changing?

7.4 OPERATIONALIZING EUROSCEPTICISM

The 'Political Representation in Europe' study includes three questions that allow an initial general assessment of Euroscepticism in the European and national parliaments, plus a fourth that, while more specific in its orientation, addresses one of the central contemporary foci of Euroscepticism. General attitudes about deepening and broadening the EU were tapped by asking respondents to place themselves on a scale between 'very much in favour' (1) and 'very much against' (7) in response to two questions:

Q2B: One of the major issues presently facing the EU is increasing the range of responsibilities of the European Union. Do you favour or are you against increasing the range of responsibilities of the EU?

Q2C: Another major issue presently facing the EU is the inclusion of new member states within the Union. Do you favour or are you against the inclusion of new member states within the next ten years?

The third general question asked for a prospective evaluation of the EU, albeit from a specifically nationally oriented perspective:

Q9: How much confidence do you have that decisions made by the European Union will be in the interest of your country?

Responses ranged from 'a great deal of confidence' (1) to 'no confidence at all' (4). Finally, respondents were asked the question (Q12_1) already cited earlier concerning their views about a common European currency.

Table 7.2 reports the mean responses to each of these questions, broken down by country and level of parliament. Two things are apparent in the table. First, there are virtually no substantial differences between the views

Table 7.2. Mean responses to Europhilia–Euroscepticism questions, by country and level of parliament

	Q2B: Increase range of responsibilities (1–7)			Q2C: Include new members (1–7)			Q9: Decisions in national interest (1–4)			Q12_1: Common currency (1–10)		
	MEPs	MNPs	eta²	MEPs	MNPs	eta²	MEPs	MNPs	eta²	MEPs	MNPs	eta²
Austria	3.43			2.43			2.05			8.84		
Belgium	2.70	2.86	0.001	3.12	3.67	0.014	2.23	2.31	0.001	9.18	8.81	0.004
Denmark	6.03			3.30			2.78			4.48		
Finland	4.07			1.98			2.07			7.92		
France	3.81	3.88	0.000	3.46	3.42	0.000	2.48	2.41	0.001	7.69	7.79	0.000
Germany	2.20	3.46	0.080	2.59	2.59	0.000	1.42	2.06	0.135	9.46	8.80	0.016
Greece	2.83	3.22	0.007	4.25	3.09	0.057	2.24	2.91	0.177	8.97	8.65	0.003
Ireland	3.49	3.54	0.000	3.43	2.51	0.048	1.92	2.07	0.013	9.84	8.70	0.046
Italy	1.74	2.24	0.022	3.24	2.43	0.037	2.22	2.16	0.053	8.79	8.09	0.011
Luxembourg	1.44	3.31		4.70	3.22		1.72	2.41		10.00	9.34	
The Netherlands	2.95	3.59	0.014	2.74	2.63	0.001	1.64	2.17	0.101	8.00	7.85	0.000
Portugal	3.30	3.42	0.001	2.90	3.63	0.021	2.26	2.30	0.001	7.63	8.37	0.011
Spain	2.11	2.51	0.014	2.78	2.78	0.000	1.94	2.06	0.005	9.18	8.66	0.008
Sweden	5.78	4.59	0.061	2.39	1.92	0.015	2.95	2.31	0.108	4.09	5.59	0.033
UK	3.56			2.93			2.10			6.93		
Overall	2.86	3.19	0.006	2.98	2.82	0.001	1.97	2.22	0.020	8.31	8.28	0.000
eta²	0.259	0.153		0.053	0.086		0.248	0.085		0.176	0.066	

expressed by MEPs and MNPs of the same country, although there is quite a consistent tendency for the MNPs to be more Eurosceptic than the MEPs rexcept for Sweden, where this pattern is completely reversed. Four of the other eight exceptions are with regard to the question of inclusion of new members. Second, although there are only very modest differences between levels of parliament, there are quite substantial differences among countries, for both levels of parliament. In particular, although there are no national monopolies on Euroscepticism, Denmark and Sweden, followed by France, Portugal, and the UK appear to be more consistently Eurosceptic than the other countries. Again, however, the question of inclusion of new members is exceptional, with Luxembourg, Greece, and Belgium among the most Eurosceptical.

Of course, given the institutional changes expected to follow from EU enlargement, including loss of an assured seat on the Commission, it is not surprising to see MPs from small countries expressing doubts about enlargement. Nonetheless, this pattern of exceptionalism raises the more general question of whether the responses cluster sufficiently for one to conclude that there is a single dimension of Euroscepticism, or whether it is instead necessary to talk about Euroscepticisms in the plural. Inspection of the correlations among these four variables suggests that there are actually two clusters (if a single variable can be called a cluster), with the broadening variable only weakly related to the other three. This apparent pattern was confirmed by a factor analysis forced to have two factors,[4] with the post-oblique-rotation pattern matrix shown in Table 7.3. Taking this as confirmation of a single underlying factor 'causing' scores on Q2B, Q9, and Q12_1, a second factor analysis was performed on just these three variables in order to generate factor scores. The single factor constructed in this analysis accounts for 63.57 per cent of the total variance in the three input variables.

Like all factor scores, the score computed here is constrained to have a mean of 0; hence positive scores indicate Euroscepticism relative to the sample means, rather than in any substantive sense. To compensate for this, and reflective of the fact that the measures are both preliminary and crude, the factor score was trichotomized, to form a variable identified for convenience as SCEPT. This variable was coded to take the value 2 for factor scores above those that would be assigned to respondents who picked the midpoint on each of the three input variables (4 for Q2B, 2.5

Table 7.3. Pattern matrix, Euroscepticism

	Factor 1	Factor 2
Increasing responsibilities of the EU	0.711	0.222
Inclusion of new member states	0.004	0.981
Confidence in EU decisions in the interest of your country	0.823	−0.012
European currency	−0.830	0.132

for Q9, and 5.5 for Q12_1), that is who on average put themselves on the *substantively* anti-further-integration side of these questions. While this category includes many respondents who fall far short of being Hard Eurosceptics in the full sense, it still represents less than one-sixth of the sample. Since there are too few true Hard Eurosceptics among MEPs and MNPs to make a separate category useful, respondents with this score are identified in the analyses below as 'harder Eurosceptics'. SCEPT takes the value 1 for those whose factor scores are less than those of the Hard Eurosceptics, but higher than the score that would be assigned to respondents picking responses about two-thirds of the way towards the Europhile end of the scales (3 for Q2B, 1.5 for Q9, and 7 for Q12_1), that is who on average were pro-European, but with reservations. Respondents with this score are identified as Soft Eurosceptics. Finally, SCEPT takes the value 0 for the Europhiles, those who on average gave strongly pro-integration responses for all three questions.

7.5 EXPLAINING EUROSCEPTICISM

7.5.1 Nationality and party of Eurosceptics

The first three obvious questions concern the distribution of individuals with regard to the SCEPT variable. First, are there significant differences between members of parliaments (MPs) at the European and national levels? Secondly, are there significant differences among MPs at either or both levels from different countries? Third, are there significant differences that are structured by political party?

Table 7.4 shows the distribution of SCEPT by country for the two samples. First comparing the two samples, if 'where you stands depends

Table 7.4. Euroscepticism by country

	MEPs			MNPs		
	Europhile	Soft Eurosceptic	Harder Eurosceptic	Europhile	Soft Eurosceptic	Harder Eurosceptic
Austria	59.4	30.0	10.7	—	—	—
Belgium	60.2	18.2	21.6	56.4	27.7	15.9
Denmark	32.3	0.0	67.7	—	—	—
Finland	40.9	50.3	8.8	—	—	—
France	45.0	24.6	30.4	36.2	30.9	32.9
Germany	88.3	11.7	0.0	46.8	42.8	10.3
Greece	64.0	28.2	7.8	12.1	63.5	24.4
Ireland	43.1	56.9	0.0	40.9	47.9	11.2
Italy	79.4	11.5	9.1	64.6	25.8	9.6
Luxembourg	100.0	0.0	0.0	39.0	55.5	5.5
The Netherlands	59.1	25.9	15.0	40.3	42.1	17.5
Portugal	57.4	13.0	29.6	31.6	56.7	11.7
Spain	74.6	25.4	0.0	56.6	34.4	9.0
Sweden	0.0	36.9	63.2	11.3	47.8	40.9
UK	44.4	27.8	27.8	—	—	—
Total	64.5	20.3	15.2	46.6	37.0	16.5

on where you sit', one would expect MEPs to be more Europhile than MNPs. This expectation has been confirmed before with these data (e.g. Katz 1999), but those analyses assessed support for Europe in purely relative terms. What the data in Table 7.4 show further is that notwithstanding the definition of a Soft Eurosceptic as one who on balance takes a pro-European position (albeit without great certainty or enthusiasm) Europhilia is nearly the majority position among MNPs, as well as being the dominant position among MEPs. Even among the MNPs, only about one-sixth are classified as harder Eurosceptics, who might be said simply to be opposed to further Europeanization.

Looking at the distribution among countries, however, there are clear exceptions to the generally pro-European pattern. Again for the most part these data simply confirm expectations. Swedish, Danish, French, and British respondents, plus Greek, and to a lesser extent Portuguese, MNPs, have high concentrations of Eurosceptics. Indeed, while nearly two-thirds of MEPs are classified as Europhiles, among the Danes and Swedes nearly two-thirds are classified as harder Eurosceptic; similarly, although over

Table 7.5. Euroscepticism by party

	MEPs						MNPs		
	EP Party Group			National Party Family					
	A	B	C	A	B	C	A	B	C
EUL—Radical Left	30.1	38.3	31.6	30.1	38.3	31.6	5.6	43.5	50.9
PSE—Social Democrat	75.9	17.2	6.8	75.9	17.2	6.8	54.9	36.3	8.7
ARE—Radical Alliance	87.1	12.9	0.0	84.0	16.0	0.0	96.3	3.7	0.0
V—Greens	38.1	39.6	22.4	38.1	39.6	22.4	48.2	39.8	12.0
ELDR—Liberal	83.3	14.4	1.9	81.4	13.0	5.6	46.9	39.4	13.7
EDN—Nationalist	0.0	0.0	100.0	0.0	0.0	100.0	0.0	0.0	100.0
PPE—Christian Democrat	69.9	21.7	8.4	70.2	22.1	7.7	47.4	42.5	10.2
UPE—Conservative	49.6	29.3	21.1	46.1	31.3	22.6	28.2	37.5	34.3
NI—Far Right	15.8	8.2	76.0	16.7	8.7	74.6	33.0	26.6	40.4
Other	—	—	—	0.0	0.0	100.0	72.0	8.6	19.5

A: Europhile; B: Soft Eurosceptic; C: Harder Eurosceptic.

45 per cent of the full MNP sample are classified as Europhiles, for the Swedes and Greeks the corresponding figure is under 13 per cent. Looking at percentages computed the other way, and given the disparity of national populations, one finds that the Eurosceptics are concentrated in particular places: more than 56 per cent of the harder Eurosceptic MEPs are British or French, as are more than 38 per cent of the Soft Eurosceptics; 56 per cent of the harder Eurosceptic MNPs in the sample (remembering that there are no British MNPs included) are French (39.2 per cent by themselves) or German, as are nearly 48 per cent (16.4 per cent French) of the Soft Eurosceptics.

Table 7.5 breaks down the distribution of SCEPT by party, again separately for MEPs and MNPs. For the MEPs, two party classifications have been used: party group within the EP, and the (closely related, but not identical) family of the MEP's national party, classified in the same way as for the MNPs. The parties are listed in the table from left to right as indicated by the average left–right self-placement of MEPs. Most obviously, the table shows that there are quite substantial differences among the parties and party groups.

Two important points can be observed in this table. First, if one ignores the Nationalists (Europe of Nations group) and Greens as being parties for which the left–right dimension has little relevance,[5] there is a strong relationship between a party's left–right placement and the distribution of its MPs among the three categories of SCEPT. The relationship, however, is parabolic rather than linear; with the obvious exception of the EDN group, whose defining characteristic is to be Eurosceptic, the greatest concentrations of Eurosceptics are found at the ends of the scale—among the radical left and the far right—while the greatest concentration of Europhiles is found in the middle.

The second point is that the distributions among the categories of SCEPT for the Social Democrats and Christian Democrats are virtually identical. Between them, these two parties represent roughly two-thirds of the MEPs (66 per cent of all MEPs in May 1999; a weighted 68 per cent of MEP respondents to the survey) and nearly 60 per cent of the MNPs in the sample. If the ELDR MNPs, whose distribution is also nearly identical, are added, the total proportion of MNPs who are in parties with virtually the same distribution with regard to SCEPT rises to over 71 per cent.

This pattern of similarity between the major party families of Europe is, for the most part, replicated within the individual countries. The only significant differences observed between the distributions of Euroscepticism between Socialists and Christian Democrats were for the Spanish and Swedish MNPs; in the Spanish case, the Christian Democrats were more Eurosceptic (57.1 per cent, including 8.9 per cent harder Eurosceptic) than the Socialists (20.8 per cent, all Soft Eurosceptics), while for the Swedes, the Socialists were more Eurosceptic (90.2 per cent, with 36.4 per cent harder Eurosceptic) than the Christian Democratic (81.9 per cent, with 20.5 per cent harder Eurosceptic). Among the other parties, Liberal MNPs are noticeably more Eurosceptic than the Socialists and Christian Democrats in Belgium, Luxembourg, the Netherlands, and Portugal although only in the first and last of these cases is the difference statistically significant.

In other words, when the parties are considered as units (as essentially they must be by citizens deciding how to vote in systems characterized by parliamentary governments, disciplined parties, and party-list proportional representation), there basically is no Eurosceptic option available unless the voter is prepared to go completely outside of the mainstream. Whether or not this situation is the result of tacit collusion among the mainstream parties to keep the European question off the political agenda, as the cartel party thesis (Katz and Mair 1995) would suggest, the resulting equation of Euroscepticism with the political fringes probably contributes significantly to the marginalization and delegitimation of the Eurosceptic perspective.

This result is particularly significant because in a fundamental sense the picture just painted is a serious distortion. While it is true that only the parties on the left–right fringes (plus, of course, the EDN) could reasonably be characterized as Eurosceptic, that does not mean that all the Eurosceptics are located on the fringes. As with the distribution by nationality, the fact that some parties are so much larger than others means that even a small percentage of their members may be a large share of the whole. Thus, the Social Democrats and the Christian Democrats, although collectively pro-Europe, provide over 30 per cent of the harder Eurosceptics and over 60 per cent of the Soft Eurosceptics. By framing the expression of harder Eurosceptic views as internal disloyalty, Europhilic governments can not only marginalize the harder Eurosceptics within their parties, but also discourage Soft Eurosceptics from expressing their reservations.

7.5.2 Attitudinal roots of Euroscepticism

Although overt public Europhilia may be the result of party pressure, internally felt Europhilia or Euroscepticism is presumably an individual attribute, to be explained by individual characteristics, of which social/national or partisan pressures for conformity are only two. The 'Political Representation in Europe' data allow several potentially more direct individual-level explanations to be considered.

First, although Euroscepticism is defined by attitudes towards the EU, one might expect it to reflect more fundamental attitudes about Europe in general. Three questions from the surveys are particularly relevant here, each asking for response on a scale from 'agree strongly' (1) to 'disagree strongly' (7):

Q17_1: The differences between European countries are far less than the similarities

Q17_2: I feel proud to be a European

Q17_3: European unity threatens my country's cultural identity

Table 7.6. Relationship between Euroscepticism and general attitudes about Europe (Somer's d)

	MEPs	MNPs
The differences between European countries are far less than the similarities	0.232	0.183
I feel proud to be a European	0.413	0.235
European unity threatens my country's cultural identity	−0.422	−0.362

The distribution of responses to all these questions is heavily skewed towards the pro-European end of the scales, in each case slightly more for the MEPs than the MNPs. With the mid, and presumably neutral, point in each case being 4, and with low scores on Q17_1 and Q17_2, and a high score on Q17_3, representing the pro-European response, the mean responses are 2.98, 2.14, and 5.92 for the MEPs, and 3.14, 2.59, and 5.59 for the MNPs. (Unfortunately, these questions were not asked in the Swedish MNP study. Consequently, the Swedish MNPs are excluded from these figures, and from all the following analyses that involve sense of European-ness.) Table 7.6 shows the correlations of these variables with Euroscepticism (Somer's d with SCEPT as the dependent variable) for the two samples. All the correlations are highly significant, and suggest that those who see a more homogeneous Europe, positively identify themselves as Europeans, and do not feel that European unity poses a threat to their own country's culture are markedly less likely to be Eurosceptics than are those who hold the opposite views.

Obviously, these three independent variables are closely related to one another; factor analyses on the two samples indicated common variances of 59.8 and 50.1 per cent for the MEPs and MNPs, respectively. I used a single factor analysis to generate a composite indicator of 'European-ness'. I then used this measure in a generalized least squares model to predict the cumulative probabilities of the three categories of SCEPT. This procedure generated a Nagelkerke pseudo-R^2 of 0.388 for the MEPs and 0.251 for the MNPs. Overall, 70.7 per cent of the MEPs' actual scores on SCEPT were predicted accurately.

A second possible explanation of Euroscepticism is that it reflects retrospective evaluation of the EU's performance. In this case, those who think that the EU has done a good job in the past ought to be more sanguine about granting it more powers in the future, and hence be less likely to be Eurosceptics. To a limited extent, this idea has already been built into the definition of SCEPT, in the confidence that EU decisions will be in the interest of one's country in the future presumably is itself strongly conditioned by one's evaluation of the EU's performance in this regard in the past. The surveys allow further, and more nuanced, analysis of this hypothesis in two respects. Respondents were asked (Q7) to evaluate whether 'the EU has done a good or a bad job... in the last five years' (using a scale from 'very good' (1) to 'very bad' (7)) for each of seventeen policy areas. On the one hand, this both directs the respondent's attention to the general quality of performance rather than to the particular interests of his or her own country (this question preceded the question about national interests in the questionnaires) and specifically asks for retrospective rather than prospective evaluation. On the other hand, the question allows disaggregation of the overall evaluation into particular policy components.

Table 7.7 summarizes the relationships between the various policy area evaluations and SCEPT. Unlike the indicators of European-ness, which were skewed in a pro-European direction, these evaluations are predominantly negative. Of the thirty-four evaluations (seventeen for each sample), the mean evaluations for twenty-seven are above 4, which is to say that they are on the negative side of the midpoint; indeed, eight of the average evaluations are over 5. This preponderance of negative evaluations was particularly true of the MNP sample, in which fifteen of the seventeen averages are over 4; on the other hand, perhaps simply reflecting a tendency of MEPs to have stronger opinions on all questions concerning the EU, five of the averages that were over 5 were found in the MEP sample.

As Table 7.7 shows, Euroscepticism is associated with negative evaluations of past EU policy performance. As with virtually everything else, the relationships are stronger in the MEP sample. Whether this is because MEPs have stronger or more consistent attitudes regarding Europe (which would make sense, given that they are more directly involved with it) or because the different methodologies (personal interview rather than mailed questionnaire) resulted in lower measurement error for the MEPs, is impossible to tell with these data.

Looking down the columns of correlations, it is evident that the same issue areas are among the more predictive of Euroscepticism in both samples. In both cases, evaluation of the EU's performance with regard

Table 7.7. Percentage scored as 'Europhile' in the top two and bottom two categories of response for evaluations of EU policy performance

Policy Area	MEPs			MNPs		
	top 2 categories	bottom 2 categories	d	top 2 categories	bottom 2 categories	d
Agriculture and fisheries	77.8 (n = 36)	41.9 (n = 62)	0.252	57.4 (n = 190)	34.7 (n = 349)	0.097
Unemployment policies	100 (n = 2)	54.2 (n = 144)	0.222	29.8 (n = 47)	43.4 (n = 709)	0.096
Economic policy	77.3 (n = 22)	38.9 (n = 72)	0.242	55.7 (n = 79)	31.1 (n = 254)	0.158
Fighting crime	100 (n = 6)	57.4 (n = 122)	0.111	44.8 (n = 58)	43.8 (n = 397)	0.057
Regional development	86.8 (n = 53)	32.1 (n = 28)	0.236	59.9 (n = 162)	34.2 (n = 161)	0.127
Security and defence	77.8 (n = 9)	62.8 (n = 172)	0.037	45.3 (n = 117)	48.8 (n = 486)	0.006
Protection of the environment	83.3 (n = 36)	36.7 (n = 30)	0.222	49.5 (n = 103)	42.1 (n = 233)	0.052
Monetary policy	88.1 (n = 59)	34.5 (n = 58)	0.292	61.5 (n = 247)	26.2 (n = 168)	0.212
Health	78.6 (n = 14)	60.0 (n = 55)	0.088	50.0 (n = 54)	41.7 (n = 300)	0.085
Social policy	63.6 (n = 11)	52.3 (n = 86)	0.175	43.9 (n = 57)	43.5 (n = 464)	0.049
Education	75.0 (n = 16)	67.7 (n = 62)	0.030	44.4 (n = 81)	37.3 (n = 279)	0.050
Basic rules for broadcasting and press	42.9 (n = 14)	54.0 (n = 63)	0.066	39.7 (n = 78)	44.8 (n = 337)	0.034
Scientific and technological research	72.7 (n = 33)	60.0 (n = 25)	0.078	55.2 (n = 87)	43.8 (n = 203)	0.068
Foreign policy	100 (n = 3)	65.6 (n = 163)	0.018	43.2 (n = 111)	49.3 (n = 509)	0.020
Taxation policy	100 (n = 4)	54.5 (n = 101)	0.091	46.2 (n = 52)	43.8 (n = 390)	0.091
Help to developing countries	73.9 (n = 46)	52.8 (n = 52)	0.099	54.1 (n = 98)	39.0 (n = 356)	0.077
Immigrants and refugees	100 (n = 5)	55.8 (n = 113)	0.129	36.7 (n = 60)	38.6 (n = 562)	0.126

to monetary policy is the strongest predictor again with some risk of tautology, given that support for a common European currency is one of the elements of SCEPT. Evaluations of the EU's performance with regard to economic policy are also important (as indicated by a value of d > 0.150) in both samples. By that criterion, agriculture and fisheries, regional development, unemployment, protection of the environment, and social policy are important for the MEPs, but not for the MNPs, although adopting a somewhat weaker standard of (relative) importance for the MNPs shows that the first three of these are also among the stronger correlates of SCEPT in the MNP sample. (The other relatively important correlate for the MNPs is evaluation of policy regarding immigrants and refugees, for which the MNP value of Somer's d is stronger than that observed for agriculture and fisheries or unemployment, although it is lower than the corresponding value of d for the MEPs.)

These results closely parallel those reported by Marsh (1999) using the same data, although his dependent variable was only confidence that EU decisions would be in the interests of the respondent's country (Q9) rather than a composite indicator of Euroscepticism. In particular, Marsh considered two independent variables: the sum of the scores for the policy areas that he identified as 'economic' (agriculture—presumably identified as economic because of its impact on the EU budget, monetary policy, economic policy, and taxation policy) and the sum of the scores for all the other policy areas. He found that the economic policy evaluation was a significant predictor of confidence in EU decisions for both MEPs and MNPs, while the non-economic policy evaluation was a significant (but weaker) predictor only for the MEPs. Adapting this analytic line, I performed a factor analysis of the seventeen policy evaluations, generating a four-factor solution accounting for 55.6 per cent of the overall variance. The resulting component matrix after varimax rotation (showing only those loadings greater than 0.500) is reported in the top panel of Table 7.8. The bottom panel of Table 7.8 shows the estimated location parameters from an ordinal regression using the factor scores as predictors of SCEPT.

As suggested by the column headings, the four factors appear to correspond to social, international, economic, and development policies. In contrast to Marsh's operationalization, the factor analysis indicates that based on evaluations of EU performance, unemployment clusters with other questions of economic policy, while taxation policy clusters with

Table 7.8. Factor matrix, EU policy evaluations (varimax rotation)

	Social Policy	International Policy	Economic Policy	Development Policy
Agriculture and fisheries			0.623	
Unemployment policies			0.539	
Economic policy			0.723	
Fighting crime				
Regional development				0.634
Security and defence		0.740		
Protection of the environment				0.618
Monetary policy			0.653	
Health	0.684			
Social policy	0.699			
Education	0.775			
Basic rules for broadcasting and press	0.710			
Scientific and technological research				0.562
Foreign policy		0.809		
Taxation policy		0.523		
Help to developing countries		0.550		0.554
Immigrants and refugees		0.641		
Location coefficients: MEPs	−0.168	−0.083	−1.142	−0.380
Location coefficients: MNPs	−0.048	−0.046	−0.495	−0.284

international policy, perhaps because from the perspective of the EU this is perceived to relate primarily to the external tariff and questions of cross-border harmonization within the EU. Two of the factors, economic policy and development policy, appear to be significant correlates of Euroscepticism, with evaluations of economic policy being the markedly stronger correlate in both samples. The other two factors appear to make little contribution to the explanation of SCEPT.

The ordinal regression shows evaluations of EU performance to be far better predictors of Euroscepticism for MEPs than for MNPs. For the former, the pseudo-R^2 is a healthy 0.338, while for the latter it is a rather anemic 0.088. Similarly, 72 per cent of the MEPs' scores on SCEPT are accurately predicted, while for the MNPs, the figure is barely 50 per cent.

A third class of potential explanations of Euroscepticism concerns the respondents' satisfaction with the quality of democracy in the EU in general, and with the current institutional arrangements of the EU in particular. As with the specific policy evaluations, the general expectation is that those who are satisfied with the performance of democracy in the EU, and with the current institutional arrangements, will be more likely to be Europhiles than those who are not satisfied.

Looking first at general satisfaction, respondents were asked:

Q18: On the whole, how satisfied are you with the way democracy works in the European Union.

Because very few respondents chose either of the extreme responses, answers were recoded to be either 0 (very satisfied or fairly satisfied) or 1 (not very satisfied or not at all satisfied). Cross-tabulation of this variable with SCEPT shows a significant relationship in both samples, with Somer's d = 0.326 for the MEPs and 0.115 for the MNPs with SCEPT as the dependent variable.

Attitudes concerning the institutional arrangements of the EU were assessed through two paired series of questions. First respondents were asked:

Q22: How much influence do you think the institutions listed here have concerning decision-making in the European Union?

Responses were coded on an 11-point scale ranging from 'very little influence' (1) to 'very much influence' (11). They were then asked (Q23) to use the same scale to rate how much influence those institutions 'ought to have'. Eight institutions were listed, of which five (the EP, the European Commission, the European Court of Justice (ECJ), the national governments, and the national parliaments) appear to be significantly (in both statistical and substantive senses) related to Euroscepticism; the other three were the Committee of Permanent Representatives (COREPER) and the Economic and Social Committee plus, somewhat surprisingly, the Council of Ministers.

The measures of satisfaction used here are based on the differences between the two responses for each institution. Clearly a difference of 0 represents a perfect congruence of perceived and desired influence for an institution; other differences, however, can be either positive (indicating the belief that the institution should have more influence than it currently does) or negative (indicating the belief that the institution currently has too much influence). As I have shown elsewhere (Katz 1999), there is quite solid agreement in both samples that both the European and the national parliaments should have more influence;[6] for the other institutions, the mean differences were at most half the magnitude, and the balance between those favouring more and less influence was much more even.

The understanding of Euroscepticism suggested when it was hypothesized that satisfaction with EU democracy would be positively associated with Europhilia coupled with the belief that dissatisfaction with EU governance reflects the so-called democratic deficit suggests that there should be a positive relationship between SCEPT and the belief that the EP should have significantly more influence. Given that the ECJ has been a strong agent of European integration, one might have the same expectation with regard to attitudes concerning the influence of the Court, although given the general national-level experience that constitutional courts can serve as a brake on government activism (Stone Sweet 2000), there would at least be a plausible post hoc explanation were the facts to be otherwise. It is much harder to form an expectation for the signs of the relationships between SCEPT and attitudes about the influence of the national governments and parliaments and the Commission, given that dissatisfaction could be rooted in a either a proto-state or an intergovernmental conception of the proper functioning of EU-level democracy (Katz 2001). And, of course, given the findings given earlier with regard to the relationship between left–right party placement and SCEPT, it is possible that the relationships simply are non-linear, with those at both extremes of dissatisfaction more Eurosceptic than those who are relatively more satisfied.

Particularly to allow for this possibility, the relationships between SCEPT and the differences between perceived and desired influence were assessed using the ordinal regression procedure with a quadratic specification.[7] The results for the five significant institutions are summarized in Table 7.9. As is apparent from the table, most of the 'action' is in the linear term, indicating that significantly larger proportion of Eurosceptics than of Europhiles report that the European institutions (EP, EC, and ECJ) have too much power and that the national institutions (parliaments and especially governments) have too little, although the quadratic term is in general also significant. Combining the five sets of evaluations in a

Table 7.9. Ordinal regression of SCEPT with differences between perceived and desired levels of influence on EU decision-making

	Parameters			Nagelkerke Pseudo-R^2	Per cent classified correctly
	Constant	Linear term	Quadratic term		
MEPs					
European Parliament					
Harder Eurosceptic	−0.694	0.759	−0.071	0.237	68.8
Soft Eurosceptic	0.702				
European Commission					
Harder Eurosceptic	−2.633	0.243	−0.032	0.307	69.3
Soft Eurosceptic	−1.082				
European Court of Justice					
Harder Eurosceptic	−1.993	0.260	−0.012*	0.176	66.5
Soft Eurosceptic	−0.708				
National Governments					
Harder Eurosceptic	−1.838	−0.259	−0.018	0.177	66.7
Soft Eurosceptic	−0.516				
National Parliaments					
Harder Eurosceptic	−2.374	0.025*	−0.037	0.143	68.1
Soft Eurosceptic	−1.095				
MNPs					
European Parliament					
Harder Eurosceptic	−1.340	0.169	−0.014	0.019	51.1
Soft Eurosceptic	0.454				
European Commission					
Harder Eurosceptic	−2.023	0.183	−0.011	0.112	51.2
Soft Eurosceptic	−0.087*				
European Court of Justice					
Harder Eurosceptic	−1.774	0.162	−0.025	0.057	47.2
Soft Eurosceptic	0.090*				
National Governments					
Harder Eurosceptic	−1.703	−0.169	−0.002*	0.079	50.4
Soft Eurosceptic	0.183				
National Parliaments					
Harder Eurosceptic	−2.167	−0.071	−0.012	0.060	47.7
Soft Eurosceptic	−0.290				

* All coefficients except those marked by an asterisk are significant at p < .05 or better.

single model gives Nagelkerke pseudo-R^2 of 0.421 for the MEP sample and 0.204 for the MNP sample, with 73.2 per cent and 53.3 per cent of the cases predicted correctly. When the indicator of general satisfaction with democracy at the European level is added to the model, the pseudo-R^2 rises to 0.463 for the MEP sample and 0.221 for the MNP sample.

A final indicator of satisfaction with EU institutional arrangements asked:

Q11: Regardless of the current legal situation, in your view, which of the following is the best way of taking important decisions in the Council of Ministers?

Respondents were given a range of choices from 'If all member states agree' through a variety of versions of majority rule (a majority of countries, countries representing a majority of citizens, a majority of nationally weighted votes). Responses were divided into three categories: unanimity; varieties of qualified majority voting; varieties of simple majority voting. Unfortunately, this question was only asked of the MEPs, but when cross-tabulated with SCEPT for this sample, Somer's d was found to be an extremely high 0.508.

7.5.3 A joint prediction of Euroscepticism

Obviously, these three sets of potential predictors of Euroscepticism are closely related to one another. This means that their joint predictive power is far less than the sum of the individual pseudo-R^2s might suggest. As shown in the first line of Table 7.10, when all three sets of predictors are combined into a single-ordinal regression model, the pseudo-R^2 for the MEPs is 0.639, while that for the MNPs is 0.420. These figures translate into correct predictions for 74.7 per cent of the MEPs and 60.6 per cent of the MNPs.

How much of this predictive power should be attributed to which sets of variables? This question is addressed from two perspectives in lines 2, 3, and 4 of Table 7.10. First, the pseudo-R^2s already reported for each set of predictors are repeated. These figures indicate that for the MEPs, democratic satisfaction is the best predictor of Euroscepticism, with a sense of European-ness important but significantly less so, and satisfaction of EU policy performance also significant. For the MNPs, a sense of European-ness is the best predictor, followed closely by democratic satisfaction, with perceptions of EU policy performance essentially irrelevant.

Table 7.10. Influence of predictors of Euroscepticism

	MEPs		MNPs	
	Pseudo-R^2 for this block	Pseudo-R^2 drop excluding this block	Pseudo-R^2 for this block	Pseudo-R^2 drop excluding this block
All individual-level predictors	0.584		0.385	
Sense of European-ness	0.388	0.045	0.251	0.102
EU policy performance evaluations	0.332	0.040	0.087	0.037
Satisfaction with EU democracy and institutions	0.463	0.114	0.221	0.110
Individual-level predictors plus country	0.639		0.420	
Individual-level predictors plus party	0.622		0.426	

The minimal relevance of European policy performance is particularly significant because it was the set of predictors most likely to suffer from circularity of explanation; apparently, there is little cause for concern. The second approach is to ask how much of the joint explanatory power is lost if the block of variables is deleted from the overall model.[8] These figures suggest the greatest marginal difference in predictive power to come from democratic satisfaction, with a sense of European-ness making a substantial marginal contribution for the MNPs, but not for the MEPs. Again, policy performance appears to be of little importance for either sample.

The next questions are whether (to what extent) national and party differences remain significant after these individual-level characteristics are controlled. These questions are addressed in lines 5 and 6 of Table 7.10. Looking first at country, inclusion of this variable increased the pseudo-R^2 by roughly 0.055 for the MEPs and 0.035 for the MNPs, increasing the proportion of SCEPT scores predicted correctly to 78.4 per cent and 62.5 per cent respectively. Taking the Italians as the reference category, for the MEPs, the only statistically significant national differences were found for the Swedish and British respondents. Among the MNPs (remembering that neither British nor Swedish MNPs are included), the French, Greek, and Spanish respondents remain significantly more Eurosceptical than other nationalities. Adding party as an explanatory variable also increased the pseudo-R^2, a bit less than country for the MEPs, and a bit more than country from the MNPs; in both samples, the proportions of SCEPT scores correctly predicted (75.3 per cent and 60.9 per cent) are lower than for country.[9] MEPs of the far right and nationalist MEPs are significantly more likely to be Eurosceptics than are MEPs of other parties (among which there are no statistically significant differences once the individual-level predictors have been controlled). For the MNPs, however, the parties appear to cluster into three groups. The most Eurosceptical are the nationalists, the far right, the Conservatives, and the radical left—that is, the nationalists plus the extremes of the left–right spectrum. The second group, consisting of the Christian Democrats and Liberals, is slightly more Eurosceptic than the Socialists (significantly so for the Christian Democrats). The Socialists, as the reference category in the analysis, and the Greens, who are slightly more Europhile than the Socialists, but not significantly so, form the third category.

7.6 EUROSCEPTICISM AND THE DEMOCRATIC DEFICIT

If dissatisfaction with the state of democracy in the EU is an important source of Euroscepticism, how do Eurosceptics think that the democratic deficit might be cured? Respondents were asked:

Q21: There is a range of proposals being discussed to deal with the 'democratic deficit' in the European Union. To what extent would you be in favour of the following proposals?

Responses were on a scale between 'very much in favour' (1) and 'very much against' (7). The specific proposals are listed in Table 7.11, together with the mean response for each category of SCEPT, and eta^2 indicating the proportion of the variance in responses explained by SCEPT.

Close inspection of the table suggests that the reforms listed are of two types, to which Eurosceptics and Europhiles respond differently. The first type are the reforms that would make the EU more like a 'typical' European parliamentary party government regime. These include: making

Table 7.11. Means of attitudes concerning EU institutional reforms to reduce the democratic deficit

	MEPs				MNPs			
	A	B	C	eta²	A	B	C	eta²
National parliaments should have a joint committee of MEPs and MPs to debate community proposals	3.53	2.84	2.71	0.025	2.94	3.04	3.11	0.001*
There should be regular joint meetings between committees of the EP and national parliaments	2.98	2.65	2.88	0.005*	2.51	2.81	2.76	0.008
National governments should have a Cabinet Minister responsible for European affairs	1.94	1.96	2.57	0.025	2.77	2.86	2.45	0.005
Debates about legislative proposals in the Council of Ministers should be a matter of public record	1.72	1.97	2.53	0.039	2.68	2.61	2.20	0.009
Ministers attending the Council should follow the instructions of their national parliaments	3.61	2.77	2.44	0.073	3.38	2.99	2.21	0.057
There should be more MEPs who are also MPs	6.18	5.67	5.25	0.050	5.55	5.52	5.30	0.003*
There should be stronger links between European Commissioners and their staff and MPs	3.25	3.33	2.56	0.018*	2.32	2.13	2.21	0.005
The same electoral system should be used in European elections in all member states	2.23	2.56	4.58	0.155	2.10	2.31	2.78	0.021
There should be compulsory voting in European parliamentary elections	5.02	5.19	5.93	0.023	5.19	5.25	5.34	0.001*
The EC should be chosen by the EP rather than by the national governments	2.19	3.00	5.36	0.295	2.93	3.94	4.57	0.089
European parties should choose the candidates for the EP rather than leaving it to the national parties	4.73	5.52	6.75	0.134	4.53	5.57	6.10	0.110

A: Europhile, B: Soft Eurosceptic, C: Harder Eurosceptic.

* Correlation not significant at p < .05.

the legislative debates of the Council of Ministers matters of public record (as the debates of any typical parliamentary body would be); standardizing the system of election for the EP and making voting in European elections compulsory; and most centrally, having European rather than national parties choose the candidates for EP elections and having the EP rather than the national governments choose the EC. With the exception of the first of these for the MNPs, in each of these cases there is a monotonic relationship between support for the proposal and Euroscepticism, with the Europhiles most, and the harder Eurosceptics least, supportive.

The other set of proposals is: for the national parliaments to have joint committees of MEPs and MNPs; for national ministers to be bound by instructions from the national parliaments; for there to be stronger links between the EC and MNPs; for there to be more dual mandates. In general terms, these proposals would reduce the democratic deficit by increasing the role of the national parliaments in EU affairs. With regard to these proposals (again with the exception of the first of them for the MNPs), it is the harder Eurosceptics who are most, and the Europhiles who are least, in favour.

The implication is that Europhiles and harder Eurosceptics differ not only with regard to their perceptions of the current level of democracy in the EU, but also in their conceptions of what a more democratic EU would be like. That this is so is demonstrated by the distribution of responses to a question asking about the proper source or meaning of democratic legitimacy in the EU.

Q20: Some people regard the European Parliament as the democratic heart of the Union, because democratic legitimacy of the Union can only be based on a supranational parliament. Others say that this is a wrong ambition because the legitimacy of the Union is already based on the national parliaments.

Respondents were asked to locate their own opinions on a scale ranging between 'The democratic legitimation of the EU should be based on...' the EP (1) and the national parliaments (7). As Table 7.12 shows, the relationship for the MNPs is reasonably strong, while that for the MEPs can only be described as overwhelming. Europhiles appear to subscribe, in the case of the MEPs quite strongly, to the 'Euro-federal' model of EU democracy; harder Eurosceptics on the other hand appear to subscribe

Table 7.12. Mean responses concerning the proper basis of democratic legitimation in the EU

	Europhile	Soft Eurosceptic	Harder Eurosceptic	eta^2
MEPs	1.96	3.02	6.25	0.616
MNPs	3.05	3.90	5.04	161

even more strongly to the intergovernmental model. As is perhaps appropriate, given their definition as a group that is supportive of European integration, but with reservations, the Soft Eurosceptics appear to cluster near the midpoint, although slightly on the side of legitimation through the EP.

This, then, suggests a qualification to the common claim that the best way to reduce Euroscepticism is to cure the democratic deficit in the minds of the Eurosceptics. While this may be true, to do so may require a two-step process. To be sure, it will be necessary to increase the democratic responsibility and transparency of the EU. It will also be necessary, however, to resolve the question of whether that means moving towards a more or a less federal model of Europe. Indeed, as the Laeken meeting of the European Council seems to indicate, this is a question that is taking on increasing significance even among the most enthusiastic Europhiles.

7.7 CONCLUSION

To return to the questions posed at the beginning of this chapter, it appears that Euroscepticism can be explained in large measure by two primary sets of attitudinal variables. On the one hand, those who feel themselves to be 'European' are less Eurosceptical than those who do not. On the other hand, those who are more satisfied with the 'democraticness' of the EU are less Eurosceptical than those are not. Once these attitudes are controlled, both partisan and national differences continue to be significant. The question of how much of the individual attitudinal differences among MPs are themselves the result of national or party influences has been left for further research.

Although the analysis here is by no means dispositive, it strongly suggests that the neo-functionalist faith that support for European integration will flow simply and directly from good performance is misplaced. While it may still be true, as Bryce opined and Sartori echoed, that men prefer to be governed well more and before they prefer self-government, at least with regard to the elites studied here, it would appear that approval of the process is more important than approval of the outcome in accounting for Europhilia. If this is more fundamentally true, amelioration of the democratic deficit is a necessary precondition for reduction of Euroscepticism, and technocratic arguments for the 'necessity' of increased Europeanization may only serve to confirm the fears of the Eurosceptics.

NOTES

1. Although the term is obviously older, the first reference to it in *Social Science Citations Index*, for example, is to Paul Taggart's 1998 article in the *European Journal of Political Research* (Taggart 1998). The earliest use found in a search of the Lexis/Nexis database is in a January 1993 article in *The Economist*, which is obviously introducing a new term for British 'anti-marketeers'. The term is also used in the title of Bernard Benoit's (1997) *Social Nationalism: An Anatomy of French Euroscepticism*.

2. As Anne McElvoy wrote of 'Euro-Brussels' in the *Sunday Telegraph* (9 November 1997: 39): 'For a start, there is a single, unquestioned approach to European affairs—namely that the EU's momentum towards a political union, its arcane structures, unelected commissioners and placebo parliament represent the best of possible options. To disagree is to be labelled deviant, perverse or stupid.' Similarly, 'The European Union has often been likened to a bicycle, which its leading politicians feel compelled to pedal forward for fear that if they stop, the whole enterprise might lose momentum and topple over' (Peter Norman, *Financial Times*, 30 May 2001: 8).

3. For example, the headline 'Eurosceptics in Sight of Victory' reporting early vote tallies, *The Times* (London; 8 June 2001).

4. Using the 'standard' criterion of eigenvalues greater than 1 yields only one factor (eigenvalue 1.999), but the second eigenvalue is nearly 1, and nearly twice the next eigenvalue.

5. One indicator of the irrelevance of the left–right dimension for the Nationalists and Greens is that their distributions of self-placements have the largest standard deviations of any of the parties.

6. The mean differences between desired and perceived influence (on the 11-point scale) for the European and national parliaments were respectively 3.30 and 2.20 for the MEPs, and 3.88 and 3.09 for the MNPs. The corresponding ratios of proportions favouring more versus less influence were 86.3:6.1, 68.8:16.6, 86.9:4.8, and 79.8:9.7.

7. In particular, I used the ordinal regression procedure with the difference between desired and observed influence and the difference squared as covariate predictors of SCEPT.

8. The figures shown in the table are the differences between the pseudo-R^2 computed for the model with all three blocks of explanatory variables and the pseudo-R^2 for a model omitting the block of variables corresponding to the line in which the figure appears. The figures shown in Table 7.10 are not entirely consistent, because patterns of missing data mean that each analysis was performed on a slightly different set of cases.

9. National party was used for both samples. If EP party group is used instead as the predictor for the MEPs, the pseudo-R^2 is 0.626 and the proportion of cases correctly predicted is 75.7 per cent.

8

How Deep Is the Wider Europe? Elites,
Europeanization, and Euroscepticism
in the CEECs

James Hughes, Gwendolyn Sasse, and Claire Gordon

8.1 INTRODUCTION

European Union (EU) enlargement has been a decade-long process that
still leaves undecided the debate of the early 1990s over whether there
should be a deepening or widening of the EU. Enlargement has certainly
provided an impetus for renewed debate over deepening in the EU, most
notably in the constitutional treaty which resulted from the convention
on Europe. The question remains, however, to what extent the enlargement to the Central and Eastern European countries (CEECs), the so-
called new Europe, will spread thin the ideal of European integration.
The critique that the CEECs constitute an obstacle to the deepening of
integration has normative and pragmatic dimensions. On the normative
dimension, these states are viewed as still being 'less European', or at
least being less committed to integration, due to path-dependent factors
concerning their historical legacies of communism and the transition
experience of overcoming these legacies. On the pragmatic dimension,
the fact that these states had considerable adaptational difficulties with
the process of adjusting to, and complying with, the *acquis communautaire* is seen as a serious practical 'technical' hurdle to these states
achieving the capacity for deeper integration in the medium term. The
discussion of these dimensions both in the scholarly and policymaking
worlds tends either to hover at the level of unverified abstraction, or is
focused on a narrow segment of the actors involved, namely national elites

and Commission bureaucrats. While the referendums on EU membership in the CEECs demonstrated the commitment of the majority of voters to the EU project, the level of commitment varied significantly from country to country. They also provided a vehicle for the mobilization of Euroscepticism either in its 'Hard' or 'Soft' form (Taggart and Szczerbiak 2002*a*: 7).

The campaigns and results of the referendums on membership indicated further that the political debate in the CEECs over EU membership had transcended the 'Euro-idealism' of the early post-communist period when membership of the EU was almost universally associated with the break from the communist past, the ideal of a 'return to Europe', and the absence of national policy alternatives. By the late 1990s, the CEECs had switched to a much higher level of realism about the short-term costs of membership with regard to the massive legal realignment, further fiscal restraint, and economic adjustment. Thus, a decade of the trials of transition and accession steadily eroded the idealism of the early post-communist years. The question is whether the early idealism about 'Europe' has been supplanted with more pragmatic considerations over the potential benefits of EU membership or outright Euroscepticism.

While the other chapters in both the volumes focus on overt party-based Euroscepticism, we focus on the Europeanization of elite actors and the extent to which this may reveal Euroscepticism. The weakness of parties as mobilizational and linkage mechanisms at the sub-national level in the states under consideration means we need to turn our attention to the roles of elites. The actors considered here are mostly public and private sector elites, of whom only a minority identified themselves as party members, and an even smaller number belonged to parties which espouse Eurosceptic positions. Consequently, the party political space for the articulation of Eurosceptical views at the local level is limited. To identify Euroscepticism is, therefore, highly problematic and so we have focused on the degree to which sub-national elites have been Europeanized and the nature of that Europeanization and whether this process reveals values that may be plausibly evaluated as Eurosceptic.

This chapter evaluates the extent of 'Europeanization' in the CEECs by testing the connectedness of sub-national elites to the EU in the run-up to accession. By a comparative study of regional and local elite values towards the EU in four CEEC states it demonstrates the weakness of Europeanization and provides empirical evidence for high levels of political pragmatism toward the EU.

8.2 EUROPEANIZATION AND THE NORMATIVE DIMENSION OF 'CAPACITY'

While there is no common understanding of the term 'Europeanization', at its most fundamental it suggests the diffusion of common political rules, norms, and practices or 'ways of doing things' which are first defined and consolidated in the making of EU decisions and then incorporated into the logic of domestic political systems (Radaelli 2000: 3; Olsen 2001: 3; Featherstone 2003: 19–20). While the theory is based on research into EU member states, it does not a priori exclude its application to non-EU states, in particular the accession countries. A widely employed model of Europeanization holds that the greater the familiarity of some actors with the EU and the more frequent their interaction with its policy activities, the more likely it is that they will benefit from a 'differential empowerment' vis-à-vis other domestic actors because their Europeanization generates a redistribution of domestic power resources towards them. This trend creates a cost–benefit calculus and incentive structure which is favourable to further Europeanization, as well as providing a mechanism for 'a socialization and collective learning process resulting in norm internalization and the development of new identities' (Börzel and Risse 2000: 268–70). Theories of institutional, policy, and normative convergence of this kind require not only proofs of connectivity to the EU integration process, but also of cognitive adaptation to common European values, a collective understanding of how policies are to be framed, and the deployment of both in policymaking and implementation. It presupposes two key conditions: firstly, it requires that some actors in a particular country have some level of connectedness to EU policy processes; secondly, it requires that some actors in a country are captured by EU norms and a European identity.

The extent to which elite and mass values in the CEECs became Europeanized during enlargement has important theoretical and policy implications beyond the ideological aspirational issue of whether this promotes or hinders EU integration. On the one hand, the study of the CEECs may confirm or challenge the assumptions about Europeanization. The assumption of differential empowerment, in particular, makes significant claims about the outcome of power games at the domestic level. What is missing from these approaches is an understanding of the important role of positional or functional power irrespective of levels of Europeanization and, furthermore, a recognition of the significance of the time factor in transition—by definition a process over time. These weaknesses in the theory are demonstrated by the study of the role of the sub-national elites in the CEECs. For, as we shall see, not only are these elites weakly Europeanized, but this weakness is outweighed by their positional and functional power in key policy areas. This is not to say that levels of Europeanization will not result in differential empowerment but rather that this is an effect that evolves over time, and may vary depending on the domestic politics and international influences on a particular country.

The sub-national level of the elite also had critical policy implications for evaluating the broader issue of concern to the Commission with regard to the 'weak capacity' in the CEECs to manage the responsibilities of EU membership. The issue of capacity is one of the most emblematic markers of the EU's shifting positions on enlargement. Whereas the 'Copenhagen criteria' of the European Council in December 1993 stipulated only that the candidates must implement the *acquis*, the Madrid European Council in December 1995 reformulated this into a vague condition that the candidate countries must have the 'administrative capacity' to implement the *acquis* (European Council 1995). This terminology became a mantra for the Commission and was restated in the Commission's report 'Agenda 2000 For a Stronger and Wider Europe', and the Commission's 'Opinions' on the candidate countries' readiness to join published contemporaneously in July 1997. Consequently, the Commission targeted its instruments for managing the enlargement process such as the 'reinforced pre-accession strategy', 'Accession Partnerships' between the EU and applicant states, and the National Programme for the Adoption of the *Acquis* (NPAA) to be implemented in each candidate country, and Poland and Hungary: Assistance for Restructuring their Economies (PHARE; included eight more member states apart from Poland and Hungary) aid, to the goal of building the required 'capacity' in the

CEECs, though without ever clarifying exactly whether the term required organizational, institutional, or personnel changes and, if so, on what scale.

In the Regular Reports on the progress of the candidates the Commission sporadically gave some further clarification as to what administrative capacity entailed by linking it to the requirements of the *acquis* in specific policy areas, such as sectoral capacity, effective structures for coordinating the negotiation process, administrative and judicial reforms, and the preparation for the implementation of structural policies (Dimitrova 2002; Hughes, Sasse, and Gordon 2004*a*). The Commission generally did not provide transparent or easily testable benchmarks for measuring progress toward the appropriate level of administrative capacity. For example, weak administrative capacity at the regional level in relation to chapter 21 of the *acquis*, was repeatedly highlighted in the Regular Reports as one of the key shortcomings of the candidate countries throughout the negotiation process. The Commission defined this as the capacity to 'define the tasks and responsibilities of all the bodies and institutions involved in the preparation and implementation', and ensure 'effective inter-ministerial coordination'. Moreover, the candidates had to show sound financial and budgetary management that complied with the provisions for structural funds and demonstrate 'additionality' in their co-financing arrangements. Moreover, it was only in the final accession reports in 2002 that the Commission linked capacity problems with 'implementation' (European Commission 1998–2002).

The Commission's clarifications of what capacity meant tended to emphasize organizational and management structures. This is an overly bureaucratic understanding of capacity and significantly underestimates its normative dimension. Getting the appropriate administrative structures in place is an important but partial step towards the implementation of the *acquis*. Equally important was ensuring that the structures were staffed with personnel who were imbued with the appropriate norms and knowledge to make them operate effectively in the implementation of the *acquis*. Some aspects of the enlargement process were concerned with the normative conversion of the CEEC elites and knowledge transfer about the EU. The 'structured dialogue' of the early 1990s and the accession negotiations themselves, for example, helped to acculturate the post-communist CEEC national elites into European elite discourse, accelerating in the first instance their presentational capacity to 'speak European'. The rapid increase in elite interactions between the EU and the CEECs, whether channelled through the inclusion of the CEEC national elites in EU fora and activities, or through more penetrative EU instruments that involved sub-national elites such as PHARE, Special Accession Programme for Agriculture and Rural Development (SAPARD), Structural Pre-Accession Instrument (ISPA), and scientific and educational exchanges, were attempts to promote Europeanized thinking in the CEECs and, therefore, in effect, to minimize the space of Euroscepticism. The 'twinning' instrument developed from 1999, whereby EU advisers and practitioners were seconded to ministries in the CEECs to assist with their accession negotiations, was also potentially an important step in the fostering of normative transfer to the CEECs. If we assume that the policy push in the CEECs for accession demonstrated a broad national elite consensus on membership irrespective of ideological position, it is equally important to consider whether this consensus extended to other levels of the elite, principally the regional and local elite segments. For just as it would be erroneous to assume that the referendums' results in favour of EU membership indicated a mass consensus with national elite values towards the EU, so we should not assume that the sub-national elite values concured with those of the national elite.

8.3 PARTY WEAKNESS AT THE SUB-NATIONAL LEVEL

One of the critical aspects of institutional debilitation during transition is that political parties, the key mechanism of political communication, mobilization, and representation in democracies, are organizationally weak in the CEECs, particularly as regards their penetrative strength from national to local level. Consequently, the importance of regional and local elites as gatekeepers and mediators astride the institutional levels between national elites and grass-roots public opinion is enhanced. The level of elite membership of political parties varied considerably in the cities analysed (Figure 8.1). Although almost two-thirds of elite respondents in Maribor (64 per cent) were members of political parties (perhaps in part because there was a less negative view of political party membership

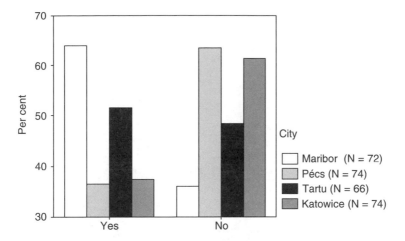

Figure 8.1. Elite membership of political parties

given that the League of Communists of Yugoslavia was a less tainted political organization than communist parties elsewhere in the East European region), in Pecs and Katowice only just over a third of local elites were members of parties (36.5 and 37.8 per cent respectively). Tartu fell somewhere in the middle with roughly half the elite belonging to political parties (51.5 per cent). As a considerable proportion of our elite sample was composed of members of local and regional executive and legislative bodies (64 per cent), the lower levels of party membership in Pecs and Katowice are surprising (Hughes, Sasse, and Gordon 2004*b*: 218). Levels of party membership in Eastern Europe as a whole remain rather low which underlines the weakness of parties as potential mobilizational and linkage mechanisms between the national and the sub-national level, thus reinforcing the need to look beyond elite party affiliation at individual attitudes and values to better understand attitudes to Europe, the degree of Europeanization, and the potential for the future emergence of Euroscepticism at this level.

The significance of looking beyond party affiliation and degree of support among sub-national elites for Eurosceptic parties is further underscored upon examination of the party breakdown of our elite respondents. An extremely small number of local elites belonged to those

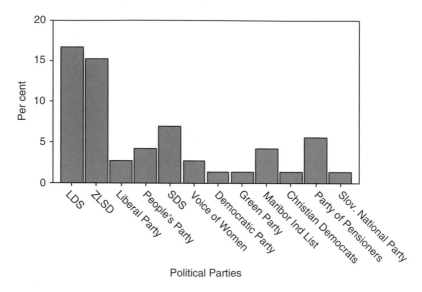

Figure 8.2. Elite membership of political parties (Maribor)

parties with Eurosceptic programmes according to the 'Soft' and 'Hard' Eurosceptic typology outlined by Taggart and Szczerbiak (2002*a*: 14) (Figures 8.2, 8.3, and 8.4). Although we have used this framework to inform our analysis here, it should be noted that at the time when the interviews were conducted in Maribor, Pecs, and Tartu (1999), for the most part party positions on the EU had not been clearly formulated. Party leaderships had not yet identified the Eurosceptic position as a potential vote-winning electoral strategy. In Tartu, for example, of those local elite respondents who were members of political parties, only 6 per cent belonged to the Centre Party classified by Taggart and Szczerbiak as a Soft Eurosceptic party.[1] As far as Pecs is concerned, the representation of Eurosceptic parties among our local elite members did not figure prominently, with only 5 per cent belonging to the Soft Eurosceptic party Fidesz.[2] In the case of Maribor, only one of our local elite members belonged to the Slovenian National Party, a Soft Eurosceptic fringe party. Finally in the case of Katowice (Figure 8.5), none of our local elite respondents belonged to parties classified as Eurosceptic. The overwhelming majority of elite respondents were not affiliated with any Eurosceptic parties.

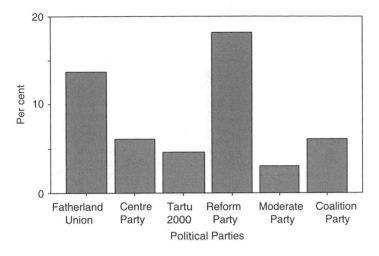

Figure 8.3. Elite membership of political parties (Tartu)

Furthermore, our research found no clear correlation between attitudes to Europe and party membership. This finding supports our argument that the positions on Europe during the enlargement process tended to be a second-order issue (Mair 2000; Hughes, Sasse, and Gordon 2004*b*). In view of the weakness of party affiliation both as a potential source of

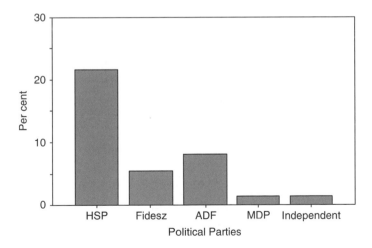

Figure 8.4. Elite membership of political parties (Pécs)

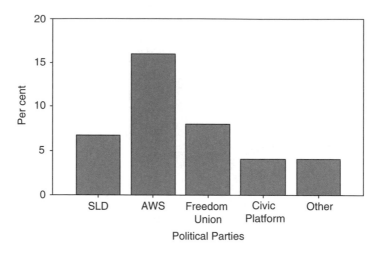

Figure 8.5. Elite membership of political parties (Katowice)

mobilization and as an identifier of values on the EU, our examination of the values of key elites at the sub-national level is more relevant. This is not to overlook the fact that in some countries there was a later crystallization of more Eurosceptic views, including the emergence of outright Eurosceptic parties, as the formal negotiations process over accession progressed and elites and publics developed informed opinions (Bielasiak 2004). The belated debates about the costs and benefits of membership of the EU were partly a result of the fact that the most contentious chapters of the *acquis* such as those on structural funds and agriculture were left to the final stages of the negotiations process in 2001–2. Moreover, we must be wary of confusing the tough negotiating positions of parties when in government and engaged in the negotiations for EU membership with 'Euroscepticism' (e.g. Fidesz in Hungary).

8.4 WHY THE SUB-NATIONAL ELITE MATTERS

The values of the sub-national level of the elite in the CEECs are immensely significant for two key reasons. First, sub-national elites occupied a positional centrality for the successful implementation of key aspects of the *acquis*. In particular, their role was critical for delivering successful outcomes in the implementation of key policies, such as regional policy, in the post-enlargement period. The enlargement to the CEECs in 2004 has brought a sharp increase in budgetary subventions from the EU to the new members. Compared with EU funding to the CEECs during the accession process, membership will result in an eightfold increase of expenditure. The financial package agreed at the Copenhagen Council in December 2002 committed €40.8 billion to the ten CEECs in 2004–6, over half of which amount (€21.7 billion) was to be spent on 'structural actions' which would largely be shaped by and benefit regional policy (European Council 2002). It was the Commission's concerns over these strategic financial impacts and incentives that made it stress capacity at the sub-national level in its Regular Reports on the CEECs. Thus, irrespective of whether financial programmes were managed centrally, as the Commission demanded, or were decentralized, the outcomes in terms of efficient implementation required an engaged and knowledgeable elite at the sub-national level.

Secondly, the regional and local elites were increasingly of normative political importance for the EU's project of democratic self-legitimation. Studies of regional policy and territorial politics suggest that the Commission's understanding of 'partnership' and multilevel governance was concerned with the correlation between regional participation in the programming of Objective 1 funds, successful economic growth and development, and the strength of regional governance (Hooghe and Marks 2001: 102). During enlargement, however, the Commission's views on what constituted best practice for the CEECs was contradictory and shifted over time, alternating between decentralized and centralized approaches to regional policy (Hughes, Sasse, and Gordon 2004a). Nevertheless, the White Paper on European Governance espoused rhetoric about the need for a 'multilevel partnership' to involve the regional and local level of governance more fully in EU decision-making (European Commission 2001b: 12). This normative commitment was much diluted in the draft constitutional treaty drawn up by the European Convention (see European Convention 2003, article 9 and the protocol on the application of the principles of subsidiarity and proportionality).

The paradox is that despite the financial implications and thus pivotal importance of sub-national elites in the CEECs for the EU, and despite the Commission's use of language about institutionally embedding partnership in regional policy and demanding greater regional capacity, the participation of the regional and local elites and institutions of the CEECs in the enlargement process was minimal. Enlargement was structurally flawed in that it was regarded by the member states, the Commission, and the candidate countries as a matter for governing national elites to negotiate. Consequently, while the Commission and the CEEC governments had a strong interest in the particular institutional territorial–administrative arrangements established for managing regional policy, and on the capacity of these institutions to access and manage the EU funds efficiently, a key layer of the delivery mechanism, namely, the actors who would be responsible for implementing this policy at the sub-national level, were largely excluded from the accession process.

What are the implications of this exclusivist approach to the accession negotiations? First, there are serious implications for the Europeanization question in the CEECs. The exclusion meant that the sub-national elites were denied one of the potentially most powerful Europeanizing influences on their norms. The structure of the accession process created a scissors effect in the norms of the CEEC elites, with a disjuncture between the more Europeanized values acculturated into the national elites and the largely unaffected sub-national elites. A significant fragmentation of norms between national and sub-national elites is obviously not conducive to policy coherence and good governance, indeed it may lead to dysfunctional governance, particularly where the sub-national elites play a key role in policy implementation. We can also hypothesize from theory that such different levels of Europeanization in the domestic setting may result in 'differential empowerment' in domestic politics though, as noted earlier, this is a factor that will take time to develop. Of more immediate concern is whether it will generate compliance and commitment problems in the implementation of policy. To demonstrate the weak Europeanization of the sub-national in the CEECs let us examine some of the key values held with regard to the EU.

8.5 THE EUROPEANIZATION OF ELITE VALUES[3]

8.5.1 Knowledge and relevance of EU activities

A reasonable hypothesis derived from the assumptions about Europeanization is that elites that are embedded in policy transfer or policy learning processes relating to the EU would have high levels of commitment to the values of membership and therefore low levels of Euroscepticism and good knowledge about the activities of the EU in their own spatial or functional domain. Although there is no area of local or regional government that is not affected by European regulation as a result of accession, our research reveals that there were low levels of engagement and poor knowledge about the EU among the sub-national elites in CEECs. Our results show that EU enlargement was not a salient issue for the sub-national elites. Rather, these elites were most concerned with the social and economic problems arising from the domestic transition process. In Maribor, not one of our elite interviewees cited EU enlargement as an issue of pressing concern for the city. In the case of Pécs, only 4 per cent considered it to be an important issue, and in Tartu and Katowice less than 2.5 per cent thought so. The focus on domestic socio-economic policy issues is understandable given the trauma of transition in the CEECs after 1989. What is surprising, however, is the absence of any recognition of the relevance of the enlargement process and EU membership to alleviating the local problems of transition, in particular through either PHARE or the potential of structural funds even though formal enlargement negotiations were already underway at the time the interviews were conducted. The disconnectedness of these elites from the EU is reinforced by their lack of understanding of how the EU is relevant for their level of governance.

Although approximately one-third to a half of our elite respondents had been involved in an EU-funded project of some kind, in general the levels of knowledge of EU programmes are low (Figure 8.6).

We found the highest levels of knowledge about EU programmes in Maribor, though even here just under half of the local elite members (51 per cent) still had poor or limited knowledge of EU-funded projects underway in their city. The high score was also influenced by knowledge of just one highly visible project ongoing in the city (the modernization of a waste-water treatment plant, partly with EU funds).[4] In Katowice, 55 per cent had poor or limited knowledge of city-based EU programmes; in Pécs, the equivalent figure was 63.5 per cent; and in Tartu, a striking 77 per cent had poor or limited knowledge of EU-funded programmes currently underway in their locale. This suggests that there was a major communication and recognition problem with the way that EU programmes were delivered at the local level. One plausible reason for this low recognition of the role of the EU is the design of EU/PHARE programmes, which were

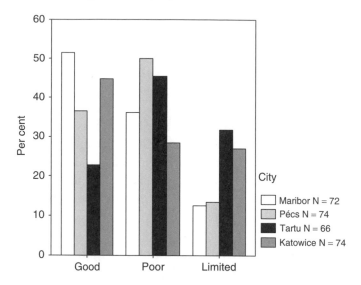

Figure 8.6. Elite knowledge of EU-funded activities in the locale

Note: Respondents were asked: *Can you name (up to) three (or more) current EU-funded (wholly or partly) projects in your city?* (Answers were coded 'good' if respondents were able to name any project and the source of funding; 'poor' if respondents were unable to name any projects or sources of funding; 'limited' if respondents showed knowledge of projects, but were unable to identify the source of funding.)

organized and funded through central ministries, were sectorally driven and rarely delivered on a territorial basis. EU funding was associated with the spending of national ministers (and by implication—political patronage) who supervised the dispersal to sectors (and indirectly to areas) identified as programme priorities. The exception to this trend was where EU funds were spent on infrastructural improvements that affected the locale, for example, on new roads or waste-water treatment plants. These were the kind of EU activities that registered most prominently among local elites.

It is difficult to assess accurately the level of correlation between the EU financial assistance that went into the cities/regions studied and the level of elite knowledge about these EU programmes. The Commission does not disperse its aid on a territorial basis and does not keep records of the amount of EU aid dispersed to particular cities or regions. EU aid, primarily PHARE, was organized and dispersed sectorally rather than territorially, and this factor, we believe, contributed to the lack of elite knowledge and association with EU activities at the local level. Regional development agencies established as part of the enlargement process in the CEECs did not promote elite connectedness because they were in most cases skeletal and highly politicized and often corrupt structures with limited administrative capacity. We attribute the significantly weak elite knowledge about the EU primarily to the structural disengagement of sub-national actors in the accession process combined with the failure on the part of the Commission and national political elites to prioritize the communication of knowledge of the benefits of membership within the CEECs. The higher level of elite knowledge of the EU exhibited in Katowice was, we believe, a result of institutional factors. In this case, the devolution of power to the regional level appears to have acted as an institutional vehicle for connecting the sub-national elite to the EU. Katowice is also a region with a strong historical regional identity and connectedness with Germany. Both factors, we believe, contributed to a deepening of the process of European integration beyond the capital in Poland.

8.5.2 Understanding the meaning of EU membership[5]

An elite that is connected to the EU is one that should have a good understanding of what the EU stands for, and what its main policy functions are. We sought to test this level of knowledge in the CEEC sub-national elites by offering our interviewees a list of twelve policy statements, some of which were relevant to EU activities and some of which were not, and some of which indicated integration, and some of which did not.[6] We asked them to select five preferences which for them best encapsulated what the EU stood for. We grouped the responses into four broad categories (Figure 8.7):

1. *Economic integration*: Free Trade, Economic Cohesion, Economic and Monetary Union (EMU), Common Agricultural Policy (CAP)
2. *Political integration*: Europe of Nation States (ENS), Federal Europe, Common European Home (CEH)
3. *Security integration*: Common Foreign and Security Policy (CFSP), Partnership for Peace (PFP)
4. *Regional integration*: Europe of Regions, Structural Funds, Subsidiarity

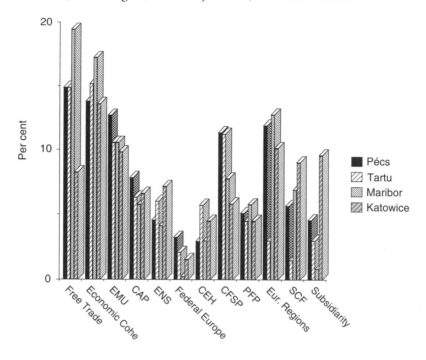

Figure 8.7. Elite perceptions of what the EU 'stands for'

Note: Respondents were asked: *Which five of the following phrases best sums up the European Union for you?* (The maximum possible score is 20 per cent.)

The overwhelming perception among the elites was that the EU stood for economic integration with free trade and economic cohesion receiving especially high scores. It is striking that the elites lacked any vision of the EU as a political integration project. Where respondents did select statements referring to the political project of the EU they tended to choose 'Europe of Nation States'. This preference reflects the determination of the CEEC elites to retain their recently regained sovereignty in the face of pressures for deeper political integration in an enlarged EU. This finding is substantiated further by the fact that the idea of a federal Europe consistently ranked very low in terms of the elites' understanding of what the EU stood for. Moreover, the Gorbachevian concept of a 'Common European Home' was significant only in Tartu (which had been part of the Soviet Union) albeit still a weak preference. In many cases, particularly Maribor and Tartu, countries which at the time the interviews were conducted

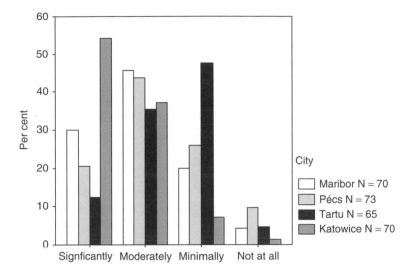

Figure 8.8. Elite opinions on the benefit of EU enlargement to the city

Note: Respondents were asked: *How much do you think EU enlargement has benefited your city?*

remained outside North Atlantic Treaty Organization (NATO), the elites attached high importance to the security dimension of the EU. Even in Pécs (Hungary already being in NATO at the time of the interviews) the security dimension was significant given its proximity to Serbia. Once more Katowice formed an exceptional case in that the elites here selected regional-level referents such as 'subsidiarity', 'Europe of the Regions', 'Structural Funds', and ranked them much higher than in other cases. Elsewhere, only 'Europe of the Regions' received a relatively high ranking (in Pécs and Maribor), though the term was poorly understood.

While the elite preferences discussed above emphasized the potential economic benefits of entry into the EU, further exploration of the meaning of the EU and the benefits of membership revealed that the elites in most cases saw most benefits accruing to the national level rather than the regional or local levels (Figures 8.8 and 8.9). It might be argued that this provided the raw material for the emergence of Soft Euroscepticism on the part of local elites whereby European integration is negatively perceived for its differential impact.

The gap between the perceptions of the benefits of enlargement at the national versus the local level was most pronounced in Pécs and Tartu. In

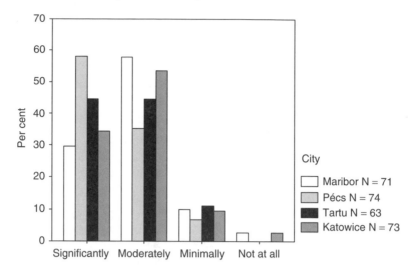

Figure 8.9. Elite opinions on the benefit of EU enlargement to the country

Note: Respondents were asked: *How much do you think your country benefits from its relationship with the EU?*

Pécs, 93 per cent of the members of the local elite considered that Hungary benefited 'significantly' or 'moderately' from its relationship with the EU, whereas 36 per cent felt that Pécs had only benefited 'minimally' or 'not at all' from the relationship. Similarly, in Tartu, 89 per cent of the local elite considered that Estonia benefited 'significantly' or 'moderately' from its relationship with the EU, whereas 52 per cent felt that Tartu had only benefited 'minimally' or 'not at all'. This confirms that the sub-national elites were poorly informed about the potential economic benefits that the EU could bring, and about structural funds in particular (Figure 8.10). Even the elite respondents in Katowice, who were more positive about the benefits of EU membership at the local level, felt that in general the EU benefited more from its relationship with Poland rather than vice versa.

In Katowice, 55 per cent of respondents felt that the EU was the main beneficiary of the relationship, and only 17 per cent considered that both Poland and the EU benefited equally. In the other cases, clear majorities considered that their countries were the key beneficiaries from the relationship with the EU. Even in Tartu, notwithstanding the fact that Estonia was consistently among the most Eurosceptic of candidate countries, and that the local elite in Tartu remained ambivalent about the potential

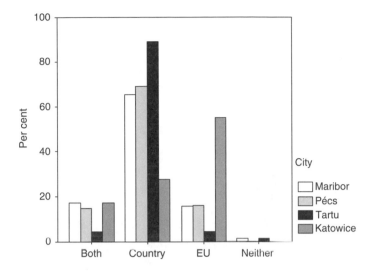

Figure 8.10. Elite opinions on who benefits most from EU enlargement?

Note: Our respondents were asked: *Who do you think benefits most out of the relationship between your country and the European Union?*

benefits at the local level, 89 per cent of our respondents were of the opinion that their country was the key beneficiary in its relationship with the EU. The evidence suggests that the sub-national elites were far from hostile to the EU or opposed to their countries' impending accession. Rather they were excluded from the enlargement process and, consequently, were poorly informed about the process and its implications.

Despite their lack of knowledge of the EU, and their failure to understand its relevance for their level of governance, they were in general pragmatically and positively predisposed to the economic benefits of membership of the EU at the macro level. These elites were pragmatic Soft Eurosceptics rather than active Hard Eurosceptics and therefore were potentially open to a greater level of engagement and connectedness with the EU in the future. The elites generally expressed a positive opinion of the EU, with large majorities seeing the future of their country closely tied to the EU. In Tartu, 71 per cent of respondents saw their country's future most closely tied to the EU (with a further 22 per cent citing Scandinavia and Germany). In the cases of Pécs, Maribor, and Katowice, 82 per cent of respondents saw their country's future most closely tied to the EU (with a further 5, 7, and 9 per cent respectively specifically highlighting Germany).

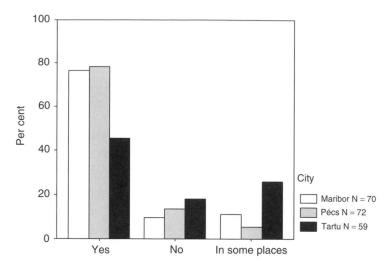

Figure 8.11. Elite opinions on the redrawing of administrative boundaries

Note: Respondents were asked: *Do you agree with the proposition that traditional administrative boundaries should be redrawn, if necessary, to comply with EU funding criteria?*

This indicates that the sub-national elites have consolidated views about the future external orientation of their economic and security relations.

The elites were also receptive to policy changes emanating from EU pressures if they were perceived to promote accession, even such intrusive proposals as the reform of internal territorial administrative boundaries— except in those cases where the potential empowerment of territorialized ethnic minorities is an issue (as in Tartu). Responses to this question may also have contained an implicit aspiration on the part of the sub-national elite members for greater involvement in the EU enlargement process (Figure 8.11).[7]

In Pécs, just under 80 per cent were prepared to accept the redrawing of administrative boundaries in compliance with EU-funding criteria. In the case of Maribor, an equally high number (79 per cent) was prepared to accept the redrawing of administrative boundaries in compliance with EU-funding criteria with a further 11 per cent prepared to countenance such administrative changes 'in some places'. These results suggest a receptiveness to changes that would accommodate accession. Conversely, though the city of Tartu does not have a large ethnic Russian population, given the

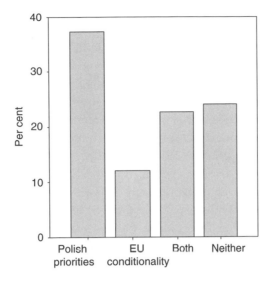

Figure 8.12. Katowice elites' opinions on EU influence on Polish regional reform (N = 72)

Note: Respondents were asked: *Do you think that the reform of regional and district governance structures in Poland in 1999 was on the whole the result of 1. Polish priorities, 2. EU conditions, 3. both, 4 neither?*

apprehension about Russian ethnic empowerment in the country, some 20 per cent of local elite members disagreed outright with the redrawing of administrative boundaries in compliance with EU-funding criteria, and 29 per cent would agree to such changes only 'in some places'.

Given that Poland's regional reform had already occurred by the time of our interviews in 2000, the elite respondents in Katowice were asked a different question in an attempt to gauge their perceptions of the influence of the EU on the process of regional reform. The Polish regional reforms of 1998 were the result of an inherently endogenous political process and EU influence was marginal (Hughes et al. 2004). Nevertheless, our findings in Katowice show that a significant number of the elite in the city (64 per cent) still felt that the 'design' of the reform was influenced by EU conditionality or at least a combination of Polish priorities and EU conditionality. At the same time, the elites recognized that the role of the EU was considerably less important for the outcome of the reform, with a large number (39 per cent) concluding that the reform overwhelmingly reflected Polish priorities (Figure 8.12).

8.5.3 Identity and 'Europeanization'

In this final section we examine the linkage between identity and Europeanization. Theory suggests that greater connectedness to EU activities promotes normative acculturation and the collective embrace of a European identity leaving little space for the emergence of Euroscepticism. What is less clear is whether this is merely a correlation or is there some causative effect at work. Is it that elites which identify themselves as being European are more predisposed to assimilate Europeanized norms and values? Or is it that those elites which engage in EU activities become Europeanized by the process of involvement. In both cases elites may be subject to reinforcing effects? To gauge the level of identification with Europe among the sub-national elites in the CEECs, our respondents were asked to select and rank their identity from a list of options. They were offered a range of options with some variations to take account of country and local particularities. In general, all elites were offered preferences including Europe, Central Europe, their country, the region, and the city. The results reveal a wide variation across countries.

The European identity is primary, that is, had most first preferences, only in Pécs. It was the secondary identity, after country, in Maribor, and was tertiary in Katowice and Tartu, after country and region/city. Thus, 27 per cent of respondents in Pécs opted for European as their primary identity compared to 21 per cent in Maribor, 17 per cent in Katowice, and a mere 9 per cent in Tartu. This result shows that the degree of identification of sub-national elite members with Europe is not necessarily indicative of their level of connectedness with the 'EU'.

Regional identities are relatively strong. In Katowice, where the elites were among the most positively predisposed towards the EU, regional identity is ranked second after the national identity. Maribor also has a more pronounced regional identity (8 per cent chose regional identity as their primary identity and a further 18 per cent chose the Stajerska region as a second identity) and perceived that it benefited more at the local level from its relationship with the EU than either Pécs or Tartu. The case of Katowice might suggest that a combination of democratized regional government and strong regional identity contributed to a strengthening of positive attitudes to the EU. Some 25 per cent of respondents in Katowice chose the locale (whether regional or city) as their

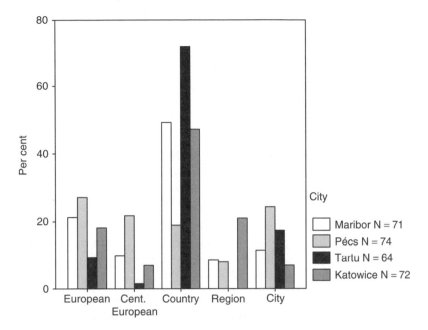

Figure 8.13. Sub-national elite identity

Note: Respondents were asked: *In your opinion, which of the following words best describes you (in order of preference)?*

primary identity. This was a striking difference from the elites elsewhere. Regional identity is virtually non-existent in Tartu (Tartumaa), where no respondents claimed primarily to have a regional identity. Only 8 per cent chose this level of identity as their first preference in Pécs (Baranya). The latter result is surprising given the much-trumpeted 'thousand-year history' of the county level in Hungary. Moreover, it is precisely in these locales where identity is weak that the gap in knowledge about the EU is greatest.

National identity is primary in three of the four cases: in Katowice, Maribor, and especially high in Tartu. In small centralized countries, such as Slovenia and Estonia, where the capital city and the national level is so predominant, it is to be expected that the country identity was the primary identity. In the case of Estonia, the city level scored highly as a secondary identity, whereas in Slovenia secondary identities were broadly spread (Figure 8.13).

8.6 CONCLUSION

Eurosceptic and pro-EU positions are two extremes of a continuum which do not capture adequately the attitudes and behaviour of sub-national elites. We view the weak connectedness of the sub-national elites in the CEECs to the EU as evidence of a very shallow level of Europeanization at this dimension of governance. This reflects the fact that the sub-national elites were deliberately and structurally excluded from the accession process by the EU and the national governments, thus, allowing an *écart* or scissors gap to develop between national and sub-national elite values. Accession to the EU, consequently, was generally perceived by the sub-national elites as a national elite project. The research demonstrates a weak knowledge of the EU's activities, a weak normative commitment to Europeanized values, and a weak European identity at the sub-national level. Given that this level of the elite was expected to play a pivotal role in the management and implementation of key enlargement policy objectives—particularly in the areas of regional policy and structural funds, agriculture, and the environment—its weak connectedness to the EU project may well have undermined compliance and hindered implementation of policy.

One of the many paradoxes of enlargement has been that the EU Regular Reports consistently criticized the weak capacity at the regional level to implement the *acquis*, while failing to structurally engage the elites at this level in the enlargement process. This gap between 'state-level' compliance with EU accession conditionality and the weak implementation capacity at the sub-national level was likely to persist until the sub-national elites became more connected to the EU in the post-enlargement period through their involvement in policy implementation. Theory suggests that greater connectedness to EU activities not only provides incentives and advantages for Europeanization in domestic-level political games by promoting differential empowerment but also progresses norm acculturation and the collective embrace of a European identity. This assumes, however, that those EU policies that are pivotal for the sub-national level, such as structural funds, are managed in the CEECs in a way which promotes wider cognitive change through greater sub-national elite participation. As we know from the experience of the pre-enlargement EU member states, structural funds are managed in a variety of ways from the highly centralized to highly decentralized. Thus, ultimately, the extent to which Europeanization proceeds to close the gap between the values of national and sub-national elites in the CEECs depends immensely on the organizational structures that are selected for the management of structural funds, and whether the new member states invest more of their sparse resources in building more capacity, both organizational and normative, at the sub-national level of governance. Presently, the limited financial resources of the CEEC transition states constrain this kind of capacity-building. Furthermore, in the final years of the negotiations process, the European Commission concentrated its attention on encouraging the enhancement of capacity at the central level to the neglect of the sub-national level. Consequently, sub-national elites who were disengaged from the enlargement process and failed to see the benefits for them, are the bedrock of a potential crisis of implementation in the post-enlargement period.

It is clear from the data presented earlier that the decisional calculus of sub-national elites in accession states was distorted by their focus on managing the immediate problems of transition, and as a consequence it was difficult for them to connect to the strategic political vision of European integration. While this does not yield Euroscepticism as such, it does have implications for the way in which these sub-national elites were Europeanized. The 'normative gap' in Europeanization at the sub-national level identified here did not appear to have significant ramifications for the referendums on EU accession, but it does not follow that we should similarly discount its impact on the implementation of deep integration. It is striking that the one case where the evidence for the normative gap among elites was consistently weaker was in Katowice. This suggests that a democratizing regionalization, that involves significant regional self-government rather than a stress on administrative capacity for policy implementation per se, may foster a higher level of norm connectedness of elites with the EU. The concomitant knock-on effect of promoting positive cognitive change among elites in their attitudes to Europe is that generates a higher level of commitment and compliance with a further deepening of the process of EU integration and constrains the space for Euroscepticism.

NOTES

1. According to Evald Mikkel, the position of the Centre Party is less clear-cut as for a long time it was trying to hedge its bets on Europe in a bid to attract support across the political spectrum and it was only at the August 2003 Party Congress that the Centre Party adopted a more overtly Eurosceptic position. Personal communication.

2. There is some disagreement in the academic literature over the classification of Fidesz. Contrary to Taggart and Szczerbiak (2002*a*), Kopecký and Mudde (2002) in their study of Euroscepticism in Eastern Europe have categorized Fidesz as a Euro-enthusiast party. What is clear is that former Prime Minister Viktor Orban found it expedient to adopt an increasingly Euro-cautious rhetoric as the membership negotiations progressed.

3. Our analysis is based on a large-scale cross-national comparative study of sub-national elites in key regional cities in the CEECs conducted in 1999–2002. The results presented here are based on an analysis of elite interviews (N = 287) conducted using a standardized questionnaire in the following CEEC cities: Pécs in Hungary (N = 74), Maribor in Slovenia (N = 72), Tartu in Estonia (N = 66), and Katowice in Poland (N = 75). We sought equivalence in our cases by using two main criteria in the selection. First, we chose key regional 'second' cities in each country case. By opting for the category second cities we aimed to minimize the effect of variation in terms of the size and importance of the cities relative to the hierarchy of cities within each country. In countries where there was more than one potential option for second city we selected cities that we considered were most geographically oriented to the EU and/or had a reputation for being 'Europeanized' (culturally, economically, politically, and historically). Elite members in each city were selected as follows. First, we used positional criteria to identify an initial selection of 20–5 individuals for interviewing, who were drawn from senior elected and appointed officials in the executive and legislative bodies of each city. After this initial selection, we snowballed out to other elite members using reputational criteria, by asking our initial selection of elites to identify other leading individuals. Using this method we interviewed as many as possible of the elite members identified, most of whom came from regional and local government, business, the mass media, and, to a lesser extent, the cultural intelligentsia, up to a maximum of 75 in each city. The interviews in Pécs, Maribor, and Tartu were conducted in the summer of 1999. The interviews in Katowice were conducted in late 2001 and early 2002 at a more advanced stage of the enlargement process. We recognize that this difference in timing may affect the comparability of the

data but on the whole we do not believe that it has a significant impact on most of the questions that we asked. We have attempted to take account of timing and contextual differences by redefining some questions. In addition to collecting key sociological information about the elite members, their activities and networks, the interviews also included a range of questions to test elite opinions on economic and political transition at the national, regional, and local level, on the expansion of NATO, as well as their attitudes to the EU and the enlargement process. The research findings are fully elaborated in Hughes, Sasse, and Gordon (2004*b*).

4. In Maribor, 17 per cent of respondents knew of the waste-water plant that was being built in the city though in fact the financing of this project was arranged by the European Bank for Reconstruction and Development (EBRD) and the EU funded only the construction of a water collector outside the plant.

5. The weak knowledge of the EU was also evident from the difficulty the interviewers experienced with certain terms, such as 'subsidiarity' and 'structural funds', which interviewees did not understand even when translated.

6. The interviewees were offered the following options: economic cohesion, partnership for peace, subsidiarity, Europe of Nation States, Free Trade, Common Agricultural Policy, Europe of the Regions, Monetary Union, A Federal Europe, Common Foreign and Security Policy, Common European Home, and Structural Funds.

7. This perception appears to have been widespread. A public opinion survey conducted in 2000 by Central European Opinion Research Group Foundation (CEORG) revealed a significant perception of a need for greater involvement of the sub-national level in the enlargement process. When asked at which level of administration EU financial resources should be distributed in the first instance, only 13 per cent of those asked in the Czech Republic, 8 per cent in Poland, and 26 per cent in Hungary thought funds should be distributed centrally. Whereas 39 per cent in the Czech Republic, 49 per cent in Poland, and 44 per cent in Hungary though funds should be primarily distributed locally or regionally. A further 31 per cent in the Czech Republic, 32 per cent in Poland, and 19 per cent in Hungary supported a more or less equal distribution between the two levels.

9

There is Not Much Eurosceptic Non-Voting in European Parliament Elections

Hermann Schmitt and Cees van der Eijk

9.1 INTRODUCTION

Participation in European Parliament (EP) elections is low, and increasingly so over the five elections since 1979. While considerable research effort has been invested to explore the causes of the meagre turnout in EP elections, the results so far are somewhat inconclusive. On the aggregate level, we know quite well that context matters. It does make a difference, of course, whether voting is compulsory or not; but it matters as well whether EP elections are held concurrently with national first-order (or other 'more important' second-order) elections or whether this is not the case; whether national first-order elections are close or not; and whether or not voting is restricted to Sundays (van der Eijk and Franklin 1996: ch. 19).

On the individual level, things seem to be less clear. Traditional predictors of individual turnout in EP elections (as well as in any other election) are hardly disputed: the effects of social integration, political mobilization, and party attachment. One controversial question remains which carries, in addition, some political dynamite. This question is whether abstentions in EP elections carry a hidden political message—like 'I don't agree with the whole European business', or 'Why do we need a EP. Let's get things right at home', and so on.

The chapter sets out to determine the relative importance of 'Eurosceptic' non-voting in EP elections as compared to what may be called 'Euro-neutral' abstentions. Based on the 1999 European Election Study, two factors that may cause 'Eurosceptic' non-voting are distinguished: (*a*) the (lack of) support for the European Union (EU) ('I don't like

Europe'), and (*b*) the (lack of) EU policy appeal of political parties ('If it comes to Europe there is no reasonable choice'). Four categories of Euro-neutral abstentions are controlled for: (lack of) support for national politics ('I don't like the way politics is run in this country'); (lack of) political parties' general appeal ('There is no party I can support'); (lack of) involvement ('I don't care'); and (lack of) efficacy ('My vote does not matter'). Social structure is also considered as a more remote social factor which precedes the political ones. Finally, the evolution of Eurosceptic causes of abstention is determined in a diachronic cross-national perspective by analysing survey evidence from the three recent EP elections of 1989, 1994, and 1999.[1]

Most of these factors which potentially have an impact on whether people turn out and cast their vote in EP elections are closely associated with the structure of party competition that is discussed in other chapters of this volume. And for many of them, not least for Eurosceptic non-voting, this association goes both ways—from voters to parties, and from parties to voters. Parties obviously shape the degree of electoral mobilization through their campaign activities: the less effort they invest in mobilization, the less citizens will participate in the election. Parties sometimes also do the opposite of electoral mobilization by calling their voters to abstain and boycott an EP election. But cause and effect may also be reversed. Parties which find themselves confronted with large numbers of Eurosceptic abstentions might want to reconsider their EU policies and pull in a more Eurocritical direction in order to strengthen their electoral appeal.

9.2 THEORETICAL CONSIDERATIONS

9.2.1 Eurosceptic abstention as a form of strategic voting

Research on strategic voting[2] is usually restricted to matters of party choice. Electoral participation is not considered in these terms. Stephen Fisher, for example, in his work on Britain defines a strategic (he says tactical) voter as 'someone who votes for a party they believe is more likely to win than their preferred party, in order to vote effectively' (Fischer 2000: 1). Referring to McKelvey and Ordeshook (1972) and ultimately to Riker and Ordeshook (1968), Alvarez and Nagler go beyond that by adding characteristics of the voters' individual preference order and of the competitive context of the electoral decision. For them, a strategic voter chooses 'her second most preferred party if the more preferred party is unlikely to win and there is a close contest between the second and third ranked party' (Alvarez and Nagler 2000: 58).

In these and similar accounts, non-voting is not considered to be a choice option for 'strategic' behaviour.[3] However, the act of voting is based on two decisions: (*a*) the decision to turn out or not, and (*b*) the decision to choose one (or more, depending on the electoral system) of the alternatives on offer.[4] It is not very plausible that voters would restrict strategic considerations to only one of these two decisions. On the contrary, if (and to the degree that) voters behave strategically, there is every reason to expect them to do so for turnout as well as for party (or candidate) choice.

For EP elections in particular, it might be useful to expand existing notions of strategic behaviour so that they apply not only to party choice but to non-voting as well. This, in turn, requires some initial understanding of the motives and political aims which, by abstaining from the election, a strategic non-voter might pursue. The motives for strategic behaviour are related to different possible outcomes of an election. For present purposes, it suffices to distinguish two kinds of outcome: policies and legitimacy.

Almost every election installs a new, or confirms the old, government. The government's political agenda ultimately results in a set of governmental policies. This is the policy outcome of elections. Based on past performance and on election programmes, voters form expectations about likely policy outcomes of an election. EP elections are different from most other elections because they do not contribute to the formation of a government. The policy consequences of different outcomes of a EP election are therefore difficult to determine (which is not to say that they do not exist). In any case, those consequences are not expected to cause strategic non-voting.

However, general elections are not only a way to collectively decide about future policies.[5] They also add to the legitimacy of the political regime. This is the second outcome of elections that is relevant here. Citizens' participation in the electoral process is often taken to indicate system support, while abstentions may signify two things—indifference as well as system opposition or alienation (Pappi 1996).[6] The context of available choice options seems to matter here a great deal. The smaller the number of anti-system choice options available on the ballot, *ceteris paribus*, the more likely abstention is to express system opposition.[7]

Abstaining because of system opposition, or more generally due to the lack of appropriate choice options, is therefore an indirect manifestation of substantive political preferences, in many ways comparable to what previous research of party choice has called 'strategic voting'. In the following sections, we will apply this notion to the motives of non-voting in EP elections and try to assess how important strategic non-voting actually is in this particular type of election.

9.2.2 Eurosceptic abstentions in European Parliament elections

By politicians and the media alike, participation rates in EP elections are seen as a crucial indicator of political support for the EU. When the first direct election was called in 1979, the EP launched a broad non-partisan mobilization campaign in all member countries of the EU (Reif 1985). Those efforts have been repeated in subsequent elections. In spite of this, turnout was widely considered disappointingly low in 1979, and has declined since. The trend generally points down. EU-wide participation dropped from some 60 per cent in 1979 and 1984, to around 55 per cent in 1989 and 1994, and down again to 50 per cent in 1999 (Table 9.1).

This decline in turnout is probably less alarming than it might seem at first sight. At least to some degree, it is the consequence of successive enlargements of the EU with countries where factors promoting high turnout are absent or weak. As a case in point, the proportion of the EU citizenry 'operating' under conditions of compulsory voting has declined.

In addition to compulsory voting, turnout is also affected by the timing of EP elections relative to that of first-order national elections. Turnout is highest when European and national elections are held concurrently. It is lowest immediately after a first-order national election, and increases slowly with the passing of the domestic electoral cycle. The effects of these factors are not immediately apparent, but they generate problems of comparability with respect to 'raw' turnout figures.

When composition effects (i.e. the decline of the proportion of citizens under compulsory voting) and timing effects (i.e. the unequal closeness to

Table 9.1. Participation in European Parliament elections, 1979–99 (in %)

	1979	1984	1989	1994	1999
Austria	—	—	—	68[3]	49
Belgium	**92**	**92**	**91**	**91**	**90**
Denmark	47	52	46	53	50
Finland	—	—	—	60	30
France	61	57	49	53	47
Germany	66	57	62	60	45
Greece	**79**[1]	**77**	[80]	**71**	**70**
Ireland	[63]	48	[68]	44	[51]
Italy	**86**	**84**	**82**	**75**	**71**
Luxembourg	[89]	[87]	[87]	[89]	[86]
Netherlands	58	51	47	36	30
Portugal	—	72[3]	51	36	40
Spain	—	69[2]	55	59	[64]
Sweden	—	—	—	42[3]	38
UK	32	33	36	36	23
EU-9	62	—	—	—	—
EU-10	64	59	—	—	—
EU-12	—	61	56	57	—
EU-15	—	—	—	57	50

Notes: (1) Election of 1981 (2) Election of 1987 (3) Election of 1995. Bold figures signify elections under compulsory voting; figures in [] indicate that national elections were held concurrently with EP elections.

Source: http://europa.eu.int, Angé et al. 1999; Grunberg, Perrineau, and Ysmal (2000).

national first-order elections) are removed, participation in EP elections is relatively stable (see, e.g. Weßels and Schmitt 2000; Franklin 2001). But stable as 'in reality' turnout may be, it is also particularly low. This brings us back to our question of strategic non-voting in EP elections in general, and to that of Eurosceptic abstentions in particular.

Past research is somewhat inconclusive with regard to Eurosceptic abstentions. Schmitt and Mannheimer (1991: 50), in their 1991 analysis of the 1989 European Election Study data, find that participation in EP elections is virtually unrelated to attitudes about European integration. In 1989, at least, electoral participation was mostly a matter of habitual voting—'people went to the polls because they are used to doing so on election day'. Later analyses based on the same 1989 European Election

Study included, in addition to individual-level factors, systemic and contextual characteristics and their interaction with individual-level variables (see Franklin, van der Eijk, and Oppenhuis 1996). While this strategy of research meant a big step forward (accompanied by a considerable raise of explained variance), attitudes about European integration and the European Community were again found to be virtually unrelated with electoral participation.

Blondel, Sinnott, and Svensson in their 1994 participation study conclude, by contrast, 'voluntary Euro-abstention to be significantly affected by attitudes to European integration, by attitudes to the European Parliament, and by attitudes to the parties and candidates in the election, and that it is not significantly affected by second-order considerations and calculations' (Sinnott 2000: 70 summarizing Blondel et al. 1998: 222–36). While this obviously conforms much better with conventional wisdom of politicians and journalists,[8] the validity of those claims has to be questioned on methodological grounds.

Blondel et al. (1998: 50) call *voluntary Euro-abstainers* those respondents who, in the course of the interview, gave one or more of the following reasons for their abstention: 'Lack of interest, distrust of, or dissatisfaction with politics and politicians, lack of knowledge and dissatisfaction with the EP electoral process'. Two objections can be made to such a self-reporting intentions methodology. First, survey respondents are themselves not the most reliable source of comparable information about the causes of their behaviour.[9] Secondly, the approach yields non-falsifiable and therefore non-scientific propositions as it is impossible to assess whether the same causes (i.e. Eurosceptic attitudes) exist among those who do not manifest the expected effect (i.e. who report to have turned out). Put somewhat differently, Blondel et al. may be seen to have 'stacked the deck' because they defined (i.e. selected) the category of respondents that was found to be 'dissatisfied with the EP electoral process' on the basis of this very characteristic.

Although we are sceptical about the validity of the conclusions of Blondel *cum suis*, we still cannot rule out that things might have changed since we first explored the issue for the 1989 election. Over the last decade, the EU has changed in many important ways. National sovereignty has been further transferred to EU institutions and authorities (e.g. in the currency domain). The political consequences of EU policymaking are more widely felt (like during the BSE crisis and the foot and mouth disease epidemic). Last but not least, the dynamics of EU membership—that is, the repeated broadening of the EU citizenry—is a source of concern for many citizens (like the eastward enlargement as it was approved in the Nice Treaty).

These and other developments may have changed the relation between mass political orientations towards the EU and electoral behaviour in EP elections. Eurosceptic abstentions in EP elections might have become more numerous and hence, strategic non-voting in the EU more important than in the past. Whether this is the case is the question which we will try to answer in this chapter, first with an in-depth analysis of the 1999 election and then in a diachronic analysis over the three elections from 1989 on.

9.3 DATABASE AND STRATEGY OF ANALYSIS

9.3.1 The database

The analyses reported below are based on the European Election Studies (EES) 1989, 1994, and 1999. While the data of the 1989 and 1994 study were collected within the Eurobarometer survey operation of the European Commission, the EES group has archived them separately (see van der Eijk et al. 1993 and Schmitt et al. 1997). The data for the 1999 study were obtained independently from the Eurobarometer in a series of nationally representative mass surveys administered by telephone (except in Italy) immediately after the EP election of June 1999.[10] The 1999 data have recently been made available for secondary analysis through the social science data archives (van der Eijk et al. 2002).

9.3.2 Scheme of analysis

In contrast to the earlier work, we will concentrate here on individual-level relationships. As our research questions do not involve multilevel relationships, no test for interactions of individual factors and systemic or contextual ones will be performed. In contrast to the work of others, such as that by Blondel et al. (1998), we refrain from subdividing our sample of non-voters into voluntary and circumstantial. There is always a certain number of citizens who, due to personal circumstances, is prevented from participation. This is equally so, no matter which election is called. Circumstantial non-voting, therefore, cannot add to our understanding of non-voting in EP elections if no epidemic diseases or other natural catastrophes are observed which could help explain the elevated abstention levels. Other methodologically inspired reasons aside, there is simply no good reason to continue on that road.

9.3.2.1 The 1999 study

Having said what we will not do, we might as well say a few words about what we intend to do. We start with the in-depth analysis of the 1999 study. The dependent variable is participation in the 1999 EP election as reported in the post-electoral survey of the EES 1999.[11] In addition to social-structural predictors of electoral participation,[12] six genuinely 'political' constructs will be used as predictors:

1. Support for EU politics[13]
2. Support for national politics[14]
3. Parties' general appeal[15]
4. Parties' policy appeal[16]
5. Political efficacy[17]
6. Political involvement (see Figure 9.1).[18]

Our central indicator of Euro-hostility is (the lack of) *support for EU politics* (construct 1). We maintain that the stronger the (positive) correlation is between support for EU politics and participation in EP elections, the more room exists for strategic Eurosceptic non-voting, and that consequently the incidence thereof *ceteris paribus* will be high.[19]

The policy appeal of political parties (construct 4) is an additional and in a way more general indicator of strategic non-voting in EP elections. If the policy appeal of political parties is very low, citizens may feel that there is no appropriate 'positive' choice option to them, causing them to abstain. A strong negative correlation of parties' policy appeal with abstention should therefore signal a substantial amount of strategic non-voting. Parties' policy appeal increases as the distance between the (non-)voter and the closest

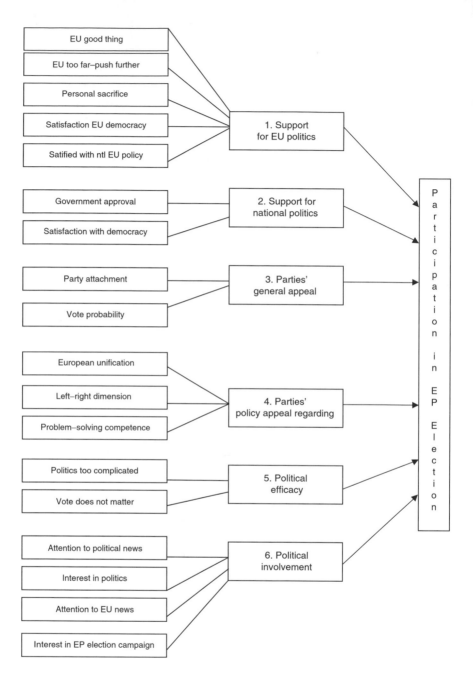

Figure 9.1. Indicators, constructs, and the dependent variable: The analytical scheme

of the relevant national parties regarding European integration and left–right becomes smaller. We also included a measure of party competence to the effect that parties' policy appeal is lacking if none of the national parties are felt competent to solve the political problem that the citizens regard as most important.[20]

Support for national politics (construct 2), *parties' general appeal* (construct 3), *political efficacy* (construct 5), and *political involvement* (construct 6) are all in a way indicators of 'Euro-neutral' (or sincere) participation or abstention. There is no 'hidden' political or substantive message behind the act of non-voting when people abstain due to a lack of mobilization or involvement, party attachment, or political powerlessness and alienation. In particular, there is no hidden Euro-hostility behind these possible causes of non-voting. Among these four, past research has identified political involvement and parties' general appeal as particularly strong predictors of electoral participation.

Strategy of analysis

We first report for each of the countries[21] in our survey the correlations between electoral participation and all independent variables we employ, which were listed in Figure 9.1, plus a few socio-demographic background variables. From these we can gauge to which extent the pattern of bivariate relationships provides a basis for expecting strategic non-voting to occur.

As our survey contains different numbers of cases for the different political systems of the EU, we decided to correct for this by weighting the respective country samples to an identical number of effective cases. In this way we avoid the risk that relationships that are found to be significant in one system fail to be so in another only for reasons of a smaller sample size.[22]

As a second step in our analyses, we focus only on the variables that pertain to the first construct identified in Figure 9.1, that is, (lack of) support for EU politics. We assess the strength of this set of five variables in explaining electoral turnout. We do so by means of multivariate regression analysis, a technique quite appropriate as we do not assume any particular causal sequence between these explanatory variables themselves. The limitation of this analysis is that no other controls are employed, and that their true causal importance may therefore be overstated. Yet, this analysis provides us with an upper limit of the causal importance of these variables in accounting for differences in electoral participation.[23]

In a third step of analyses we add relevant controls. The aim of this third step is to assess the relative explanatory importance of each of the constructs depicted in Figure 9.1, plus the socio-demographics. Here, however, we cannot use multivariate regression. That would assume equal causal status between all the independent variables, an assumption we do not subscribe to. It does not seem sensible, for example, that socio-demographics and EU-attitudes are equally proximal to electoral participation. Rather, it seems appropriate to look at attitudes as mediating (part of) the effect of background characteristics of respondents, in addition to adding explanatory power to them.[24] Therefore, we use causal analysis methods (structural equation modelling) instead.

The general structure of the model to be tested is depicted in Figure 9.2, which displays the theoretical expectations included in the model that is estimated for each of the political systems of the EU. From these models different kinds of results are important. First, whether or not the causal structure imposed on the models that are estimated is falsified by the structure of the empirical data; this is reflected in so-called fit indices. Secondly, the extent to which all these variables in combination are able to explain individual-level variation in electoral participation, that is, explained variance. Third, the causal importance of each of the constructs shown in Figure 9.1. This is expressed in so-called (standardized) total effects. These express in a way similar to standardized regression coefficients the sum of the direct as well as indirect causal effects of each of the constructs on electoral participation.

As the total number of independent variables is twenty-four, a structural equation model becomes more complex than necessary for the research question we address here. We are *not* primarily interested in the relative importance of each and every individual variable—let alone in the specification of their interrelationships—but rather in the importance of clusters of variables, each representing a construct as illustrated in Figure 9.1. Therefore, each of these constructs has been operationalized in the form of a single empirical measure. Each construct is measured by the optimal linear transformation and addition of the variables involved. This is obtained by taking the predicted value of the dependent variable (electoral participation) from a multivariate linear regression with only

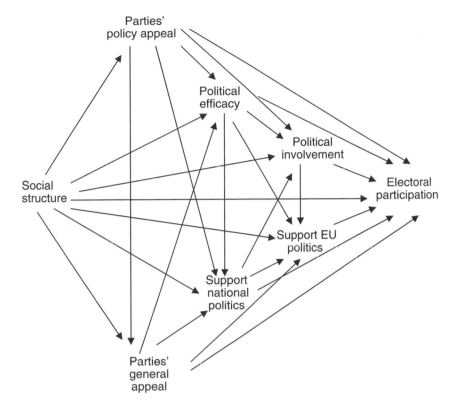

Figure 9.2. Determinants of electoral participation in the 1999 European election: 'Permissible' arrows

the variables pertaining to a single construct. In contrast to methods such as factor analysis, this ensures that *all* explanatory power of this set of variables is retained. All constructs have been measured in this way, as well as the entire set of socio-demographic background variables.

9.3.2.2 Comparing Eurosceptic non-voting over time

Our analytical scheme inevitably becomes more modest when we move on from the analysis of one study to the analysis of several. The reason is that the survey instrumentation usually differs somewhat from one election to the next, leaving the analyst with a relatively small common denominator of indicators that are available in each of three consecutive EES. Three sets of independent variables have been included in every EES post-election survey since 1989 that can be employed here, two structural and one attitudinal. On the structural side, there are the social-structural position of respondents[25] and their general political involvement.[26] These structural factors will be used to isolate the true effects of Eurosceptic attitudes on turnout. Two basic indicators of respondents' support for Europe and the EU[27] will then be utilized to determine the evolution of Eurosceptic abstentions. If it comes to the dependent variable, respondents have been asked in each study whether they participated in the preceding election and which party they voted for. The format of these questions differs slightly from study to study; but that would probably be of greater concern if we were estimating levels of participation rather than identifying causes of abstention.

Strategy of analysis

A strategy for determining the effects of EU attitudes on participation in three consecutive EP elections must be both theoretically grounded and empirically parsimonious. With regard to theory, we refer to the conventional wisdom that non-voters are 'peripheral' socially[28] and politically.[29] Both these peripheral locations are of a structural—that is, not election specific—nature. They are supposed to impact on turnout no matter what election is analysed. The potential relevance of support for Europe and the EU, by contrast, is of an attitudinal nature and is very election specific. While both structural position and political attitudes may be interlinked, we decided for the diachronic analysis—with an eye on parsimony—to control for structural factors first and then move on and assess the behavioural relevance of EU attitudes. This can be done by a procedure known as block-recursive regression. Stepwise regressions are performed with electoral participation as the dependent variable. Social-structural factors are entered first, and their explanatory power is determined. Indicators of political involvement are entered second, and the proportion of additional variance explained is determined. Attitudes about Europe and the EU are entered third and again the proportion of additional variance explained is determined (together with the proportion of variance explained overall).

9.4 FINDINGS

9.4.1 Bivariate relationships

In Table 9.2 we present for each of the political systems of the EU the bivariate correlation between electoral participation on the one hand and each of the independent variables on the other hand. For presentational purposes, correlations not significant at the 0.05 level were omitted. The independent variables have been ordered according to the construct or cluster they belong to.

By looking at the rows of Table 9.2, one sees immediately in how many of the systems each of these variables is significantly correlated with electoral participation. Three clusters stand out in this respect: political parties' general appeal, political involvement, and political efficacy. With only a few exceptions, we find correlations of indicators of these constructs with electoral participation in all political systems under study.[30] Moreover, the signs of these correlations are all the same, and in the expected direction.

For the other clusters, we find considerable differences between EU member countries. The 'support for EU politics' variables, for example, are all quite strongly correlated with electoral participation in Sweden. In a number of countries only some of these variables show significant correlations. There these correlations are also weaker than in Sweden. In five countries—Greece, Ireland, Italy, Luxembourg, and Portugal—none of these variables is significantly correlated with electoral participation. The correlations from this cluster of indicators are almost all positive, which indicates that 'supportive' attitudes towards the EU are more prevalent among voters than among non-voters. This seems to be in line with a hypothesis of strategic non-voting, motivated by anti-EU attitudes. Three coefficients are, however, negative, and indicate that sometimes Eurosceptics of one kind or another are more, not less, prevalent among those who turn out to cast their vote. Obviously, contextual differences, such as the way in which political parties are aligned with these attitudes have to be taken into account to understand these differences. Although we will not do such analyses in this chapter, the mere fact that in Britain and (to some extent) in Flanders, it is the Europhiles that are more prone to abstain should serve as a warning against hasty conclusions that abstention can only be motivated by a *lack* of support for the EU.

Table 9.2. Correlates of participation in European Parliament elections, 1999

	Au	Be F	Be W	De	Fi	Fr	Ge	GB	Gr	Ir	It	Lu	Ne	Po	Sp	Sw
Support for EU politics																
EU membership bad or good	0.110	−0.138	0.069	0.078	0.102	—	0.131	—	—	—	—	—	—	—	0.116	0.270
Integration gone too far vs. push further	0.081	—	0.121	—	0.113	—	0.142	—	—	—	—	—	0.130	—	—	0.245
Personal sacrifice to help other EU country	0.145	0.102	—	0.088	0.190	0.089	0.191	—	—	—	—	—	0.186	—	—	0.198
Satisfaction with EU democracy	—	0.078	—	—	—	—	—	−0.097	—	—	—	—	—	—	0.090	0.145
Satisfaction with national EU policy	—	—	0.130	—	0.096	—	0.119	−0.082	—	—	—	—	—	—	—	0.188
Support for national politics																
Approval of government record to date	—	−0.131	—	—	—	—	—	—	—	—	—	—	—	—	—	0.084
Satisfaction with democracy in country	—	—	—	—	—	—	0.096	—	0.078	0.078	—	—	—	—	0.108	0.202
Parties' general appeal																
Party attachment strength	0.223	0.128	—	0.158	0.312	0.207	0.182	0.130	0.155	0.147	0.250	0.074	0.274	0.335	0.183	0.282
Highest ptv score given	0.217	0.302	—	0.106	0.221	0.203	0.163	0.208	0.161	0.231	0.311	0.219	0.184	0.316	0.259	0.256
Parties' policy appeal																
Distance of closest party on integration scale	—	—	0.082	—	—	−0.117	—	—	—	—	—	—	—	—	—	—
Distance of closest party on left-right scale	—	—	−0.134	—	—	−0.172	—	—	—	—	—	−0.090	−0.083	−0.158	−0.076	—

No party felt competent to solve MIP	−0.125	—	—	—	—	—	—	—	—	—	—	—	—	—	—	—
Political efficacy																
Politics too complicated	−0.098	—	−0.151	−0.191	−0.109	—	−0.101	−0.168	−0.144	−0.086	—	−0.099	−0.166	−0.121	−0.120	−0.235
Vote does not matter	−0.094	—	−0.159	−0.245	−0.119	−0.206	−0.122	−0.178	−0.156	−0.088	—	−0.256	−0.180	—	−0.160	−0.195
Political involvement																
Attention to news about politics	0.183	0.226	0.120	0.286	0.275	0.220	0.251	0.248	0.076	0.206	0.169	0.130	0.280	0.188	0.152	0.365
Interest in politics	0.159	0.142	0.178	0.312	0.299	0.178	0.268	0.248	0.137	0.096	0.199	0.196	0.273	0.239	0.134	0.317
Attention to news about Europe	0.162	0.118	0.142	0.230	0.119	0.218	0.189	0.268	0.057	0.147	—	—	0.122	0.122	—	0.283
Interest in election campaign	0.260	0.135	0.148	0.432	0.393	0.238	0.279	0.336	0.285	0.228	—	—	0.377	0.328	0.278	0.386
Socio-demographics																
Sex	—	0.079	—	—	—	—	−0.099	—	—	—	—	—	—	—	—	—
Age	−0.276	0.162	0.122	−0.258	−0.174	−0.158	0.191	−0.190	−0.147	−0.239	—	−0.149	−0.194	−0.121	−0.216	−0.261
Education	0.158	—	—	0.085	0.114	0.165	0.084	0.180	0.122	0.122	—	—	0.074	—	—	0.072
Union membership	—	−0.112	—	—	0.098	—	−0.100	—	—	—	—	—	−0.096	—	—	0.101
Church attendance	—	−0.100	0.108	0.160	0.124	0.159	—	0.107	—	0.255	—	0.175	—	—	0.185	0.158
Rural–urban residence	—	—	−0.070	—	0.079	—	—	—	−0.183	—	−0.071	—	−0.134	—	−0.084	0.133

Source: European Elections Study 1999. Findings are based on weighted data (political weight 2). Figures are bivariate Pearson's correlation coefficients. Coefficients not significant at the 0.05 level are not reported.

The construct 'support for national politics' appears everywhere to be of limited importance at best. In ten countries neither of the two variables involved shows any significant correlation, and in the remaining countries the significant correlations are weak (with the exception of—again—Sweden where the correlation of electoral participation with (lack of) satisfaction with democracy in the country is of medium strength).

The variables measuring 'parties' policy appeal' are also only weakly related to electoral participation, and quite differently so in the various political systems. As the construct is related to contextual phenomena such as the format of the party competition in the different political systems, the differences we find between the systems do not come as a surprise. What is surprising, however, is the general weakness of these correlations.

The correlations of socio-demographics with turnout also show considerable country differences. Age is almost everywhere significantly related to electoral participation. Most often this correlation is negative, but in three systems it is positive. All correlations with education are positive, but in seven of the sixteen systems education is *not* significantly related to participation. Similar remarks can be made about the other background variables. Interesting as these differences may be, they are not central to our research question in this chapter. The main reason for looking at these variables at all is to use them as controls in later analyses.

9.4.2 EU-attitudes and electoral participation

The bivariate correlations presented in Table 9.2 do not tell us how much of the variance of electoral participation can conceivably be explained by sets of variables. In this section we focus on the set of five indicators that make up the construct '(lack of) support for EU politics', one of the 'usual suspects' in political and journalistic interpretations of low turnout in European elections. In academic circles the importance of these attitudes is contested, as discussed earlier in this chapter.

Table 9.3 reports a multiple regression in each of the political systems, in which electoral participation is the dependent variable and the five different EU-attitudinal variables are used as independents. In this table, the systems are ordered on the basis of the variance that is explained by these variables (bottom row: adjusted R^2). Inspection of this table leads to the following conclusions.

Table 9.3. Electoral participation and attitudes towards European integration and the EU: Results from multiple ordinary least squares (OLS) regressions (figures are unstandardized regression coefficients and significance levels)

	Sw	BF	Ge	Ne	Fi	BW	Au	De	Sp	GB	Fr	Lu	It	Po	Gr	Ir
Constant	−0.082	0.908	0.172	.067	0.058	0.870	0.382	0.530	0.549	0.383	0.587	0.903	0.764	0.636	0.799	0.600
	0.312	0.000	0.096	0.584	0.538	0.000	0.000	0.000	0.000	0.000	0.000	0.000	0.000	0.000	0.000	0.000
EU membership Bad or good thing	0.092	−0.057	0.034	−0.025	0.014	0.003	−0.043	0.058	0.080	0.025	0.037	0.030	−0.009	−0.023	0.015	0.020
	0.002	0.000	0.358	0.537	0.619	0.821	0.159	0.043	0.006	0.376	0.286	0.210	0.783	0.622	0.489	0.607
Personal sacrifice for member country	0.081	0.065	0.144	0.147	0.211	−0.002	0.115	0.073	−0.010	0.072	0.079	−0.041	0.058	−0.009	0.010	0.008
	0.058	0.001	0.000	0.000	0.000	0.928	0.005	0.063	0.742	0.073	0.045	0.045	0.145	0.841	0.700	0.848
Satisfaction with EU democracy	0.006	0.039	−0.035	−0.050	−0.034	−0.020	−0.003	−0.029	0.039	−0.046	−0.010	−0.001	0.005	0.004	0.006	0.009
	0.823	0.001	0.203	0.047	0.269	0.115	0.276	0.268	0.095	0.055	0.752	0.952	0.841	0.902	0.691	0.771
Integration 'too far' or 'push further'	0.019	0.009	0.013	0.018	0.012	0.007	0.000	0.007	−0.008	−0.012	−0.003	−0.002	−0.004	−0.008	0.001	−0.001
	0.025	0.016	0.090	0.035	0.182	0.017	0.974	0.404	0.168	0.147	0.728	0.538	0.628	0.194	0.804	0.930
Satisfaction with national EU policy	0.063	−0.016	0.049	0.037	0.041	0.033	0.015	−0.071	0.016	−0.036	−0.028	0.016	0.028	0.026	0.009	−0.0040
	0.026	0.193	0.079	0.173	0.210	0.004	0.580	0.014	0.438	0.153	0.274	0.297	0.221	0.382	0.537	0.218
Adjusted R^2	0.094	0.049	0.044	0.041	0.037	0.022	0.019	0.016	0.014	0.012	0.004	0.002	−0.001	−0.003	−0.004	−0.005
	0.000	0.000	0.000	0.000	0.000	0.001	0.002	0.006	0.014	0.027	0.201	0.286	0.453	0.681	0.753	0.895

Source: European Elections Study 1999. Findings are based on weighted data (political weight 2). All independent variables are coded such that the higher values are pointing in a Euro-positive direction.

First and foremost, the extent to which voting or abstention can be explained by support (or lack thereof) for the EU is extremely limited in most of the EU systems. In six systems there is no statistically significant contribution whatsoever to explaining variance in participation. In no less than eleven out of sixteen systems, R^2 falls below 0.025. This includes such countries as Britain and Denmark, where Euroscepticism (possibly even Europhobia) is very strong and possibly dominant, as well as traditionally Europhile systems such as Italy and Luxembourg. In all systems but one, the explained variance is less than 5 per cent, and that is an upper limit as controls for additional or rivalling explanations have not been included. The only real exception to this *pervasive marginality* of the effect of EU-support is Sweden. More than anywhere else in the EU, electoral participation may be (partly) explained by support or lack of support for the EU.

A second conclusion to be drawn from Table 9.3 is that of the five variables involved, one stands out in terms of the number of systems where it reaches significance. The willingness to sacrifice some of one's own wealth to help another country in the EU experiencing economic difficulties shows a significant regression coefficient in seven systems (plus two borderline cases). This variable relates more directly than other ones to respondents' attachment to a EU-wide political community.

As already discussed, the degree to which electoral participation can be explained by EU-support may be different than indicated in Table 9.3, as no controls have been included in these analyses for potentially rivalling explanations of voting and abstention. To the extent that these effects merely mirror spurious correlations, they are overstated. In principle, they can also be understated, namely in the case of spurious zero correlations, a rare but not impossible phenomenon. Their importance as shown here is not affected when they are an intermediate variable in a causal chain leading towards electoral participation.

9.4.3 Causal effects of the different constructs

The explanatory power of the constructs shown in Figure 9.1, and of the cluster of socio-demographic background variables has each been captured in a single variable, using the method described in section 9.2.3. With the resulting seven independent variables and electoral participation as the dependent one, a series of causal models (structural equation models) has been estimated, using the hypothesized direction of potential effects that was depicted in Figure 9.2.

A first question to be addressed with this kind of modelling is whether or not the empirical observations contradict the hypothesized model, that is, the total set of hypothesized effects. This is indicated by so-called fit coefficients, which are reported in the bottom rows of Table 9.4. The value of these coefficients is in each case satisfactory, which implies that empirical observations did not falsify the assumptions of causal effects implied in the model, and no significant portions of covariance between the variables are left unaccounted.[31]

The next question that we can address with the analyses reported in Table 9.4 is how well they explain electoral participation. In Table 9.4 we ordered the political systems again on the basis of explained variance. This order is different than that in Table 9.3, a difference that is caused by the inclusion of other constructs and variables that contribute to the explanation of voting and abstention. The explanatory power of the same set of independent variables varies considerably between the political systems of the EU. Greece ranks lowest, with a mere 6.7 per cent explained variance, Sweden ranks highest with 30.9. Why these differences? The coefficients of the independent variables may help elucidate these contrasts.

In a EU-wide perspective, three constructs or clusters stand out as the most powerful: social structure, political involvement, and parties' general appeal. The first of these, social structure, has by far the weakest (but still significant) effects in those systems where voting is compulsory (Belgium—Flanders and Wallonia—and Luxembourg), or where a quasi-compulsory regime is in place (Italy and Greece).

This underscores the observation by Franklin, van der Eijk, and Oppenhuis (1996) that system characteristics can constrain the playing room for individual-level factors when it comes to electoral participation. It also confirms the expectation of Verba, Nie, and Kim (1978) that compulsory voting diminishes the effect of social inequality on political participation. In line with the reduced impact of social structure under conditions of (semi-)compulsory voting, we also see that in these same systems the effect of involvement is much weaker than elsewhere. So, the differences between systems in terms of the explanatory power of the model are at least in part a

Table 9.4. Determinants of participation in the European Parliament elections of 1999: Standardized total effects (STEs), explained variance, and model fit indices

	Sw	Fi	Ne	Po	Ir	BF	De	GB	Sp	Au	Ge	Fr	It	Lu	BW	Gr
Support EU politics	0.117	0.082	—	—	—	0.142	—	0.089	0.085	—	—	—	—	0.132	0.075	—
Support national politics	0.089	—	—	—	—	—	—	0.054	—	—	—	—	—	—	—	—
Parties' general appeal	0.261	0.300	0.247	0.359	0.222	0.383	0.094	0.171	0.242	0.246	0.200	0.219	0.332	0.197	0.077	0.163
Political involvement	0.354	0.319	0.281	0.224	0.197	0.174	0.412	0.278	0.201	0.186	0.247	0.184	0.103	0.170	0.196	0.115
Parties' policy appeal	0.167	0.089	0.248	0.131	—	—	0.086	—	0.083	—	0.142	—	—	—	0.203	—
Political efficacy	0.100	—	—	—	—	—	—	—	—	—	—	0.143	—	0.106	—	—
Social structure	0.312	0.279	0.257	0.223	0.380	0.175	0.235	0.305	0.281	0.303	0.271	0.220	0.102	0.173	0.171	0.172
% explained variance	30.9	26.0	24.8	23.8	22.9	22.6	21.7	19.5	18.8	18.3	18.1	14.4	12.9	12.6	10.7	6.7
NFI (1)	0.978	0.987	0.978	0.938	0.932	0.997	0.998	0.955	0.972	0.974	0.976	0.937	0.968	0.955	0.990	0.947
NNFI (2)	1.000	0.996	0.996	1.000	1.000	1.000	1.000	1.000	1.000	1.000	0.993	1.000	1.000	1.000	1.000	1.000
CFI (3)	1.000	0.999	0.998	1.000	1.000	1.000	1.000	1.000	1.000	1.000	0.998	1.000	1.000	1.000	1.000	1.000

Source: European Elections Study 1999. The structural equations program used is EQS. Findings are based on weighted data (political weight 2). For the EU-wide analysis, sample sizes are additionally adjusted to the proportions of national electorates. (1) Bentler and Bonett's Normed Fit Index. (2) Bentler and Bonett's Non-Normed Fit Index. (3) Comparative Fit Index. STEs > 0.05 are not reported.

direct consequence of the limited opportunity for some kinds of variables to exert the effects they would have when voting is a voluntary act and abstention is legitimate.

Of the other variables, efficacy and parties' policy appeal are the most important, although their effects vary considerably between systems. Support (or lack thereof) of national or EU politics are factors that do generate significant coefficients in only a few of the political systems. Support of national politics is the weakest of these two, which indicates that non-participation in EP elections can hardly be accounted for by citizens' alienation from their domestic political systems. Support of EU politics also fails to add significantly to explanations of voting or abstention in nine out of sixteen systems, and is significant, but weak in the other seven. It is strongest in Flanders, Luxembourg, and Sweden, but even in those three systems inferior by far to the three most powerful factors: social structure, political involvement, and general party support.

9.4.4 The importance of Eurosceptic abstentions over time

We move on, finally, and consider possible changes in the frequency of Eurosceptic abstentions over time. Did the phenomenon increase, or decrease, or was there not much of a change? Are particular country patterns standing out? And what about the evolution of structural determinants of electoral participation? Some of these questions can be answered on the basis of information provided in Table 9.5.[32] The first observation is that attitudes about Europe and the EU do not play much of a role for the decision to go and vote, or to abstain, after structural determinants of electoral participation have been considered. This is so across the board; no countries are really standing out here as exceptions to the rule; and we find not much development over time either.

However, we see some evolution in the explanatory power of the structural determinants of turnout. Social-structural factors are loosing some of their importance for electoral participation. This is most visible in France, but can be traced elsewhere too. It seems to suggest that more and more of those whose social profile traditionally promoted electoral participation abstain nevertheless. Even more pronounced is the downturn of political involvement as a facilitator of participation in EP elections. Increasingly, people abstain no matter whether they are interested in politics or not,

Hermann Schmitt and Cees van der Eijk

Table 9.5. Participation in European Parliament elections: The effects of social structure, political involvement, and attitudes towards Europe (figures are R^2 and R^2 changes from block-recursive multiple OLS regressions)

Election	1989				1994				1999			
Country	A	B	C	C-B	A	B	C	C-B	A	B	C	C-B
Au	—	—	—	—	—	—	—	—	0.09	0.13	0.14	0.01
Be	0.09	0.12	0.12	0.00	0.08	0.14	0.14	0.00	0.04	0.06	0.09	0.03
De	0.09	0.17	0.18	0.00	0.08	0.20	0.20	0.00	0.05	0.12	0.13	0.00
Fi	—	—	—	—	—	—	—	—	0.07	0.19	0.20	0.01
Fr	0.16	0.21	0.21	0.00	0.13	0.24	0.24	0.01	0.09	0.12	0.12	0.00
Ge	0.07	0.15	0.16	0.01	0.07	0.18	0.21	0.03	0.08	0.12	0.12	0.00
Gr	0.22	0.24	0.24	0.00	0.23	0.32	0.32	0.01	0.04	0.06	0.06	0.00
Ir	0.18	0.20	0.20	0.00	0.11	0.19	0.19	0.00	0.13	0.14	0.14	0.00
It	0.08	0.15	0.15	0.00	0.17	0.24	0.25	0.01	0.02	0.10	0.10	0.00
Lu	0.07	0.08	0.08	0.00	0.04	0.11	0.16	0.04	0.07	0.13	0.15	0.01
Ne	0.08	0.15	0.17	0.02	0.10	0.15	0.17	0.02	0.08	0.16	0.17	0.01
Po	0.07	0.17	0.18	0.01	0.09	0.23	0.23	0.00	0.04	0.16	0.16	0.00
Sp	0.09	0.15	0.16	0.00	0.11	0.21	0.22	0.02	0.08	0.12	0.13	0.01
Sw	—	—	—	—	—	—	—	—	0.12	0.20	0.23	0.03
UK	0.12	0.20	0.21	0.01	0.08	0.16	0.17	0.01	0.12	0.15	0.16	0.00
Country Average	0.11	0.17	0.17	0.00	0.11	0.20	0.21	0.01	0.08	0.13	0.14	0.01

Source: *European Election Studies* 1989, 1994, and 1999. Missing values have been deleted pairwise. In the above table heading, 'A' symbolizes the proportion of variance explained in turnout by social structural factors; the sex of respondents, their age, education, marital status, union membership, and church attendance are used as predictors in this block. 'B' stands for a model where in addition to social structural factors those of political involvement are entered; political involvement is measured as interest in politics and party attachment. 'C' represents a model where in addition to social structural factors and factors measuring political involvement a third block of variables has been entered: attitudes towards European unification (for–against unification) and the EU (is EU membership of one's country good or bad); note that in 1999, the unification question has been asked in a somewhat different form than in the earlier surveys.

or whether they feel attached to a political party or not. Both trends accelerated between the 1994 and the 1999 election.

Could it be that controlling for the two structural dimensions conceals a stronger direct ('gross') association between turnout and (lack of) support for Europe and the EU? Table 9.6 compares gross and net effects of European attitudes on electoral participation. It appears that there are, indeed, examples where social integration and political involvement shield a substantial gross effect of European attitudes on participation in EP elections: Germany in 1994 and Sweden in 1999 belong in that class

Table 9.6. Attitudes towards Europe and participation in European Parliament elections: Direct impact and effect when social structure and political involvement is controlled for (figures are proportions of explained variance from multiple OLS regressions)

Election year	1989		1994		1999	
Country	R^2	ΔR^2	R^2	ΔR^2	R^2	ΔR^2
Austria	—	—	—	—	0.02	0.01
Belgium	0.00	0.00	0.01	0.00	0.03	0.03
Denmark	0.00	0.00	0.01	0.00	0.01	0.00
Finland	—	—	—	—	0.02	0.01
France	0.02	0.00	0.02	0.01	0.00	0.00
Germany	0.04	0.01	0.09	0.03	0.02	0.00
Greece	0.00	0.00	0.00	0.01	0.00	0.00
Ireland	0.00	0.00	0.00	0.00	0.00	0.00
Italy	0.01	0.00	0.01	0.01	0.00	0.00
Luxemburg	0.00	0.00	0.05	0.04	0.01	0.01
The Netherlands	0.05	0.02	0.04	0.02	0.02	0.01
Portugal	0.01	0.01	0.00	0.00	0.00	0.00
Spain	0.01	0.00	0.03	0.02	0.02	0.01
Sweden	—	—	—	—	0.08	0.03
United Kingdom	0.03	0.01	0.03	0.01	0.01	0.00
Country average	0.02	0.00	0.02	0.01	0.02	0.01

Source: European Election Studies 1989, 1994, and 1999. Missing values have been deleted pairwise. In the above table heading, OLS R^2 symbolizes the gross effect of attitudes towards European unification (for–against unification) and the EU (is EU membership of one's country a good or bad thing) on electoral participation; note that in 1999, the unification question has been asked in a somewhat different form than in the earlier surveys. ΔR^2 symbolizes the net effect of these same variables— after the effect of social structural factors (sex, age, education, marital status [not available in 1999], union membership, and church attendance) and political involvement (interest in politics and party attachment) has been removed.

of cases. But on average, 'gross' and 'net' effects of political support for Europe and the EU do not differ much—mainly because the gross effects are very modest themselves.

9.5 SUMMARY AND PERSPECTIVES

How much 'strategy' is behind the motives for non-voting in EP elections? Do people stay home because they disagree with the EU and European integration? Or is it the more general problem that non-voters do not have a 'supportable choice option', that is, that they do not see (at least) one political party which expresses their policy concerns reasonably well? The answer, in a nutshell, is no. Nowhere does anti-EU sentiment play a major role in the decision to participate in, or abstain from EP elections. Compared to that, the policy appeal of political parties is somewhat more important (in the Netherlands and in Wallonia in particular). But this second cluster of 'strategic' motives of non-voting is not really pervasive either. Given the weight that is attributed to policy orientations in 'economic' models of party choice, the limited impact on non-voting of policy-based relative 'choicelessness' is actually quite surprising.

Among the individual-level constructs considered in the present chapter, social-structural locations are clearly the single most important predictor of electoral participation. It is the strongest standardized total effect in seven of our sixteen political systems. General party support and political involvement together come in second, with four first ranks each. Strategic considerations—be it the Eurosceptic or the choicelessness variant of it—are defeated, together with support for national politics and political efficacy.

This in a way is good news for the prospects of EU democracy. Growing levels of abstention in EP elections are not the result of a growing alienation with the EU political system or hostility towards the politics of European integration. They rather seem to result from the fact that those who used to go and vote on election day—the socially integrated and politically involved—stay home in ever-greater numbers when the members of the EP are elected. The lack of excitement that comes with these elections, which itself is largely a function of the shortage of political consequences that can be associated with the election result, may be the main reason for this phenomenon. The second-order logic of EP elections thus seems to diffuse the impact of factors that cause (non-)participation in first-order elections.

But there is another, darker side to it. Due to the limited turnout, EP elections do not contribute to the legitimation of the EU political system as much as they possibly could. And in the long run, low turnout figures might contribute to the erosion of political involvement and political support in more general terms. There is a danger of spillover of apathy and disaffection to the politics at national and sub-national levels although so far this seems not to have materialized (Franklin 2001).

Having ruled out Eurosceptic non-voting as a major factor in explaining abstention in EP elections is one thing, a satisfactory explanation is quite another. Two kinds of extensions of the analyses reported here should result in more satisfactory models, at least as far as explanatory power is concerned. First of all, low R^2's to some extent may be caused by local independence.[33] Some factors that impinge on voting versus abstaining are a constant within each of the political systems. They may have an 'across-the-board' effect, which cannot be picked up in separate analyses for each of the systems. This suggests a pooled analysis in which systemic and contextual explanatory factors (such as the timing of EP elections in terms of the domestic electoral cycle) are added to individual-level ones. A second kind of extension of our present analysis involves interactions involving subgroups of citizens. Generational differences and differences in political sophistication come immediately to mind when thinking about the possibility that the specification of an explanatory model may be different for subgroups of respondents. Both of these extensions however are beyond the confines of the present chapter and will be taken up in future work.

NOTES

1. Analyses of data produced by post-election surveys following the 2004 election largely confirm the finding to be reported in this chapter. (see Schmitt 2005; Franklin 2007; an van der Eijk and Schmitt, forthcoming).
2. Depending on the author, strategic voting is also called tactical or sophisticated voting.
3. Quite the contrary, rational choice-oriented scholarship still struggles with the question how voting can be understood as rational behaviour (Aldrich 1993). In a recent contribution Franklin (2004) argues that the classic formulation of the problem—which implies that electoral participation is not rational behavior—is based on unnecessary assumptions. A reformulation of the problem does lead to the conclusion of non-rational participation.
4. Some authors have suggested that voting implies just one decision, with not turning out as one of the options amidst the options provided by the parties on the ballot (e.g. Schram 1989). As such perspectives have failed so far to provide new insights into the bases of turnout and party choice, we do not follow them.

5. Obviously, the causal chain from elections to government formation to policies is far from deterministic, and the term 'decide' should not be taken literally.

6. Theoretically one could expect satisfaction also to generate abstentions. But empirical research so far has failed to present evidence for this claim.

7. An obvious example are elections under communist rule, for example, in the former GDR. Anti-system parties could not form and participate in general elections, and citizens opposing the regime could not directly express their preferences: they had to abstain in order to do so. A good number did, but official turnout figures were sugarcoated in order to mock mass support (Weber 1999).

8. See, for example, J. Smith who notes that 'Franklin, van der Eijk, and Oppenhuis have challenged the sort of claims made in this section...' and contends without further empirical evidence or argument that 'Despite their scepticism it seems that attitudes do have a part to play in explaining behaviour in EP elections' (Smith 1999: 123, n. 10).

9. Alvarez and Nagler (2000: 61), reviewing the strategic voting literature, cast doubt on the validity of data gathered with the *self-reporting intentions methodology*: 'Unfortunately, researchers using these survey questions do not appear to have seriously considered the quality of the survey responses obtained for questions asking for justifications of reported political behaviour.'

10. Fieldwork was carried out by IPSOS (except in Italy). Overall, 13,549 interviews were realized. The numbers of interviews carried out vary between the countries, with some 1,000 respondents interviewed in Denmark, France, Germany, the Netherlands, Spain, and the UK, and some 500 interviews in the remaining countries except Luxembourg and Italy. In Luxembourg, 300 interviews were felt sufficient. In Italy, the questionnaire was administered by ISPO (Milano) in a tele-panel and some 3,700 interviews were realized.

11. Measurements of electoral participation/abstention regularly suffer from the tendency of over-reporting (i.e. from the fact that people claim to have voted while they actually abstained). One of the reasons for this is the 'social desirability' response set, that is, that respondents say what they think is socially acceptable or desirable. We have tried to overcome this problem to some degree by lowering the 'social desirability' threshold of having participated by the following wording of the participation question: 'A lot of people abstained in the European Parliament election of June 10 while others voted. Did you cast your vote?' Answer categories are: (1) yes, (2) no, (8) don't know, (9) no answer. 8 and 9 are coded as missing. The

data reveal that the 'don't knows' are very few so that there is no need to reconsider (and possibly recode) these cases as likely non-voters. There are hardly any refusals either.

12. These are age and sex of respondents, their education, church attendance, union membership, and urban–rural residence.

13. This construct is based on the following indicators: EU membership is a good/bad thing (Eurobarometer trend variable); European integration has gone too far versus should be pushed further (10-point scale); preparedness for personal sacrifice if member country in crisis; satisfaction with the functioning of EU democracy (4-point scale); satisfaction with national EU policy (4-point scale). Note that this construct is somewhat broader than the conventional indicators of support for European integration as it involves both measures of policy satisfaction and regime support.

14. This construct is based on the following indicators: approval of the government's record to date; satisfaction with the functioning of democracy [in country] (4-point scale).

15. This class includes the following indicators: party attachment (four categories from very close to not close to any party); vote probability for the most preferred of the relevant national parties (a value approaching 10 on a scale ranging from 1 to 10).

16. This construct is based on the following indicators: the smallest of the distances to any of the nationally relevant parties in terms of European integration (see second indicator of footnote 12; this results in a value approaching 0 on a scale ranging from 0 to 9); the smallest of the distances to any of the relevant national parties in terms of left and right (this as well results in a value approaching 0 on a scale ranging from 0 to 9); perceived existence or otherwise (dichotomous coding) of a national political party which is capable of dealing with the most important political problem (party competence).

17. This construct is based on the following indicators: politics is too complicated (4-point agree/disagree scale); vote does not matter (4-point agree/disagree scale).

18. This construct is based on the following indicators: attention to political news (4-point scale from none to a lot); interest in politics (4-point scale from not at all to very); attention to EU news (4-point scale from none to a lot); interest in EP election campaign (4-point scale from not at all to very).

19. Strong negative correlations indicate that Eurosceptic citizens are more likely to participate than to abstain, and vice versa. This can occur when Eurocritical forces are particularly successful in mobilizing the vote, the result of which might be called sincere (Eurosceptic) voting.

20. See Schmitt (2001) on the extraordinary importance of party competence considerations for vote choices.

21. In these analyses we distinguish between the two parts of Belgium—Flanders and Wallonia—because of the differences in their respective party systems. For the same reason we should differentiate between respondents in Northern Ireland and in Britain. The number of respondents in Northern Ireland is too small however to be used as a separate sub-sample, so these cases were dropped from the analysis. Compared to the Belgian and the British/Northern Irish differences in the structure of party competition, the deviation from the national scheme in the two regional party systems of Scotland and Wales are minor and do not require a distinct analysis.

22. The weight used in our analyses is known in the data file as 'political weight 2'. It weights within each of the countries the data so that (weighted) distribution of electoral behaviour in the 1999 EP elections corresponds to the actual election result in that country. The specifics of this method have been reported elsewhere (Van der Eijk and Oppenhuis 1991; Appendix B in Van der Eijk and Franklin 1996). After this, the resulting weight was multiplied with a country-specific constant so that the effective number of cases after weighting is equal for each political system.

23. One could wonder why no method of analysis was used that is specifically designed for dichotomous dependent variables, such as, for example, logit or probit methods. First of all we refrained from doing so for presentational purposes, having found that such analyses do not lead to substantively different conclusions. More importantly, however, the logit model is of little use in the subsequent step of our analysis, causal modelling. Logit models are firmly embedded in the tradition of regression, in which all independent variables have equivalent causal status. The consequence thereof is that only direct effects on the dependent are estimated and that (ubiquitous) intercorrelations between the exogenous variables (i.e. all independents in the logit model) may lead to the absorption of one variable's effects into that of another one. These problems are avoided in causal analysis, albeit at the cost of not being puritan in the handling of the dichotomous dependent variable.

24. Of course, attitudinal variables can also be seen as moderators of the effect of background characteristics on electoral participation. In this chapter, however, we will not pursue this possibility.

25. Sex, age, education, marital status, union membership, and church attendance are used mainly as indicators of social integration and resource attribution.

26. Political involvement is measured somewhat differently than for the 1999 study—we include interest in politics (4-point scale from not at all to very) and party attachment (measured on a 4-point scale from not close to any party to very close to a particular party).

27. Support for Europe and the EU is measured by two indicators. One is asking for respondents support for European unification (in 1989 and 1994 on a 4-point scale from very much against to very much in favour; in 1999 on a 10-point scale from has already gone to far to should be pushed further). The other is the familiar membership 'trend' question from the Eurobarometers which establishes whether one's countries membership of the EC/EU, according to the respondent, is a good thing, neither good nor bad, or a bad thing.

28. Due to a lack of social integration; see, for example: Lipset (1959), Tingsten (1963), Lancelot (1968), and Wolfinger and Rosenstone (1980).

29. Due to a lack of political involvement; see, for example: Lazarsfeld, Berelson, and Gaudet (1944), Berelson, Lazarsfeld, and McPhee (1954), and Campbell (1962).

30. Although the EU has fifteen member states, we report on sixteen systems, because we distinguish within Belgium between Flanders and Wallonia.

31. This does not exclude the possibility that other models, with different assumptions about the direction of causal processes, are also not falsified by the data.

32. While we remain faithful to our preference for the OLS algorithm, control runs have been done with multiple logistic regression. We arrived at virtually the same results with Nagelkerke's pseudo R^2 as compared to OLS.

33. It must be recognized, however, that R^2 is an often misleading measure for the explanatory power. It seems almost impossible to eradicate the notion that the magnitude of this coefficient should be gauged in terms of the interval between 0 and 1. This is incorrect, however. Empirical distributions of categorical variables generate an upper limit that R^2 can attain that is usually far below 1.

10

Theorizing Party-Based Euroscepticism: Problems of Definition, Measurement, and Causality

Aleks Szczerbiak and Paul Taggart

10.1 INTRODUCTION

Why do political parties take the positions they do on particular issues, or use those issues in a given way as part of inter-party competition? In this concluding chapter we examine the way that parties have addressed the issue of European integration in order to try and contribute to a wider understanding of the dynamics of party politics. In doing this, we aim to assess the relative degree of influence of ideas and ideologies, the role of individuals and leadership within parties, institutional constraints and opportunities offered by the context in which they operate, and role of the interests of parties, their constituent elements, and electoral bases. We are focusing on the way in which parties take Eurosceptic positions on the project of European integration or problematize the issue as part of inter-party competition. This is an issue of low (if any) salience for many parties, but this makes the picture somewhat clearer as the issue is not, in the long sweep of history, an embedded issue which parties find themselves unable to change. In other words, the European issue is a very slippery one, amenable to very different interpretations, and one that cannot necessarily be easily read off from other party positions. This makes it, potentially, a powerful illuminator of some key processes of party positioning.

As noted in the introduction to Volume 1 of this book, recent years have seen an upsurge in academic research on the subject of political party attitudes towards European integration[1] and specifically on the emergence of party-based Euroscepticism.[2] This literature has produced some extremely valuable single country or party case studies as well as more comparative and theoretical contributions. Most of the theoretical controversies that have arisen within the various papers and seminars on this topic have focused on two linked issues. First, how does one define and measure party-based Euroscepticism? Secondly, what is it that causes parties to adopt Eurosceptic positions and/or Eurosceptic discourses in party competition?

This chapter, therefore, also seeks to address and move forward the debate on these two controversial theoretical issues. It surveys the current literature and attempts to draw conclusions in terms of where the debate has reached. Section 10.2 examines the definitional controversies and, on the basis of the various approaches surveyed, attempts to draw some tentative conclusions about how party-based Euroscepticism should be conceptualized. Section 10.3 briefly considers some of the positions and discourses that have, in our view, been wrongly categorized as party-based Euroscepticism (by ourselves, among others). Section 10.4 examines whether or not (and how) it is possible to 'measure' levels of party-based Euroscepticism and critically evaluates our own earlier attempts to try to do so. Finally, Section 10.5 reflects on the academic debate on what causes party-based Euroscepticism. This has tended to be portrayed (wrongly, in our view) in dichotomous terms as an argument between those who give priority to ideological–programmatic impulses on the one hand and those who stress the imperatives of strategic–tactical positioning on the other. It should be stressed that this is very much a summary of research in progress and that the conclusions it reaches are tentative ones. It is primarily a synthesis of, and our latest contribution to, an ongoing debate rather than the last word.

The chapter argues that analysts must be careful to ensure that definitions of party-based Euroscepticism are not over-inclusive and should refer specifically to party attitudes towards European integration through the European Union (EU) in principle and the EU's current or future trajectory. The next stage in the theorizing process is to locate party-based Euroscepticism within a broader typology of party positions on Europe that breaks down attitudes among pro-integrationist parties. However, the more complex and fine-grained the typology is, the more difficult it is to operationalize. Finally, we argue that the debate on causality (as well as that on conceptualization and definition) has been confused by the conflation of Eurosceptic party positions on the one hand, and the use of Eurosceptic discourses in inter-party competition on the other. In our view, these two phenomena need to be clearly distinguished for analytical purposes and have different causal mechanisms.[3]

10.2 WHAT IS PARTY-BASED EUROSCEPTICISM?

The term Euroscepticism has emerged relatively recently as a concept derived from journalistic discourse rather than political science.[4] Euroscepticism tends to be used as a generic, catch-all term encapsulating a disparate bundle of attitudes opposed to European integration in general and opposition to the EU in particular. Consequently, political scientists who have attempted to borrow and adapt the term to analyse the impact of European integration on domestic politics and party systems have encountered a number of conceptual difficulties. This is particularly true when they have attempted to analyse the phenomenon of Euroscepticism in a comparative (and especially pan-European) way.

In recent years, several authors have attempted to define the term with greater precision, with specific reference to its manifestation in party politics. Our own working definition developed and refined over a number of years built on Taggart's initial observation that it was used as a term that 'expresses the idea of contingent or qualified opposition, as well as incorporating outright and unqualified opposition to the process of European integration' (Taggart 1998: 365).[5] Subsequently, we attempted to break this concept down to distinguish between principled (Hard) opposition to European integration and contingent (Soft) opposition, with attitudes towards a country's membership of the EU being viewed as the ultimate litmus test of whether one fell into the first or second camp. Consequently, we arrived at the following definition of party-based Hard Euroscepticism as being

where there is a principled opposition to the EU and European integration and therefore can be seen in parties who think that their countries should withdraw from membership, or whose policies towards the EU are tantamount to being opposed to the whole project of European integration as it is currently conceived.

Party-based Soft Euroscepticism, on the other hand, was

where there is NOT a principled objection to European integration or EU membership but where concerns on one (or a number) of policy areas leads to the expression of qualified opposition to the EU, or where there is a sense that "national interest" is currently at odds with the EU trajectory. (Taggart and Szczerbiak 2008*b*)

The Hard–Soft Euroscepticism dichotomy was designed as a (in the end, rather cumbersome) working definition for the specific purpose of conducting basic, comparative empirical research on the manifestation of Euroscepticism in European party systems. Although it has been extensively applied (and critiqued) by other researchers, it is important to bear in mind that it was originally formulated very much as a work in progress with the explicit objective of stimulating further debate and we have never been theologically attached to it.

The most comprehensive alternative conceptualization, based on a critique of our Hard–Soft distinction, emerged from Kopecky and Mudde (2002).[6] Kopecký and Mudde's critique of our working definition was based on two main strands of argument (both of which, incidentally, we agree with). First, they argued explicitly that our definition of Soft party-based Euroscepticism was too inclusive and all-encompassing or, as they put it, 'defined (Euroscepticism) in such a broad manner that virtually every disagreement with any policy decision of the EU can be included' (Kopecký and Mudde 2002: 300). Secondly, and more implicitly, they argued that support for, or opposition to, EU membership was not the litmus test that we made it in our Hard–Soft dichotomy and, therefore, not the key distinction that should be drawn among critics of the European integration project.

Returning to Taggart's original 1998 conceptualization, that placed greater emphasis on attitudes towards European integration per se rather than attitudes for or against EU membership, Kopecký and Mudde argued for a two-stage distinction. First, between those parties that supported or opposed the *principle* of ceding sovereignty to supranational bodies (what they describe as the original ideas underlying the EU). Secondly, between those parties that supported or opposed the planned *further* extensions of EU sovereignty (what they call the EU's current or expected future trajectory). On the basis of these two dichotomies—party attitudes towards both

Table 10.1. Kopecký–Mudde typology of party positions on Europe

Euroenthusiasts (pro-integration and trajectory)	Europramatists (anti-integration, pro-trajectory)
Eurosceptics (pro-integration, anti-trajectory)	Eurorejects (anti-integration, anti-trajectory)

Source: Kopecký and Mudde (2002: 303).

European integration through the EU in principle and the EU's current or future trajectory—they produced a fourfold typology of party positions on Europe as shown in Table 10.1.

In many ways, Kopecký and Mudde's critique and alternative conceptualization is very well thought through and moves the debate on defining party-based Euroscepticism forward in a significant way. We accept that our definition of Soft party-based Euroscepticism may, indeed, have been too broad and included parties that were in essence pro-European integration. In particular, we find what we consider to be their most important argument to be a compelling one. That is, that the key variables in determining party attitudes should be first, underlying support for or opposition to the European integration project as embodied in the EU (rather than a party's support for or opposition to their country's membership at any given time) and, secondly, attitudes towards further actual or planned extensions of EU competencies. In particular, we accept the weakness of using attitudes towards EU membership as the key definitional variable separating different party positions towards Europe.

This is partly because of our own and others' empirical findings on this issue. This points to the fact that whether or not a party says that it is in favour of their country being a member of the EU is certainly important at particular moments such as accession referendums and potentially crucial in terms of the translation of broad party positions into specific policy outcomes. However, it also suggests that party attitudes towards EU membership may be a more conjunctural–opportunistic stance developed in response to short-term tactical and medium-term strategic domestic considerations such as the 'deal' that their country is currently being offered or relating to positioning the party during a referendum campaign. For example, Fallend's (2008) account of party-based Euroscepticism in

Austria in Volume 1 describes how the Green Party came to terms with EU membership after their country voted 'yes' to accession without really changing their underlying attitudes towards the European integration project. Similarly, in her account of party-based Euroscepticism in Hungary, Batory (2008) describes how two parties, the Justice and Life Party and Hungarian Workers' Party switched their positions on this issue with relative ease in response to short-term tactical coalition considerations. In Poland, the Peasant Party determined its attitudes towards the June 2003 EU accession referendum on the basis of a cost–benefit analysis of the terms negotiated and whether or not the government introduced some specific items of legislation effecting farmers and rural areas (Szczerbiak 2008). This suggests that a party's stance on its country's EU membership is not, in fact, such a caesura as described in our original Hard–Soft conceptualization. On other occasions, it may also be simply a paper commitment in deference to a certain political correctness about attitudes towards EU membership that masks an underlying hostility to the principle of European integration through the EU. This could almost certainly explain the attitude of some parties in Central and Eastern Europe, such as the Movement for a Democratic Slovakia, that endorse EU membership for strategic reasons and claimed to be pro-EU membership in principle but whose actions and underlying values suggested a fundamental hostility to the European integration project, a phenomena that Henderson (2008) terms dubs 'phoney Europhilia'. In other words, party attitudes towards EU membership do not necessarily tell us what that party's deeper position is on the broader underlying issue of European integration through the EU.

However, while agreeing with the broad thrust of their critique and overall argument, we also have a number of reservations about the Kopecký–Mudde classificatory schema. The first of these is a relatively less important terminological one, namely, that it departs from the existing common usage of the term Euroscepticism by confining it to a subset of what would generally be considered Eurosceptic attitudes. In the popular sense, the term Eurosceptic generally encompasses *both* principled and contingent opposition to the European integration project. Indeed, many commentators often use the term even more broadly to refer to virtually *any* criticism of the EU; something that we have been accused of on occasion. This is a point that we consider in greater detail in the next section. Kopecký and

Mudde, on the other hand, refer to principled opponents of European integration either generically as 'Europhobes' or specifically if they (logically) combine this with criticism of the EU's current/future trajectory (i.e. deepening) as 'Eurorejects'.[7] These terminological problems are highlighted when one considers that the UK Independence Party, for example, would not be categorized a Eurosceptic party according to this definition.

Secondly, we believe that Kopecký and Mudde's 'Europragmatist' category comprising parties that are opposed to European integration in principle but supportive of the further extensions of EU sovereignty and the deepening of integration project that the EU's current trajectory envisages, is illogical. The placement of certain parties such as the Movement for a Democratic Slovakia and the Hungarian Independent Smallholders Party in this particular category simply reflects the fact that they had positions on Europe that made them extremely difficult to categorize. In our view, the fact that there will be certain parties that are difficult to fit neatly into any typology is something that we simply have to accept rather than inventing separate and illogical categories for them. Moreover, we cannot think of any parties in 'old' EU member states that would fit into this category.

Thirdly, and most importantly, we believe that Kopecký and Mudde's default 'Euroenthusiast' category is too inclusive and does not really capture the full range of different approaches to the EU that are encompassed within it. In doing so, it produces strange bedfellows (in the same way that we were rightly accused of doing with our Soft Eurosceptic category) placing the Polish Peasant Party and Hungarian Fidesz party in the same box as the Polish Civic Platform and Hungarian Alliance of Free Democrats. The problem is highlighted by the fact that in 'old' EU member states this category would, presumably, have included parties such as the German Christian Democrats, French Gaullists, and Forza Italia, who clearly held different views about how they wished to see the European integration project develop. In other words, the Kopecký–Mudde classificatory does not capture the fact that just as opposition to the European integration project as embodied in the EU can be both principled and contingent so can support for it. Any classificatory schema that attempts to be comprehensive and offer a full-blown typology of party positions (as Kopecký and Mudde's typology does) must capture and reflect different degrees of enthusiasm for the European integration project as well as opposition to it.

Logically, therefore, the next step in terms of building upon our and Kopecký and Mudde's attempts to conceptualize party-based Euroscepticism (but one that goes beyond the scope of this chapter) is to further break down the category of parties that are broadly supportive of both the European integration project in principle and the EU's current trajectory. In other words, it is necessary to locate Eurosceptic party positions within a broader typology of party positions on Europe that reflect nuances among the (broadly conceived) Euro-enthusiast bloc of parties. Some commentators have already made some tentative attempts to try to do this. Conti and Verzichelli (2005), for example, have (without using this precise terminology) attempted to break down the pro-European integration camp into principled and contingent Euro-enthusiasts to mirror the principled and contingent opposition that is to be found among Eurosceptic parties. The most ambitious and comprehensive attempt to develop a classificatory schema that encompasses a range of party positions on Europe is Flood's (2002—which, interestingly, deliberately avoids the term Euroscepticism). This comprises six categories (all carrying the prefix EU- rather than Euro-):

- *Rejectionist*: Positions opposed to *either* (*a*) membership of the EU *or* (*b*) participation in some particular institution or policy.

- *Revisionist*: Positions in favour of a return to the state of affairs before some major treaty revision *either* (*a*) in relation to the entire configuration of the EU *or* (*b*) in relation to one or more policy areas.

- *Minimalist*: Positions accepting the status quo but resisting further integration *either* (*a*) of the entire structure *or* (*b*) of some particular policy area(s).

- *Gradualist*: Positions supporting further integration *either* (*a*) of the system as a whole *or* (*b*) in some particular policy area(s), so long as the process is taken slowly and with great care.

- *Reformist*: Positions of constructive engagement, emphasizing the need to improve one or more existing institutions and/or practices.

- *Maximalist*: Positions in favour of pushing forward with the existing processes as rapidly as is practicable towards higher levels of integration *either* (*a*) of the overall structure *or* (*b*) in some particular policy areas (all emphases in the original).

Apart from the epistemological problem that these categories are not necessarily mutually exclusive and some parties might comfortably be located in more than one of them, Flood's typology (together with Kopecký and Mudde's) draws our attention towards one of the generic problems of defining party positions on the European issue, including Eurosceptic ones. That is, that the more complex and fine-grained the typology, the more difficult it is to operationalize and categorize the parties. This is because parties rarely elaborate their policies on the key issues on European integration in such detail that we can properly categorize them. Put simply, both the Flood and the Kopecký–Mudde typologies require a lot of data in order to categorize broad underlying party positions with the degree of precision that is required to fully operationalize them and this kind of information is often not available. There are, of course, various strategies that researchers can adopt to circumvent this problem. For example, Baker et al. (2002) have attempted to analyse the broad underlying positions of British parties (particularly the Conservatives) by referring to their broader political economy and this approach could be generalized to other parties and party systems. Ultimately, however, all these approaches involve inferring party positions on Europe from statements on other policy areas or broader ideological positions and, therefore, involve a high degree of imprecision and second-guessing about what party positions really are.

Ironically, given that Kopecký and Mudde's empirical focus is on four Central and East European EU states that were, at the time that they published their paper, candidate countries, this kind of data is actually easier to obtain for parties in existing member states. The latter are likely to have had more time to work out elaborate stances on various EU-related issues so that the researcher can discern the kind of EU that they are in favour or against with greater precision. In candidate states, however, it is difficult to identify a party's stance on either European integration through the EU in principle or on the EU's current trajectory because most of them do not articulate them, or simply have not even considered them. Very few parties in post-communist states elaborated their positions on the kind of EU they wanted to quite the extent of Vaclav Klaus' Civic Democratic Party, the paradigmatic case of a Eurosceptic party (pro-integration in principle, but anti the EU's current trajectory) according to Kopecký and Mudde, at the time when they were candidate countries.[8]

Henderson illustrates this point very well in Chapter 5 of this volume when she argues: 'In the 1990s, "Europe" was viewed through the prism of domestic politics even more strongly in post-communist states than in Western Europe.' In most cases, parties in candidate states have, indeed, tended to view EU integration almost exclusively through the prism of the accession negotiations and the kind of 'deal' that their country is likely to be offered. The kind of EU that they want to be members of, were issues of pure abstraction to them and therefore rarely addressed in any detail in party programmes, if at all. Moreover, given the predominant role that domestic politics plays in determining party positions on Europe, criticisms of the EU in candidate states are generally couched in terms of attacking the membership terms and conditions that are being offered by the EU and that country's government's approach to the EU negotiations.[9]

Nevertheless, it is possible to overplay the differences between candidate and member states. Many parties in the latter also view the European issue primarily through the lens of domestic politics and it is possible to exaggerate the extent to which they too have elaborated detailed policy positions on a broad range of EU-related issues. For example, Lees' (2008) analysis of party programmes in the October 2002 German Bundestag election in Volume 1 of this book highlights how little detail was accorded to this issue (and therefore, of the difficulties of identifying broad, underlying party positions) even in one of the EU founder states. This is in spite of the fact that most German parties have had several decades when they have been constantly forced to confront the issue of what kind of EU they want to see.

In the short term, therefore, we would argue that Kopecký and Mudde's classificatory schema should be modified so that it so that it focuses solely on party-based opposition to European integration, rather than attempting to locate their categories within a broader classificatory schema of party positions on Europe, and adopts the more popular usage of the term/convention of referring to Euroscepticism as both principled and contingent opponents of EU integration. While we think that the basic twofold distinction based on the Kopecký and Mudde criteria is more workable than our original Hard–Soft formulation, we would reformulate it as follows. Hard Euroscepticism (what Kopecký and Mudde term Eurorejectionism) might be defined as principled opposition to the project of European integration as embodied in the EU, in other words, based on the ceding or transfer of powers to supranational institution such as the EU. Soft Euroscepticism (what they term simply Euroscepticism) might be redefined as when there is not a principled objection to the European integration project of transferring powers to a supranational body such as the EU, but there is opposition to the EU's current or future planned trajectory based on the *further* extension of competencies that the EU is planning to make. This is a piece of short-term theorizing and must, in our view, be only a first step in the larger project of developing a more comprehensive typology of party positions on Europe that offers a more nuanced approach to pro-integration as well as anti-integration stances.

10.3 OPPOSING EUROPE OR PROBLEMATIZING EUROPE? WHAT PARTY-BASED EUROSCEPTICISM IS NOT

As noted earlier, the term Euroscepticism has been used in an all-encompassing and over-inclusive way by a number of commentators, including us. Finally, therefore, on this issue of definition it is worth discussing briefly a number of problem cases that those who have been researching this topic have had difficulties with when considering whether or not to include them in the definition of party-based Euroscepticism. The examples listed below are intended to be illustrative rather than exhaustive and there are, no doubt, other such difficult areas that can be added.

10.3.1 Criticizing the EU for failing to reflect a country's national interests

Does a party criticizing the EU for failing to properly reflect its country's national interests in, for example, budget negotiations (in the case of member states) or accession negotiations (in the case of candidate states) count as Euroscepticism? We have been criticized for appearing to include this within our definition of party-based Euroscepticism ('a sense that national interest is at odds with the EU's current trajectory') and, therefore, of being over-inclusive. Clearly, it is possible at any given time for almost any party, however pro-European, to engage in this kind of rhetoric. On reflection, therefore, we believe that it was incorrect of us to include these kinds of critics of the EU within our definition of party-based Euroscepticism. In other words, we now reject the idea that criticism of the EU for simply failing to reflect their country's national interests is sufficient for a party to be described as Eurosceptic.

10.3.2 Criticizing specific EU policies

We also accept the criticism made by some commentators that our formulation of Soft party-based Euroscepticism, as outlined earlier, was in danger of including parties that only have concerns about what is going on in one or two EU policy areas. As noted above, Kopecký and Mudde (2002: 300) have argued that 'soft Euroscepticism is defined [by Taggart and Szczerbiak] in such a broad manner that virtually every disagreement with any policy decision of the EU can be included'. Similarly, in a paper discussing party-based Euroscepticism in Belgium, Deschouwer and Van Assche (2002: 24) criticized us for including 'concerns about what is going on in one or in a few policy areas' within our definition. In his discussion of party-based Euroscepticism in Finland, Raunio points out how parties can have individual policies that are against the EU's current trajectory but nonetheless remain broadly in favour of it and therefore have a broad underlying party position that is not Eurosceptic. For example, the Finnish Social Democrats and Green League who opposed a common European defence policy but broadly supported 'deepening' European integration in principle (Raunio 2002: 8, 11). Clearly if a party is broadly in favour of both European integration as embodied in the EU in principle and the EU's general current trajectory but opposes one particular extension of sovereignty (to, say, include a common European defence policy), then that does not necessarily make it Eurosceptic. All this, of course, begs a series of questions, an important one being: how many extensions of sovereignty must a party oppose before it can be categorized as Eurosceptic? In this respect, a certain amount of common sense has to be applied. There are no simple answers here and clearly further reflection on this point is necessary. The basic point is that opposing only one or two EU policy areas is clearly not sufficient to qualify a party as Eurosceptic.

A possible alternative answer is to focus on the quality of the policy being opposed rather than the quantity. We might want to ask what sorts of policies are being opposed, and to differentiate between 'core' and 'peripheral' areas of policy concern for the EU. Clearly a party opposed to Economic and Monetary Union (EMU) is more likely to be categorized as Eurosceptic than a party opposed to say the Common Fisheries Policy (CFP). Again, there will be disagreement about what constitutes core policies but it is clear that picking away at marginal policy disagreements does not necessary constitute Euroscepticism.

A logical next step would, therefore, be to specify some areas of policy that are core parts of the European project as embodied in the EU or encapsulate its current/future trajectory, although we fully appreciate that this is open to dispute. An obvious example is EMU. The idea that one could support the EU's current/future trajectory and yet be opposed to EMU seems deeply problematic to us. The Common Foreign and Security Policy (CFSP) may, on the other hand, be an area where there is fundamental disagreement about the principle and practice but where support for the EU's broad current/future trajectory is not jeopardized and, therefore, represents a non-core area.

The picture is further complicated by the fact that, arguably, the subjective lens through which they view the European project may well condition the positions that parties take on Europe. The European project as embodied in the EU can, in turn, be opposed (or, indeed, supported) on the grounds that it is, for example, a Christian democratic, social democratic, liberal, or regionalist project. Similarly, it may well be that, to simplify a little, some parties view the European project as essentially a political project. In this case the EU is good in so far as it promotes internationalism, peace, and security. Others may view the project as essentially economic. Seen through this lens, the EU is a way of either promoting prosperity, capitalism, socio-economic cohesion, or all of these things. This may well yield different subjective evaluations of what constitute the core areas of EU policy. One solution to this may be to adopt the approach implicit in Kopecký and Mudde's model, whereby it is a general subjective *pessimism* about the EU's current/future trajectory that determines classification as Eurosceptic rather than any objective stance that parties may adopt on particular policies or issues.

10.3.3 Opposing EU enlargement

Although some observers appear to have interpreted it as such (Fallend 2008), we have never explicitly included opposition to EU enlargement as evidence of party-based Euroscepticism. In our view, opposition to 'widening' the EU contains no necessary assumptions about the current or future trajectory of the European project in terms of giving the EU further competencies or 'deepening' integration. Indeed, it can be argued that (in some Eurosceptics' view, at least) widening and deepening European integration may actually have conflicting logics so that opposition to enlargement can (logically, if not necessarily correctly) be equally well adopted by those who oppose as well as support 'deeper' European integration. As Baker et al. (2002: 3) point out in their survey of British Conservative MPs, the 'strong support of some Eurosceptic Conservatives for widening the EU to well over 20 countries, carries with it the covert intent of diluting, weakening and eventually destroying the basis of the whole process of EU'. In other words, Eurosceptic parties can support EU enlargement without necessarily supporting the EU's current or future trajectory; indeed, they may see it as a way of undermining it.

10.3.4 Criticizing the EU for being insufficiently integrationist and/or undemocratic

Another problem area that has puzzled analysts is the issue of whether to categorize as Eurosceptic those parties that criticize the EU for being *insufficiently* integrationist? This is the kind of critique that is often levelled at the EU by 'New Politics' left parties such as the Greens and often combined with calls for the 'democratization' of the EU.[10] It is clearly difficult to consider parties that call for the transfer of more competencies to the EU level as being opposed to the EU's current/future trajectory in terms of deepening integration and, therefore, incorrect to categorize them as Eurosceptic. As to whether or not parties that call for the 'democratization' of the EU should be included in the Eurosceptic category, it really depends on what precisely they are referring to as the means to achieve this objective. If they are calling, for example, for treaty revisions to repatriate powers to national governments, this is clearly against the EU's current/future trajectory in terms of deepening integration and therefore indicative of a Eurosceptic stance. If, on the other hand, democratization is synonymous with strengthening supranational institutions such as the European Parliament (as is often the case with 'New Politics' left critics of the EU), this cannot be interpreted as opposed to the EU's current/future trajectory of deepening integration and, therefore, not Eurosceptic.

To sum up this part of the argument, we believe that commentators need to be careful to avoid the temptation of interpreting parties that problematize Europe, opposing whatever the EU happens to be doing at any given time (however vigorously), with party-based Euroscepticism. It is clearly perfectly possible for a party to problematize aspects of European integration without necessarily being a Eurosceptic party. To include these parties within definition of party-based Euroscepticism is, indeed, casting this net too widely. Some commentators have implicitly drawn our attention to a phenomenon that they refer to as 'Euro-criticism',[11] criticizing the EU without being opposed to European integration through the EU. We shall return to this idea of parties engaging in Euro-criticism (or, perhaps, Euro-contestation), problematizing Europe without being Eurosceptic, in our later discussion on causal mechanisms.

10.4 (HOW) CAN PARTY-BASED EUROSCEPTICISM BE MEASURED?

The question of definition is, of course, inextricably linked with issues of measurement and testing propositions about the *levels* of Euroscepticism within different party systems. Only when one knows who the Eurosceptic (and other) parties are can one begin to attempt to measure levels of party-based Euroscepticism. But even assuming that one can define party positions with any degree of precision in this way, is it possible to measure *levels* of Euroscepticism within party systems? In our previous papers, we included the party's share of the vote at the most recent parliamentary election, alongside the lists of parties that we considered to be Eurosceptic. We believe that this remains a valid exercise provided one can develop an operationalizable definition of a Eurosceptic party. Vote shares for parties can provide us with a crude but simple and clear indicator of the importance of these Eurosceptic parties within their national party systems although it does not give us a guide to levels of support for Euroscepticism.

However, we also went on to aggregate the vote share for Eurosceptic parties and, on this basis, attempted to compare levels of party-based Euroscepticism across Europe. We then tested a series of propositions on the link between levels of Euroscepticism in a party system and public opposition to EU membership, the prospects of accession to the EU of candidate states, state longevity (Taggart and Szczerbiak 2001*a*, 2002*a*, 2004), levels of trust in the political regime, institutions and political actors (Taggart and Szczerbiak 2001*c*), and the type of party system in that country (Taggart and Szczerbiak 2001*c*, 2002*b*). However, commentators such as Deschouwer and Van Assche (2002: 24–5) have questioned the extent to which electoral results can be used as an indicator of party-based Euroscepticism at the country level and, more broadly, whether party-based Euroscepticism is a phenomenon that can be measured in a hard and quantitative way.

We have become increasingly sympathetic to the arguments of these critics. While we still strongly believe that party-based Euroscepticism is a portable concept that can be compared across countries rather than just relatively within countries, we are now dubious of whether it is, in fact, possible to 'measure' levels of party-based Euroscepticism in this way. The reason for this is the varying (generally low) level of salience of the European issue in terms of: first, the extent to which parties use the issue in inter-party competition (discussed later); secondly, more generally how much it features in the public debate of political issues; and, thirdly, how much weight citizens attach to it when determining their voting behaviour.[12] For example, a Eurosceptic party in one country may (hypothetically) obtain 40 per cent of the vote in an election. However, the party may barely mention the issue in its programme and it may hardly feature either as an election campaign issue or in the rankings of issues that voters considered as important when determining how they vote. This is, arguably, much less significant than a party that obtains 10 per cent of the vote in another country where the issue was much more salient in all or any of these dimensions. Consequently, we are now dubious of the value of 'measuring' levels of party-based Euroscepticism in this way and testing comparative and theoretical propositions on the basis of such data. To sum up, varying (generally low) levels of salience of the European issue make it virtually impossible to compare aggregate vote shares across countries as a means of 'measuring' levels of party-based Euroscepticism.

10.5 WHAT CAUSES PARTY-BASED EUROSCEPTICISM?

The other major theoretical issue that has vexed analysts of party-based Euroscepticism is the question of causality. Here the causes identified in the literature can be broadly divided into those that privilege either ideological–programmatic or strategic–tactical party competition factors. For example, the approach adopted by Sitter (2001, 2002) sees party-based Euroscepticism very much as a question of strategic positioning, and closely linked to what he terms the 'politics of opposition'. Another sub-school of theorists point to the importance of incentives created by political institutions such as the electoral system (Aspinwall 2004), types of legislature (Raunio 2008), or the spatial distribution of power within the polity (Lees 2002). On the other hand, in an analysis that considers party positions on Europe more broadly, Marks and Wilson (2000) view party positions in more ideological programmatic terms. They argue that the main causes of why parties take Eurosceptic (or other) positions on Europe are to be found in the historical cleavages that Lipset and Rokkan argue gave rise to the main ideological party families: Christian democratic, liberal, social democratic, and conservative.[13] In later work with Hooghe, they expand this analysis to include the cleavages reflecting the 'New Politics' left and right (Hooghe, Marks, and Wilson 2002). In other words, party positions on Europe (particularly when broken down to individual EU policies) can often be discerned from a party's more general ideological–programmatic disposition that is, in turn, rooted in how it positions itself in terms of historical or contemporary cleavages. In their analysis, Kopecký and Mudde (2002: 319–21) have attempted to account for the different circumstances in which strategy and ideology might determine party positions. Ideology, they argue, determines broad attitudes towards European integration in principle (which they argue is a relative constant) while strategy determines whether or not a party supports the EU's current trajectory.

In our own earlier writings, although we have often been identified as belonging to the strategic–tactical party competition camp, we have not taken such an unambiguous stance on this issue. We noted that certain party families have ideological predispositions to take a Eurosceptic stance (e.g. nationalist parties) or not to take one (social democratic and Christian democratic parties). However, we also noted that our empirical survey data of parties identified as Eurosceptic (according to our earlier definitions) found a pattern of strange ideological bedfellows and no linear relationship between Euroscepticism and left- and right-wing location on the political spectrum. We also found a marked tendency for Eurosceptic parties to be located on the peripheries or extremes of party politics. Generally, therefore, we identified this as an issue on which the evidence was inconclusive and requiring further research (Taggart and Szczerbiak 2002*a*).

Having reflected on this, we feel that much of this 'ideology versus strategy' debate has been cast in incorrect terms. Much of the confusion here stems from the conflation (not least by ourselves on occasions) of 'Euroscepticism' as: (*a*) a broad, underlying party position and (*b*) whether or not (and how) parties use the European issue (in this case in a contestatory way) as an element of inter-party competition.[14] As Sitter (2008) has presciently pointed out in Chapter 19 in Volume 1 of this book discussing party-based Euroscepticism in Norway, while 'party positions have (apparently) remained relatively stable on the surface', since the 1972 EU accession referendum this is somewhat deceptive because 'parties have a degree of freedom in translating issues (or even cleavages) into party politics'. In other words, the question of how a party determines its underlying position on the European issue is often different from how that issue has been accommodated into (in this case Norwegian) party politics.

We have come across several examples of when a party holds a broad underlying position that is Eurosceptic but does not choose to give it prominence in its discourse. One was the British Conservative Party, which, following its June 2001 parliamentary election defeat decided to play down (indeed, virtually eliminated) the emphasis that it gave to the

EU issue. At the same time it retained its broad, underlying Soft Eurosceptic stance on the EU's current/future trajectory; indeed, it elected one of the
infamous 'Maastricht rebels' Ian Duncan-Smith, as its leader (Baker et al.
2008). Another example of this was the Belgian Vlaams Blok party. An
analysis of its party programme would have lead one to clearly categorize
it as a (Soft) Eurosceptic party but Euroscepticism played virtually no role
in its discourse (Deschouwer and Van Assche 2008). In her discussion
of the Hungarian Justice and Life and Workers Parties in Chapter 15,
Volume 1 of this book, Batory (2008) points out how these parties softened
or sharpened their rhetoric on the European issue to suit their electoral
strategy and coalition tactics. At the same time they retained the same
broad underlying position of ideological hostility to European integration though the EU. In our view, therefore, it is necessary for analytical
purposes to clearly separate out these two phenomena—party position
and whether or not (and how) a party chooses to use an issue in inter-
party competition. This is an important distinction not just for the sake
of conceptual and definitional clarity. We also believe that these two distinct phenomena have different causal mechanisms that explain whether
or not—and, more importantly, under what circumstances—ideological–
programmatic factors or strategic–tactical factors play a role in causing
party-based Euroscepticism.[15]

In our view, broad, underlying party positions on the issue of European
integration (including Eurosceptic ones) are determined by two factors:
firstly, the party's wider ideological profile and values and, secondly, the
perceived interests of its supporters. The relative importance of the first
or second factor is determined by the type of party in question and
whether it is primarily a more ideological, value-based goal-seeking or
a more pragmatic office-seeking party. A goal-seeking party with clear
ideological and programmatic objectives will obviously privilege the former (ideology). A clientelistic, interest-based office-seeking party, on the
other hand, will obviously privilege the latter and undertake a cruder
economic cost–benefit analysis of how European integration is likely to
benefit its supporters. In our view, these broad underlying positions are
(generally) quite firmly rooted and, therefore, whatever rhetorical shifts
parties may undertake, remain relatively fixed. This is particularly true
if primarily ideology and values determine them because change would
involve the party engaging in a potentially painful and costly ideological

volte-face. For sure, parties do undertake ideological shifts that can change their underlying positions (although, admittedly, this is unusual). Indeed, contrary to what Kopecky and Mudde have argued, parties do change their position even on the principle of European integration through the EU; the British Labour Party and Greek PASOK in the 1980s and 1990s are obvious examples. The extent to which parties find it easy to shift their underlying position on Europe, therefore, depends on the extent to which they are primarily policy-seeking or office-seeking, with the latter obviously finding fundamental ideological shifts easier than the former.

However, while ideology is a key component in determining broad underlying party positions on Europe, we also believe that there is no straightforward linear relationship between general party ideology and party position on Europe. In other words, it is not possible to 'read' a party's position from whatever ideological family it belongs to. This is partly because, as noted earlier, some parties are primarily office-seeking rather than goal-seeking and, therefore, ideology is a secondary factor in determining party positions. But there are two other reasons for this that Flood (2002: 7–11) correctly draws our attention to. Firstly, because parties can interpret their ideologies flexibly and a broad ideological orientation can lead to a range of possible outcomes in terms of party position. Secondly, because the EU, and the 'European project' more generally, are themselves extremely malleable. There are many different 'Europes' embodied in the idea of EU and the project can be interpreted (and, therefore, supported or opposed) as a liberal, Christian democratic, social democratic, conservative, or even (ethno-)regionalist one to suit one's likes or dislikes.

Whether or not parties use the European issue as an element of inter-party competition and how much prominence they give to it, is, on the other hand, determined by a combination of (electoral) strategic and (coalition) tactical factors. A party's electoral strategy is, in turn, determined by a number of variables. The list that follows is intended to be illustrative rather than exhaustive: (1) The views of the party's current supporters and potential target supporters (rather than voters as a whole) on the issue of European integration, and (critically) how much importance they accord to this the issue;[16] (2) Whether it is a catch-all party that is attempting to attract a broad swathe of the electorate or a clientelistic or fringe party with a more segmented electoral strategy;

(3) Institutional factors such as the type of electoral system and, critically, whether or not it allows parties to survive and/or secure parliamentary representation by carving out a niche electorate for themselves or if it forces them to construct a somewhat broader electoral base. Other institutional factors that may be important here include the format and dynamics of party system that the party operates in, the structure of the state in terms of the spatial distribution of power, and whether or not and how frequently that country uses referendums; (4) How its discourse on the European issue and the prominence that it gives the issue fits in with its broader electoral appeal—a fringe protest party is clearly more likely to oppose the consensus view on Europe than one that seeks to locate itself within the political mainstream; (5) The positions taken by its competitors; and, (6) The imperatives of party unity and the strength of various intra-party factional positions will also affect party electoral strategy.

A second set of variables determining the prominence that the party gives to the issue in party competition relate to coalition–tactical considerations. These include the position of its potential coalition partners (both pre- and post-election) and, specifically, whether or not the party has to 'tone down' its rhetoric in order to secure a place in government—what Sitter (2001) refers to as the 'government–opposition dynamic'.

As noted earlier, some of these factors have been identified by other theorists of party-based Euroscepticism as factors causal of party position (Sitter 2001; Lees 2002; Aspinwall 2004). However, we would argue that they cause parties to give prominence, or not, to the issue in inter-party competition rather than determining their broad, underlying positions on this issue.[17]

We also believe that the same causal mechanisms that determine whether or not, and how, a party uses the European issue in party competition can also determine whether or not a party uses what we have termed above as the rhetoric of 'Euro-contestation'. This refers to those parties that problematize Europe—use rhetoric that is critical of the EU—while retaining a broad, underlying position that is supportive of EU integration in principle or even of the EU's current/future integrationist trajectory. In other words, electoral strategic or coalition-tactical reasons may cause parties that are supportive of the EU project to use rhetoric that is highly critical of the EU on occasions.

10.6 CONCLUSION

Definitions of party-based Euroscepticism have, therefore, become sharper since we set up our initial Hard–Soft conceptualization. One of the conclusions of this is that analysts must be careful to ensure that definitions of party-based Euroscepticism are not over-inclusive and, as Kopecky and Mudde suggest, refer specifically to party attitudes towards European integration through the EU in principle and the EU's current/future integrationist trajectory. At the same time, however, we believe that the term party-based Euroscepticism should also encompass principled opponents of European integration as embodied by the EU, as it does in the popular discourse on attitudes towards European integration. We believe that the next logical step in terms of theorizing party attitudes towards European integration involves locating party-based Euroscepticism within a broader typology that breaks down pro-integrationist parties. However, it is clear that the more complex and fine-grained such a typology is, the more difficult it is to operationalize because parties often do not go into sufficient detail when elaborating their European policies for firm conclusions to be drawn. We have also come to the conclusion that while vote share gives a crude indication of a (Eurosceptic) party's significance within its party system, it is not possible to 'measure' levels of party-based Euroscepticism in a particular country (or, indeed, comparatively) by aggregating vote shares.

Finally, we believe that broad, underlying party positions on Europe need to be distinguished from whether (and how) parties use the issue in inter-party competition and that these two phenomena are driven by different causal mechanisms. A party's broad underlying position on Europe is determined by a blend of its ideology and what it perceives the interests of its members to be. The relative importance of the two causal factors depends on whether it is a more ideological, value-based, and goal-oriented party or a more pragmatic, interest-based, and office-seeking party. Whether or not (and to what extent) a party uses the issue of Europe in party competition depends on the party's electoral strategy and coalition-formation and government-participation tactics.

Moreover, we believe that this has broader implications for the analysis of why parties take the positions they do and why they give prominence to certain issues in inter-party competition that goes beyond the scope of the study of party-based Euroscepticism. It other words, it potentially provides party scholars with the first stages of a broader framework for analysing how parties determine their positions and use issues in party competition. In this sense, we believe that the study of party-based Euroscepticism can actually make a much larger contribution not simply to the debate on the impact of European integration on domestic politics but also to on the study of party politics in general. The extent to which this framework is more broadly applicable and generalizable beyond this specific case depends, of course, on just how distinctive or typical we believe the European issue is.

Finally, and even more ambitiously, we believe that the implications of the study of Euroscepticism go beyond party politics to the way we understand the nature of politics more broadly. Euroscepticism is one manifestation of a lack of support for political institutions and political elites and so our understanding of it helps to demonstrate the way new issues are entangled, embedded, and implicated in wider political concerns. It is a potential bellwether for understanding the tenor of politics in a climate of sceptical or distrusting mass public sentiment. At the same time, the European project is part of wider processes of global change involving a re-constellation of the international institutional architecture as well as a growing interaction of global and domestic issues and politics. Attitudes to European integration, therefore, may well highlight issues of how domestic politics meshes with international politics in a global context.

NOTES

1. See, for example, Gaffney (1996), Hix and Lord (1997), Marks and Wilson (1999, 2000), Ray (1999), Ladrech (2002), and Steenbergen and Marks (2002).
2. See, for example, Taggart (1998), Sitter (2001), and Kopecký and Mudde (2002).
3. The focus of this chapter is on how Euroscepticism manifests itself at the elite level, with political parties being the specific unit of analysis. It does not attempt to extrapolate these findings to the mass level in order to analyse the conceptualization, measurement, and causality of public Euroscepticism, nor does it make any claims that the analytical framework set out here is transferable in this way. The authors disagree on whether or not it is possible to do so.

4. The *Oxford English Dictionary*, which defines it as 'a person, especially a politician, who is sceptical about the supposed benefits to Britain of increasing co-operation with the fellow members of the European Union, esp. one who strongly opposes greater political or economic integration', cites its first usage to a June 1986 article in *The Times* referring to British Prime Minister Margaret Thatcher. See Flood (2002) who cites Simon Usherwood as his source for this.

5. This is the first reference to the term in the *Social Science Citation Index* and, therefore, probably the first attempt in the academic literature to define party-based Euroscepticism.

6. An earlier (slightly different) version of this paper appeared as Kopecky and Mudde (2001).

7. Other academic commentators are more sympathetic to using the terminology in this way. Katz, for example, in his contribution to this volume (Chapter 7) implies that a different term may be appropriate for principled opposition to the European project given that ' "scepticism" ordinarily refers to doubts or reservations rather than outright opposition'. See also Henderson (2008).

8. On the Czech Civic Democrats see Hanley (2004).

9. This is not the same as contesting the European integration project as such or the EU's current/future trajectory and, as Kopecky and Mudde argue, it is incorrect to classify such parties as Eurosceptic. This point is discussed in more detail in the next section.

10. In their contribution to Volume 1 of this book, Deschouwer and Van Assche (2008:) draw our attention to this issue in their analysis of the Belgian Greens who voted against the Maastricht Treaty because it was 'not European enough'.

11. Benedetto (2002: 17), for example, uses this term when discussing the Green and Radical Left groupings within the European Parliament.

12. Low salience of the European issue in party politics is also implicit in the argument developed in Mair (2000).

13. Although they term this a 'cleavage approach' we would argue that it should more accurately be described as a 'party ideology approach'. We also have some more general reservations about their methodology which uses rankings based on experts' surveys, ultimately a qualitative source of data, as the basis for a quantitative statistical analysis on which they base their conclusions.

14. This has also caused confusion in terms of conceptualization. For example, while Kopecký and Mudde (2002) were attempting to develop a typology based on party positions, much of what we were doing in our earlier surveys

was attempting to find evidence of Euroscepticism as a contestatory political discourse.

15. For this part of the analysis we draw heavily upon the ideas developed by Sitter in his various papers and set out most elaborately in his jointly authored chapter with Batory in this book, and also in Sitter and Batory (2004).

16. It is important to note here that there is no linear relationship between overall levels of public Euroscepticism and whether or not and how a party uses the issue in competition. It is the level of support for, or opposition to, European integration and the salience of this issue among the party's supporters and/or the segment of the electorate that it is attempting to attract that are the key variables here.

17. Raunio (2008), on the other hand, in Chapter 10 in Volume 1 of this book, argues that it is government coalition tactics and a policymaking system that takes the sting out of the government–opposition dynamic that determine (and moderate) parties' broad, underlying *positions* on the European issue in Finland. There are two possible (mutually incompatible) explanations for this. First, he has not got it quite right and that party positions are actually determined by other factors, including the ones we identify earlier. Secondly, he is right and we need to rethink our nascent causal model perhaps by stepping back and developing a more dynamic model of how party ideology is determined and whether this includes the kind of the factors that Raunio identifies.

References

Agardi, A. (2000). Interview. International secretary of the SMK, Bratislava, November.

Aldrich, J. H. (1993). 'Rational Choice and Turnout', *American Journal of Political Science*, 37: 246–78.

Alexandrescu, I., Bulei, I., Mamina, I., and Scurtu, I. (2000). *Enciclopedia de Istorie a Romaniei*. Bucharest: Meronia.

Alvarez, R. M. and Nagler, J. (2000). 'A New Approach for Modelling Strategic Voting in Multiparty Elections', *British Journal for Political Science*, 30: 57–75.

Anderson, C. J. and Reichert, M. S. (2000). 'Economic Benefits and Support for Membership in the EU: A Cross-National Analysis', *Journal of Public Policy*, 15: 231–49.

Angé, H., C. Van der Eijk, B. Laffan, P. Norris, H. Schmitt and R. Sinnott (1999). *Citizen Participation in European Politics*. (Demokrati Utredningens skrift nr. 32) Stockholm: Statens Offentliga Utredningar.

Arrow, K. J. (1951). *Social Choice and Individual Values*. New York: Wiley.

Arter, D. (1979). 'The Finnish Centre Party: Profile of a "Hinge Group"', *West European Politics*, 2: 108–27.

——— (1999). 'From Class Party to Catchall Party? The Adaptation of the Finnish Agrarian-Center Party', *Scandinavian Political Studies*, 22: 157–80.

Arter, D. (ed.) (2001a). *From Farmyard to City Square? The Electoral Adaptation of the Nordic Agrarian Parties*. Aldershot, UK: Ashgate.

——— (2001b). 'Conclusion', in D. Arter (ed.), *From Farmyard to City Square? The Electoral Adaptation of the Nordic Agrarian Parties*. Aldershot, UK: Ashgate.

Asgrimsson, H. (2002a). 'The European Union Fisheries Policy', The University of Akureyri, 18 January 2002, unofficial translation. Iceland: Ministry of Foreign Affairs.

——— (2002b). 'The Impact of International Co-operation on Sovereignty', University of Iceland, 15 January 2002, unofficial translation. Iceland: Ministry of Foreign Affairs.

Aspinwall, M. (2004). *Rethinking Britain and Europe: Plurality Elections, Party Management and British Policy on European Integration*. Manchester and New York: Manchester University Press.

Axelrod, R. (1970). *Conflict of Interest*. Chicago: Markham.

Aylott, N. (1999). 'Paradoxes and Opportunism: The Danish Election of March 1998', *Government and Opposition*, 43: 59–77.

Baker, D., Gamble, A., and Seawright, D. (2002). 'Sovereign Nations and Global Markets: Modern British Conservatism and Hyperglobalism', *British Journal of Politics and International Relations*, 4: 399–428.

—————— and Randall, N. (2002). 'Elite Party Based Euroscepticism in the UK: A Case of Fractured Consensus and Asymmetrical Attitudes', Paper presented at ECPR Joint Sessions workshop on 'Opposing Europe: Euroscepticism and Political Parties', Turin, Italy, 22–27 March.

—————— Randall, N., and Seawright, D. (2008). 'Euroscepticism in the British Party System: "A Source of Fascination, Perplexity and Sometimes Frustration"', in P. Taggart and A. Szczerbiak (eds.), *Opposing Europe: The Comparative Party Politics of Euroscepticism in Europe*, Vol. 1: *Case Studies and Country Surveys*. Oxford: Oxford University Press.

Barnes, I. (1996). 'Agriculture, Fisheries and the 1995 Nordic Enlargement', in L. Miles (ed.), *The European Union and the Nordic Countries*. London: Routledge.

Batory, A. (2001). 'Hungarian Party Identities and the Question of European Integration', Opposing Europe Research Network Working Paper No. 4. Brighton, UK: Sussex European Institute. Available at http://www.sussex.ac.uk/Units/SEI/pdfs/wp49.pdf

—— (2002). 'Attitudes to Europe: Ideology, Strategy and the Issue of European Union Membership in Hungarian Party Politics', *Party Politics*, 8: 525–39.

—— (2008). 'Euroscepticism in the Hungarian Party System', in P. Taggart and A. Szczerbiak (eds.), *Opposing Europe: The Comparative Party Politics of Euroscepticism in Europe*, Vol. 1: *Case Studies and Country Surveys*. Oxford: Oxford University Press.

Benedetto, G. (2002). 'Euroscepticism and the Failure of "Blackmail" Power in the European Parliament', Paper presented at ECPR Joint Sessions workshop on 'Opposing Europe: Euroscepticism and Political Parties', Turin, Italy, 22–27 March.

Benoît, B. (1997). *Social-Nationalism: An Anatomy of French Euroscepticism*. Aldershot, UK: Ashgate.

Berelson, B., Lazarsfeld, P. F., and McPhee, W. N. (1954). *Voting*. Chicago: University of Chicago Press.

Beres, B. (2000). Interview. Head of the Foreign Department of the FKGP and Chef de Cabinet to Torgyan, Hungarian Minister of Agriculture. Budapest, October.

Bergman, T. (2000). 'Sweden: Where Minority Cabinets are the Rule and Majority Coalitions the Exception', in W. C. Müller and K. Strøm (eds.), *Coalition Governments in Western Europe*. Oxford: Oxford University Press.

Berthu, G. (2000). *Europe Démocratie ou super-Etat*. Paris: F.-X. De Guibert.

Bielasiak, J. (2004). 'Party Systems and EU Accession: Euroscepticism in Eastern Europe', Paper presented at the Conference on Public Opinion about the EU in Post-Communist Eastern Europe. Bloomington, IN: Indiana University.

Bille, L. (1994). 'Denmark: The Decline of the Membership Party?', in R. S. Katz and P. Mair (eds.), *How Parties Organize: Change and Adaptation in Party Organizations in Western Democracies*. London: Sage.

Black, D. (1948). 'On the Rationale of Group Decision Making', *Journal of Political Economy*, 56: 23–34.

Blazyca, G. and Kolkiewicz, M. (1999). 'Poland and the EU: Internal Disputes, Domestic Politics and Accession', *Journal of Communist and Transition Politics*, 15: 131–43.

Blondel, J., R. Sinnott and P. Svensson, (eds.) (1998). *People and parliament in the European Union: participation, democracy, and legitimacy*. Oxford: Clarendon Press.

Bokova, I. (2001). Interview. Deputy Foreign Minister and State Secretary for European Integration, Bulgarian Government, 1995–6. Sofia, September.

Börzel, T. A. and Risse, T. (2000). 'When Europe Hits Home: Europeanization and Domestic Change', *European Integration online Paper (EioP)*, 4: 15. Available at http://eiop.or.at/eiop/texte/2000–015a.htm

Brudascu, D. (2001). Interview. PRM Spokesman and Member of Romanian Chamber of Deputies. Bucharest, May.

Budge, I., Newton, K. et al. (1997). *The Politics of the New Europe: Atlantic to Urals*. London: Longman.

Campbell, A. (1962). 'The Passive Citizen', *Acta Sociologica*, 6: 9–21.

Canovan, M. (1981). *Populism*. New York: Harcourt Brace Jovanovich.

Checkel, J. T. and Moravcsik, A. (2001). 'A Constructivist Research Programme in EU Studies?', *European Union Politics*, 2: 219–49.

Conti, N. and Verzichelli, L. (2005). 'La Dimensione Europea del Discorso Politico: Un'Analisi Diacronica del Caso Italiano (1950–2001)', in M. Cotta, P. Isernia, and L. Verzichelli (eds.), *L'Europa in Italia*. Bologna, Italy: Il Mulino, pp. 71–116.

De Swaan, A. (1973). *Coalition Theories And Cabinet Formation*. Amsterdam: Elsevier.

Deschouwer, K. and Van Assche, M. (2002). 'Why is there no Euroscepticism in Belgium?', Paper prepared for ECPR Joint Sessions Workshop on 'Opposing Europe: Euroscepticism and Political Parties', Turin, Italy, 22–27 March.

Deschouwer, K. and Van Assche, M. (2008). 'Hard but Hardly Relevant: Party-Based Euroscepticism in Belgium', in P. Taggart and A. Szczerbiak (eds.), *Opposing Europe: The Comparative Party Politics of Euroscepticism in Europe*, Vol. 1: *Case Studies and Country Surveys*. Oxford: Oxford University Press.

Dimitrova, A. L. (2002). 'Enlargement, Institution-Building and the EU's Administrative Capacity Requirement', *West European Politics*, 25: 171–90.

Downs, A. (1957). *An Economic Theory of Democracy*. New York: Harper & Row.

Draghici, V. (2001). Interview. Official Responsible for Links with Council of Europe Parliamentary Assembly, Romanian Senate. Bucharest, May.

Duhac, J. (2000). Interview. Head of the Konrad Adenauer Foundation in Hungary. Budapest, April.

Duverger, M. (1954). *Political Parties: Their Organisation and Activity in the Modern State*. London: Methuen.

Ejub, K. (2001). Interview. DPS Member of the Bulgarian Parliament. Sofia, September.

Epstein, L. (1967). *Political Parties in Western Democracies*. London: Pall Mall.

European Commission (1994). *Presidency Conclusions: Copenhagen European Council*. Brussels: European Commission

—— (1998). *Central and Eastern Eurobarometer No. 8*. Brussels: European Commission.

—— (1998–2002). *Regular Reports on Progress Toward Accession*, Brussels: Office for Official Publications of the European Communities. Available at http://europa.eu.int/comm/enlargement/candidate.htm

—— (2001*a*). *Applicant Countries Eurobarometer*, December. Brussels: European Commission.

—— (2001*b*). *White Paper on European Governance*, Com (2001) 428. Brussels: Office for Official Publications of the European Communities.

—— (2003). *Draft Treaty Establishing a Constitution for Europe*, Conv. 850/03. Brussels: The European Convention Secretariat. Available at http://register.consilium.eu.int/pdf/en/03/cv00/cv00850en03.pdf

European Council (1995). *Presidency Conclusions*, Madrid European Council, 15–16 December. Luxembourg: Office for Official Publications of the European Communities. Available at http://europa.eu.int/european_council/conclusions/index_en.htm

—— (2002). *Presidency Conclusions*, Copenhagen European Council 12 and 13 December. Luxembourg: Office for Official Publications of the European Communities. Available at http://ue.eu.int/presid/conclusions.htm

Fallend, F. (2008). 'Euroscepticism in Austrian Political Parties: Ideologically Rooted or Strategically Motivated?', in P. Taggart and A. Szczerbiak (eds.), *Opposing Europe: The Comparative Party Politics of Euroscepticism in Europe*, Vol. 1: *Case Studies and Country Surveys*. Oxford: Oxford University Press.

—— (2003). 'Introduction: In the Name of Europe', in: C. Radaelli and K. Featherstone (eds.), *The Politics of Europeanization: Theory and Analysis*. Oxford: Oxford University Press, pp. 3–26.

Fisher, S. (2000). *Tactical Voting in England—1987 to 1997.* Mimeo.

FKgP (1995). *Hazánk honop.*

—— (2002). *Program 2002.*

Flood, C. (2002). 'Euroscepticism: A Problematic Concept,' Paper presented at the UACES 32nd Annual Conference and 7th Research Conference, Queen's University, Belfast, 2–4 September.

Franklin, M. N. (2001). 'How Structural Factors Cause Turnout Variations at European Parliament Elections', *European Union Politics*, 2: 309–28.

—— Van der Eijk, C., and Oppenhuis, E. (1996). 'The Institutional Context: Turnout', in C. Van der Eijk and M. N. Franklin (eds.), *Choosing Europe*. Ann Arbor, MI: The University of Michigan Press, pp. 306–31.

—— (2004). *Voter Turnout and the Dynamics of Electoral Competition in Established Democracies*. Oxford: Oxford University Press. New York: Cambridge University Press.

—— (2007). 'Turning out or turning off?' In *European after Eastern Enlargement*, eds. Michael Marsh, Slava Mikhaylov and Hermann Schmitt. Mannheim: MZES, University of Mannheim [CONNEX Report Series No. 01], pp. 53–70.

Gabel, M. and Palmer, H. D. (1995). 'Understanding Variation in Public Support for European Integration', *European Journal of Political Research*, 27: 3–19.

Gaffney, J. (ed.) (1996). *Political Parties and the European Union*. London: Routledge.

Gahrton, P. (1998). *The New EU After Amsterdam—From a Swedish Point of View*. Lund, Sweden: Gröna Böcker.

GfK, S. (1998). SR 9516 02 02 Public Awareness Campaign. Bratislava, April–July.

Gilljam, M. and Oscarsson, H. (1996). 'Mapping the Nordic Party Space', *Scandinavian Political Studies*, 19: 25–43.

Glasberg, R. (2001). Interview. Official at ELDR Headquarters. Brussels, February.

Goetz, K. and Hix, S. (eds.) (2000). *Europeanised Politics?: European Integration and National Political Systems*. London: Frank Cass.

Goldsmith, J. (1994). *The Trap*. London: Macmillan.

Grabbe, H. and Hughes, K. (1998). *Enlarging the EU Eastwards*. London: Royal Institute of International Affairs.

—— —— (1999). 'Central and East European Views on EU Enlargement: Political Debates and Public Opinion', in K. Henderson (ed.), *Back to Europe: Central and Eastern Europe and the European Union*. London: UCL Press, pp. 185–202.

Grunberg, G. (2008). 'Euroscepticism in France, 1992–2002', in P. Taggart and A. Szczerbiak (eds.), *Opposing Europe: The Comparative Party Politics of Euroscepticism in Europe*, Vol. 1: *Case Studies and Country Surveys*. Oxford: Oxford University Press.

Grunberg, G., Perrineau, P., and Ysmal, C. (2000). *Le Vote des Quinze*. Paris: Presses de Science Po.

Gyarfasova, O. and Velsic, M. (2000). *Foreign Policy Orientations in Slovakia*. Bratislava: Institute for Public Affairs.

Haas, E. B. (1958). *The Uniting of Europe: Political, Social, and Economic Forces, 1950–57*. Stanford, CA: Stanford University Press.

Hall, P. (1986). *Governing the Economy*. Oxford: Oxford University Press.

—— (1989). *The Power of Economic Ideas*. Princeton, NJ: Princeton University Press.

Handl, V. and Zaborowski, M. (1999). *Comparative Czech and Polish Perspectives and Policies on the Eastern Enlargement of the EU and the Prominence of the 'German Factor'*. Birmingham, UK: Institute of German Studies, University of Birmingham.

Hanley, S. (2004). 'From Neo-Liberalism to National Interests: Ideology, Strategy, and Party Development in the Euroscepticism of the Czech Right', *East European Politics and Societies*, 18: 513–48.

—— (2008). 'Embracing Europe, Opposing EU-rope?: Party-Based Euroscepticism in the Czech Republic', in P. Taggart and A. Szczerbiak (eds.), *Opposing Europe: The Comparative Party Politics of Euroscepticism in Europe*, Vol. 1: *Case Studies and Country Surveys*. Oxford: Oxford University Press.

Heidar, K. and Saglie, J. (2002). *Hva skjer med partiene?* Oslo: Gyldendal Akademisk.

Helms, L. (1997). 'Right-Wing Populist Parties in Austria and Switzerland: A Comparative Analysis', *West European Politics*, 20: 37–52.

Henderson, K. (1999). *Back to Europe: Central and Eastern Europe and the European Union*. London: UCL Press.

—— (2000). 'The Challenges of EU Eastward Enlargement', *International Politics*, 37(1): 1–15.

—— (2001). 'Euroscepticism or Europhobia: Opposition Attitudes to the EU in the Slovak Republic', Opposing Europe Research Network Working Paper No. 5. Brighton, UK: Sussex European Institute. Available at http://www.sussex.ac.uk/Units/SEI/pdfs/wp50.pdf

—— (2008). 'The Slovak Republic: Eurosceptics and Phoney Europhiles' in P. Taggart and A. Szczerbiak (eds.), *Opposing Europe: The Comparative Party Politics of Euroscepticism in Europe*, Vol. 1: *Case Studies and Country Surveys*. Oxford: Oxford University Press.

Hinckley, B. (1981). *Coalitions And Politics*. New York: Harcourt Brace Jovanovich.

Hix, S. and Lord, C. (1996). 'The Making of a President: The European Parliament and the Confirmation of Jacques Santer as President of the Commission', *Government and Opposition*, 31: 62–76.

—— —— (1997). *Political Parties in the European Union*. Basingstoke, UK: Macmillan.

Hoffmann, S. (1966). 'Obstinate or Obsolete: The Fate of the Nation State and the Case of Western Europe', *Daedelus*, 95: 862–915.

Hooghe, L. and Marks, G. (2001). *Multi-Level Governance and European Integration*. Lanham, MD: Rowman & Littlefield.

—— —— and Wilson, C. J. (2002). 'Does Left/Right Structure Party Positions on European Integration?', *Comparative Political Studies*, 35: 965–89.

Hughes, J., Sasse, G., and Gordon, C. (2004*a*), 'Conditionality and Compliance in the EU's Eastward Enlargement: Regional Policy and the Reform of Sub-National Governance', *Journal of Common Market Studies*, 42: 523–51.

—— —— —— (2004*b*), *Europeanization and Regionalization in the EU's Enlargement to Central and Eastern Europe, The Myth of Conditionality*. Basingstoke, UK: Palgrave.

—— —— —— and Majcherkiewicz, T. (2004). 'Silesia and the Politics of Regionalisation in Poland' in: T. Zarycki and G. Kolankiewicz (eds.), *Regional Issues in Polish Politics*. London: School of Slavonic and East European Studies/UCL, pp. 83–111.

Ikenberry, G. J. (1988). 'Conclusion: An Institutional Approach to American Foreign Economic Policy' in G. J. Ikenberry, D. A. Lake, and M. Mastanduno (eds.), *The State and American Foreign Economic Policy*. Ithaca, NY: Cornell University Press.

Integrace (2002). 'Podpora vstupu do EU podle jednotlivých sociálních skupin', 4.

Johansson, K. M., and Raunio, T. (2001). 'Partisan Reponses to Europe: Comparing Finnish and Swedish Political Parties', *European Journal of Political Research*, 39: 225–49.

Kanev, D. (2001). Interview. New Bulgarian University and Former Head of Parliamentary Research Department, Bulgarian Parliament. Sofia, September.

Katz, R. S. (1999). 'Representation, the Locus of Democratic Legitimation, and the Role of the National Parliaments in the European Union', in R. S. Katz and B. Wessels (eds.), *The European Parliament, the National Parliaments, and European Integration*. Oxford: Oxford University Press, pp. 21–44.

—— (2001). Models of Democracy: Elite Attitudes and the Democratic Deficit in the European Union', *European Union Politics*, 2: 53–79.

—— and Mair, P. (1995). 'Changing Models of Party Organisation and Party Democracy: The Emergence of the Cartel Party', *Party Politics*, 1: 5–28.

—— —— (2002). 'The Ascendancy of the Party in Public Office: Party Organizational Change in Twentieth-Century Democracies', in R. Gunther, J. R. Montero, and J. J. Linz (eds.), *Political Parties: Old Concepts and New Challenges*. Oxford: Oxford University Press.

Katz, R. S. and Wessels, B. (1999). *The European Parliament, the National Parliaments and European Integration.* Oxford: Oxford University Press.

Keltosova, O. (2000). Interview. HZDS Member of Slovak Parliament and Member of the Joint Parliamentary Committee with the EP. Bratislava, October.

Kerr, H. H. (1987). 'The Swiss Party System: Steadfast and Changing', in H. Daalder (ed.), *Party Systems in Denmark, Austria, Switzerland, the Netherlands and Belgium.* London: Frances Pinter.

King, D. S. (1995). *Actively Seeking Work. The Politics of Unemployment and Welfare Policy in the United States.* Chicago: University of Chicago Press.

Kirchheimer, O. (1966). 'The Transformation of West European Party Systems', in J. LaPalombara and M. Weiner (eds.), *Political Parties and Political Development.* Princeton, NJ: Princeton University Press.

Kitschelt, H. (1986). 'Political Opportunity Structures and Political Protest: Anti-Nuclear Movements in Four Democracies', *British Journal of Political Science,* 16: 57–85.

—— (1992). 'The Formation of Party Systems in East Central Europe', *Politics and Society,* 20(1): 7–50.

Knudsen, A-C. L. (2008). 'Euroscepticism in Denmark' in P. Taggart and A. Szczerbiak (eds.), *Opposing Europe: The Comparative Party Politics of Euroscepticism in Europe,* Vol. 1: *Case Studies and Country Surveys.* Oxford: Oxford University Press.

Knudsen, T. and Rothstein, B. (1994). 'State Building in Scandinavia', *Comparative Politics,* 26: 203–20.

Koga, K. and Nagatani, H. (1974). 'Voter Antagonism and the Paradox of Voting', *Econometrica,* 42: 1045–67.

Kohutiar, J. (1995). Interview. International Secretary of the KDH. Bratislava, November.

Kopecký, P. and Mudde, C. (2001). 'Empty Words or Irreducible Core? Euroscepticism in East Central Europe', Paper presented at the 97th Annual Meeting of the American Political Science Association, San Francisco, 30 August–2 September.

—— (2002). 'The Two Sides of Euroscepticism: Party Positions on European Integration in East Central Europe', *European Union Politics,* 3: 297–326.

Körösényi, A. (1992) 'Revival of the Past or a New Beginning? The Nature of Post-Communist Politics', in A. Bozóki, A. Körösényi, and G. Schöpflin (eds.), *Post-Communist Transition: Emerging Pluralism in Hungary.* London: Pinter.

—— (1999). *Government and Politics in Hungary.* Budapest: Central European University Press.

Kramer, G. H. (1973). 'On a Class of Equilibrium Conditions for Majority Rule', *Econometrica,* 41: 285–97.

Krasner, S. (1988). 'Approaches to the State: Alternative Conceptions and Historical Dynamics', *Comparative Political Studies*, 21: 223–46.

Kristinsson, G. H. (1991). *Farmers' Parties: A Study in Electoral Adaptation*. Reykjavik: Social Science Research Institute.

—— (2001). 'The Icelandic Progressive Party: Trawling for the Town Vote', in D. Arter (ed.), *From Farmyard to City Square? The Electoral Adaptation of the Nordic Agrarian Parties*. Aldershot, UK: Ashgate.

Kucia, M. (1999). 'Public Opinion in Central Europe on EU Accession: The Czech Republic and Poland', *Journal of Common Market Studies*, 37: 143–52.

Kystpartict (2001). *Partiprogram*.

Ladner, A. (2001). 'Swiss Political Parties: Between Persistency and Change', *West European Politics*, 24: 123–44.

Ladrech, R. (ed.) (2002). 'Special Issue: The Europeanization of Party Politics', *Party Politics*, 8.

Lancelot, A. (1968). *L'Abstentionisme électoral en France*. Paris: Colin.

Lane, J-E. and Ersson, S. (1999). *Politics and Society in Western Europe*. London: Sage.

Laver, M. (1994). 'Party policy and Cabinet Portfolios in Ireland 1992: Results from an Expert Survey', *Irish Political Studies*, 9: 157–64.

—— (1995). 'Party Policy and Cabinet Portfolios in the Netherlands 1994: Results from an Expert Survey', *Acta Politica*, 30: 3–28.

—— and Schofield, N. (1990). *Multi-Party Government: The Politics Of Coalition In Europe*. Oxford: Oxford University Press.

—— and Shepsle, K. A. (1995). *Making and Breaking Governments: Cabinets and Legitimacy in Parliamentary Democracies*. Cambridge: Cambridge University Press.

Lazarsfeld, P. F., Berelson, B., and Gaudet, H. (1944). *The Peoples Choice*. New York: Duell, Sloan & Pierce.

Ledenyi, A. (1993). Interview. International Secretary, Fidesz. Budapest, March.

Lees, C. (2001). 'Social Democracy and Structures of Governance in Britain and Germany: How Institutions and Norms Shape Political Innovation', in L. Martell et al. (eds.), *Social Democracy: Global and National Perspectives*. Basingstoke, UK: Palgrave.

—— (2002a). 'Dark Matter: Institutional Constraints and the Failure of Party-Based Euroscepticism in Germany', *Political Studies*, 50: 243–67.

—— (2002b). '"Dark Matter": Institutional Constraints and the Failure of Party-Based Euroscepticism in Germany', Opposing Europe Research Network Working Paper No 8/SEI Working Paper No 4. Brighton, UK: Sussex European Institute, June.

Lees, C. (2008). 'The Limits of Party-Based Euroscepticism in Germany' in P. Taggart and A. Szczerbiak (eds.), *Opposing Europe: The Comparative Party Politics of Euroscepticism in Europe*, Vol. 1: *Case Studies and Country Surveys*. Oxford: Oxford University Press.

Lindberg, L. N. (1963). *The Political Dynamics of European Economic Integration*. Oxford: Oxford University Press.

—— and Scheingold, S. A. (eds.) (1970). *Europe's Would-Be Polity: Patterns of Change in the European Community*. Englewood Cliffs, NJ: Prentice-Hall.

Lipset, S. M. (1959). *Political Man*. New York: Doubleday.

—— and Rokkan, S. (eds.) (1967*a*). *Party Systems and Voter Alignments: Cross-National Perspectives*. London: The Free Press.

—— and Rokkan, S. (1967*b*). 'Cleavage Structures, Party Systems, and Voter Alignments: and Introduction', in S. M. Lipset and S. Rokkan (eds.), *Party Systems and Voter Alignments: Cross-National Perspectives*. London: The Free Press.

Lupia, A. and McCubbins. (1994). 'Learning from Oversight: Fire Alarms and Police Patrols Reconstructed', *Journal of Law, Economics, and Organisation*, 10: 96–125.

Madeley, J. (1994). 'The Antinomies of Lutheran Politics: The Case of Norway's Christian People's Party', in D. Hanley (ed.), *Christian Democracy in Europe: A Comparative Perspective*. London: Pinter.

—— (1998). 'The Politics of Embarrassment: Norway's 1997 Election', *West European Politics*, 21: 187–94.

Madsen, R. (2001). *Motstraums: Senterpartiets Historie, 1959–2000*. Oslo: Det Norske Samlaget.

Mair, P. (1990). 'Introduction', in P. Mair (ed.), *The West European Party System*. Oxford: Oxford University Press.

—— (2000). 'The Limited Impact of Europe on National Party Systems', *West European Politics*, 23: 27–51.

—— and Mudde, C. (1998). 'The Party Family and Its Study', *Annual Review of Political Science*, 1: 211–29.

Major, T. (2000). Interview. International Secretary of Fidesz. Budapest, April.

Malikova, A. (2000). Interview. Chairperson of the SNS. Bratislava, May.

March, J. G. and Olsen, J. P. (1984). 'The New Institutionalism: Organisational Factors in Political Life', *American Political Science Review*, 78: 734–49.

Marks, G. and Wilson, C. (1999). 'National Parties and the Contestation of Europe', in T. Banchoff and M. P. Smith (eds.), *Legitimacy and the European Union*. London: Routledge, pp. 113–33.

—— —— (2000). 'The Past in the Present: A Cleavage Theory of Party Response to European Integration', *British Journal of Political Science*, 30: 433–59.

Marsh, M. (1999). 'Policy Evaluations', in R. S. Katz and B. Wessels (eds.), *The European Parliament, the National Parliaments, and European Integration.* Oxford: Oxford University Press, pp. 197–212.

McKelvey, R. D. and Ordeshook, P. C. (1972). 'A General Theory of the Calculus of Voting', in J. F. Herdon and J. L. Bernd (eds.), *Mathematical Applications in Political Science VI.* Charlottsville, VA: The University of Virginia Press, pp. 32–78.

McKenna, P. (1997). *Amsterdam Treaty: The Road to an Undemocratic and Military Superstate.* Dublin: Green Party.

Mikkel, E. (2008). 'Emerging Party-Based Euroscepticism in Estonia,' in P. Taggart and A. Szczerbiak (eds.), *Opposing Europe: The Comparative Party Politics of Euroscepticism in Europe,* Vol. 1: *Case Studies and Country Surveys.* Oxford: Oxford University Press.

Miles, L. (1994). 'Sweden and Finland: From EFTA Neutrals to EU Members', in J. Redmond (ed.), *Prospective Europeans: New Member States for the European Union.* London: Harvester Wheatsheaf.

Mueller, D. C. (1996). *Constitutional Democracy.* Oxford: Oxford University Press.

Müller, W. C. and Strøm, K. (1999). *Policy, Office or Votes? How Political Parties in Western Europe Make Hard Decisions.* Cambridge: Cambridge University Press.

Mylly, J. (1984). 'The Agrarian Center Party in Finnish Politics', in J. Mylly and R. M. Berry (eds.), *Political Parties in Finland: Essays in History and Politics.* Turku, Finland: Garia Oy.

Nelsen, B. F. (1993). 'The European Community Debate in Norway: The Periphery Revolts Again', in B. F. Nelsen (ed.), *Norway and the European Community: The Political Economy of Integration.* London: Praeger.

Niemi, R. G. (1969). 'Majority Decision Making with Partial Unidimensionality', *American Political Science Review,* 63: 488–97.

Normington, R. (1996). Interview. Head of International Office, British Conservative Party. London, January.

Nugent, N. (1999). *The Government and Politics of the European Union.* Durham, NC: Duke University Press.

ODS. (2001). *Manifest českého eurorealismu (dokument k ideové konferenci ODS).* Available at http://www.ods.cz.

Offe, C. (1996). *Varieties of Transition: The East European and East German Experience.* Cambridge: Polity Press.

Olsen, J. (2001). 'The Many Faces of Europeanization', ARENA Working Paper 01/02. Available at http://www.sv.uio.no/arena/publications/wp02_2.htm

Ostrom, E. (1986). 'An Agenda for the Study of Institutions', *Public Choice,* 48: 3–25.

Pappi, F. U. (1996). 'Political Behaviour: Reasoning Voters and Multi-Party Systems', in R. E. Goodin and H.-D. Klingemann (eds.), *A New Handbook of Political Science*. Oxford: Oxford University Press, pp. 255–75.

Peters, B. G. (1998). 'Political Institutions: Old and New', in R. E. Goodin and H. -D. Klingemann (eds.), *A New Handbook of Political Science*. Oxford: Oxford University Press.

Peters, D. (2001). 'The Debate about a New Foreign Policy after Unification', in V. Rittberger (ed.), *German Foreign Policy after Unification*. Manchester, UK: Manchester University Press.

Pierre, J. and Widfeld, A. (1994). 'Party Organizations in Sweden: Colossuses with Feet of Clay or Flexible Pillars of Government', in R. S. Katz and P. Mair (eds.), *How Parties Organize: Change and Adaptation in Party Organizations in Western Democracies*. London: Sage, pp. 332–56.

Porter, M. (1980/1998). *Competitive Strategy: Techniques for Analyzing Industries and Competitors*. New York. Free Press.

Preston, C. (1997). *Enlargement and Integration in the European Union*. London: Routledge.

Pridham, G. (1999*a*). 'The European Union, Democratic Conditionality and Transnational Party Linkages: The Case of Eastern Europe', in J. Grugel (ed.), *Democracy without Borders: Transnationalisation and Conditionality in New Democracies*. London: Routledge.

—— (1999*b*). 'Complying with the European Union's Democratic Conditionality: Transnational Party Linkages and Regime Change in Slovakia, 1993–98', *Europe-Asia Studies*, 51: 1221–44.

—— (2001). 'Patterns of Europeanisation and Transnational Party Cooperation: Party Development in Central and Eastern Europe', in P. Lewis (ed.), *Party Development and Democratic Change in Post-Communist Europe: The First Decade*. London: Frank Cass.

—— (2002). 'Transnational Party Co-operation and Post-Communist Politics: Evaluating Euroscepticism in Comparative Perspective', Paper presented at ECPR Joint Sessions Workshop on 'Opposing Europe: Euroscepticism and Political Parties', Turin, Italy, 22–27 March.

Prisacaru, G. (2001). Interview. Chairman of the Foreign Policy Committee, Romanian Senate. Bucharest, May.

Radaelli, C. (2000). 'Whither Europeanization? Concept Stretching and Substantive Change', *European Integration online Paper (EioP)*, 4(8). Available at http://eiop.or.at/eiop/texte/2000–008a.htm

Ransdorf, M. (1995). Interview. KSCM Vice-Chairman for International Relations. Prague, November.

Raunio, T. (1999). 'Facing the European Challenge: Finnish Parties Adjust to the Integration Process', *West European Politics*, 22: 138–59.

—— (2002). 'The Difficult Task of Opposing EU in Finland', Paper presented at ECPR Joint Sessions Workshop on 'Opposing Europe: Euroscepticism and Political Parties', Turin, Italy, 22–27 March.

—— (2008) 'The Difficult Task of Opposing Europe: The Finnish Party Politics of Euroscepticism' in P. Taggart and A. Szczerbiak (eds.), *Opposing Europe: The Comparative Party Politics of Euroscepticism in Europe*, Vol. 1: *Case Studies and Country Surveys*. Oxford: Oxford University Press.

Ray, L. (1999). 'Measuring Party Orientations towards European Integration: Results from an Expert Survey', *European Journal of Political Research*, 36: 283–306.

Reif, K. (ed.) (1985). *Ten European Elections*. Aldershot, UK: Gower.

—— and Schmitt, H. (1980). 'Nine Second-Order National Elections: A Conceptual Framework for the Analysis of European Election Results', *European Journal of Political Research*, 8: 3–44.

Riker, W. H. (1964). *Federalism: Origin, Operations Significance*. Boston: Little Brown.

—— (1980). 'Implications from the Disequilibrium of Majority Rule for the Study of Institutions', *American Political Science Review*, 74: 432–46.

—— (1983). 'Political Theory and the Art of Heresthetics' in Finifter, A. W. (ed.) *Political Science: the State of the Discipline*, 47–67. Washington: American Political Science Association.

—— and Ordeshook, P. H. (1968). 'The Theory of the Calculus of Voting', *American Political Science Review*, 62: 25–42.

Rokkan, S. (1966). 'Norway: Numerical Democracy and Corporate Pluralism', in R. A. Dahl (ed.), *Political Oppositions in Western Democracies*. New Haven, CT: Yale University Press.

—— and Urwin, D. (1982). 'Introduction: Centres and Peripheries in Western Europe', in S. Rokkan and D. Urwin (eds.), *The Politics of Territorial Identity: Studies in European Regionalism*. London: Sage.

———— (1983). *Economy, Territory, Identity: Politics of West European Peripheries*. London: Sage.

Roll, F. (2001). Interview. Official of the PES. Brussels, February.

Ryden, L. L. (2000). *Ett Svenskt Dilemma: Socialdemokraterna, Centren och EG-Frågan 1975–1994*. Göteborg, Sweden: Avhandlingar från Historiska institutionen i Göteborg.

Šafaříková, K. (2001). 'Lobbování na špatné adrese', *Integrace*, 9. Available at http://www.integrace.cz.

Saglie, J. (2000). *Standpunkter og strategi: EU-saken i norsk partipolitikk, 1989–1994*. Oslo: Universitetet i Oslo.

Sartori, G. (1968). 'The Sociology of Parties: A Critical Review', in O. Stammer (ed.), *Party Systems, Party Organisations, and the Politics of New Masses*. Berlin: Free University of Berlin.

—— (1976). *Parties and Party Systems: A Framework for Analysis*. New York: Cambridge University Press.

Scharpf, F. W. (1985). 'Die Politikverflechtungs-Falle: Europäische Integration und deutscher Föderalismus im Vergleich', *Politische Vierteljahresschrift*, 26: 346–50.

—— (1988). 'The Joint-Decision Trap: Lessons from German Federalism and European Integration', *Public Administration*, 66: 239–78.

Schmitt, H. (2001). *Politische Repräsentation in Europa*. Frankfurt, Germany: Campus.

Schmitt, H. (2005). 'The European Parliament elections of June 2004: Still second-order?' *West European Politics* 28: 650–679.

—— and Mannheimer, R. (1991). 'About Voting and Non-voting in the European Parliament Elections of June 1989', *European Journal of Political Research*, 19: 31–54.

—— and Thomassen, J. (eds.) (1999). *Political Representation and Legitimacy in the European Union*. Oxford: Oxford University Press.

—— Van der Eijk, C., Pappi, F.U. et al. (1997). *European Elections Study 1994: Design, Implementation and Results*, (Computer file and codebook). Köln, Germany: Zentralarchiv für Empirische Sozialforschung.

Schram, A. J. C. (1989). *Voter Behavior in Economic Perspective*. Alblasserdam, The Netherlands: Kanters.

Shepsle, K. A. and Weingast B. R. (1995). 'Studying Institutions: Lessons from the Rational Choice Approach', *Journal of Theoretical Politics*, 1: 131–47.

Sinnott, R. (2000).'European Parliament Elections: Institutions, Attitudes, and Participation', in H. Angé, C. Van der Eijk, B. Laffan, et al. (eds.), *Citizen Participation in European Politics*, SOU 1999: 151, Demokrati Utredningens skrift nr. 32. Stockholm: Statens Offentliga Utredningar, pp. 57–74.

Sitter, N. (2001). 'The Politics of Opposition and European Integration in Scandinavia: Is Euro-Scepticism a Government-Opposition Dynamic?', *West European Politics*, 24: 22–39.

—— (2002). 'Opposing Europe: Euro-Scepticism, Opposition and Party Competition', Opposing Europe Research Network Working Paper No 9/SEI Working Paper No 56. Brighton, UK: Sussex European Institute. Available at http://www.susx.ac.uk/Units/SEI/pdfs/wp56.pdf.

—— (2008). 'The European Question and the Norwegian Party System since 1961: The Freezing of a Modern Cleavage or Continent Opposition' in P. Taggart and A. Szczerbiak (eds.), *Opposing Europe: The Comparative Party Politics of Euroscepticism in Europe*, Vol. 1: *Case Studies and Country Surveys*. Oxford: Oxford University Press.

—— and Batory, A. (2004). 'Cleavages, Competition and Coalition Building: Agrarian Parties and the European Question in Western and East-Central Europe', *European Journal of Political Research*, 43: 523–46.

Skocpol, T. (1992). *Protecting Soldiers and Mothers: The Political Origins of Social Policy in the United States*. Newbury Park, CA: Sage.

Smith, A. (1986). *The Ethnic Origins of Nation*. Oxford: Blackwell.

Smith, J. (1999). *Europe's Elected Parliament*. Sheffield, UK: Sheffield Academic Press.

SNS. (1998). *Programme of the SNS for 1998–2002*. Bratislava: SNS.

Stanishev, S. (2001). Interview. International Secretary of the BSP. Sofia, September.

Štebe, J. (2001). 'Support for the European Union from a Comparative Perspective: Stability and Change in the Period of Transition', *Central European Political Science Review*, 2(3): 92–111.

Steenbergen, M. and Marks, G. (2002). 'Special Issue: Dimensions of Contestation in the European Union', *Comparative Politics*, 35.

STEM (2000). *Veřejnost ke vstupy ČR do EU*. Prague: STEM.

Stepan, A. (2001). *Arguing Comparative Politics*. Oxford: Oxford University Press.

Stone Sweet. A. (2000). *Governing with Judges: Constitutional Politics in Europe*. Oxford: Oxford University Press.

Svåsand, L. and Lindström, U. (1996). 'Scandinavian Political Parties and the European Union', in J. Gaffney (ed.), *Political Parties and the European Union*. London: Routledge.

SVP (1999). Partiprogramm 1999–2003.

Swedish Left Party (2000). *A Socialist Offensive*.

Szczerbiak, A. (1999). 'Interests and Values: The New Polish Parties and their Electorates', *Europe-Asia Studies*, 51: 1401–32.

—— (2001*a*). 'Europe as a Re-aligning Issue in Polish Politics? Evidence from the October 2000 Presidential Election', Opposing Europe Research Network Working Paper No. 3/Sussex European Institute Working Paper No. 48. Brighton, UK: Sussex European Institute.

—— (2001*b*). 'Party Structure and Organisational Development in Post-Communist Poland', *Journal of Communist Studies and Transition Politics*, 17: 94–130.

Szczerbiak, A. (2001*c*). 'Polish Public Opinion: Explaining Declining Polish Support for EU Membership', *Journal of Common Market Studies*, 39: 105–22.

—— (2008). 'Opposing Europe or Problematizing Europe? Euroscepticism and "Eurorealism" in the Polish Party System', in P. Taggart and A. Szczerbiak (eds.), *Opposing Europe: The Comparative Party Politics of Euroscepticism in Europe*, Vol. 1: *Case Studies and Country Surveys*. Oxford: Oxford University Press.

—— and Taggart, P. (2000). 'Opposing Europe: Party Systems and Opposition to the Union, the Euro and Europeanisation', Opposing Europe Research Network Working Paper No 1/Sussex European Institute Working Paper No. 36. Brighton, UK: Sussex European Institute. Available at http://www.susx. ac.uk/Units/SEI/pdfs/wp36.pdf.

Taggart, P. (1995). 'New Populist Parties in Western Europe', *West European Politics*, 18: 34–51.

—— (1998). 'A Touchstone of Dissent: Euroscepticism in Contemporary West European Party Systems', *European Journal of Political Research*, 33: 363–88.

—— and Szczerbiak, A. (2001*a*). 'Parties, Positions and Europe: Euroscepticism in the EU the Candidate States of Central and Eastern Europe', Sussex European Institute Working Paper No. 46/Opposing Europe Research Network Working Paper No. 2. Brighton, UK: Sussex European Institute. Available at http://www.susx.ac.uk/Units/SEI/pdfs/wp46.pdf.

—— —— (2001*b*). 'Crossing Europe: Patterns of Contemporary Party-Based Euroscepticism in EU Member States and the Candidate States of Central and Eastern Europe', Paper presented at American Political Science Association, San Francisco, CA, 29 August–2 September.

—— —— (2001*c*). 'Party Politics, Political Support and Europe: Mapping Euroscepticism in EU Candidate States of Central and Eastern Europe', Paper presented at the Seventh Biennial International Conference of the European Community Studies Association, Madison, WI, 31 May–2 June.

—— —— (2002*a*). 'The Party Politics of Euroscepticism in EU Member and Candidate States', Sussex European Institute Working Paper No 51/Opposing Europe Research Network Working Paper No 6. Brighton, UK: Sussex European Institute. Available at http://www.susx.ac.uk/Units/SEI/pdfs/wp51.pdf.

—— —— (2002*b*). 'Europeanisation, Euroscepticism and Party Systems: Party-based Euroscepticism in the Candidate States of Central and Eastern Europe', *Perspectives on European Politics and Society*, 3: 23–41.

—— —— (2003). 'Europeanisation, Euroscepticism and Party Systems,' in P. G. Lewis and P. Webb (eds.), *Pan-European Perspectives on Party Politics*. Leiden, The Netherlands: Brill, pp. 207–25.

—————— (2004). 'Contemporary Euroscepticism in the Party Systems of the EU Candidate States of Central and Eastern Europe', *European Journal of Political Research*, 43: 1–27.

—————— (2008*a*). 'Opposing Europe? Three Patterns of Party Competition Over Europe', in P. Taggart and A. Szczerbiak (eds.), *Opposing Europe: The Comparative Party Politics of Euroscepticism in Europe* Vol. 1: *Case Studies and Country Surveys*. Oxford: Oxford University Press.

—————— (2008*b*). 'The Politics of Euroscepticism in Europe', in P. Taggart and A. Szczerbiak (eds.), *Opposing Europe: The Comparative Party Politics of Euroscepticism in Europe*, Vol. 1: *Case Studies and Country Surveys*. Oxford: Oxford University Press.

Tarrow, S. (1994). *Power in Movement: Social Movements, Collective Action and Politics*. Cambridge: Cambridge University Press.

Tiersky, R. (2001). 'Introduction: Euro-skepticism and "Europe"', in R. Tiersky (ed.), *Euro-skepticism: A Reader*. Oxford: Rowman & Littlefield, pp. 1–6.

Tiilikainen, T. (1996). 'Finland and the European Union', in L. Miles (ed.), *The European Union and the Nordic Countries*. London: Routledge.

Tingsten, H. (1963 [1937]). *Political Behavior*. New York: Bedminster Press.

Tsebelis, G. (1990). *Nested Games: Rational Choice in Comparative Politics*. Berkeley, CA: University of California Press.

Tullock, G. and Campbell, C. D. (1970). 'Computer Simulation of a Small Voting System', *Economics Journal*, 80: 97–104.

Urwin, D. W. (1980). *From Ploughshare to Ballot Box: The Politics of Agrarian Defence in Europe*. Oslo: Universitetsforlaget.

Van der Eijk, C. and Oppenhuis, E. (1991). '"European Parties" Performance in Electoral Competition', *European Journal for Political Research*, 19: 55–80.

—————— Schmitt, H., et al. (1993). *European Elections Study 1989: Design, Implementation and Results* (Computer file and codebook). Amsterdam: Steinmetz Archives.

—————— Franklin, M. N., et al. (1996). *Choosing Europe? The European Electorate and National Politics at the Eve of Unification*. Ann Arbor, MI: The University of Michigan Press.

—————— Schönbach, K., Schmitt, H., Semetko, H., et al. (2002). *European Election Study 1999: Design, Data Description, and Documentation*. Amsterdam: Steinmetz Archives.

—————— and H. Schmitt. (Forthcoming). 'Electoral Participation.' In *The Legitimacy of EU Politics After Eastern Enlargement*, ed. Jacques Thomassen. Oxford: Oxford University Press.

Verba, S., Nie, N. H., and Kim, J. (1978). *Participation and Political Equality.* Cambridge: Cambridge University Press.

Von Beyme, K. (1985). *Political Parties in Western Democracies.* Aldershot, UK: Gower.

Von Solemacher, H-F. (2000). Interview. Head of the Hanns Seidel Foundation for Hungary and Slovakia. Budapest, April.

Weale, A. (1992). *The New Politics of Pollution.* Manchester: Manchester University Press.

Weber, H. (1999). *Die DDR, 1945–1990.* München, Germany: Oldenbourg.

Weingast, B. R. (1998). 'Political Institutions: Rational Choice Perspectives' in Goodin, R. E. and Klingemann, H.-E. (eds.). *A New Handbook of Political Science*, Oxford: Oxford University Press.

Welle, K. (1996). Interview. Secretary-General of the EPP. Brussels, January.

Welle, K. (2001). Secretary-General of the EPP group in the EP. Brussels, February.

Wessels, B. and Schmitt, H. (2000). 'Europawahlen, Europäisches Parlament und nationalstaatliche Demokratie', in H.-D. Klingemann and F. Neidhardt (eds.), *Die Zukunft der Demokratie.* Berlin: Sigma, pp. 295–320.

Widfelt, A. (1996). 'Sweden and the EU: Implications for the Swedish Party System', in L. Miles (ed.), *The European Union and the Nordic Countries.* London: Routledge.

Williams, K. (2000). 'Introduction: What was Mečiarism?', in K. Williams (ed.), *Slovakia after Communism and Mečiarism.* London: SSEES, pp. 1–16.

Wolfinger, R. and Rosenstone, S. (1980). *Who Votes?* New Haven, CT and London: Yale University Press.

Wolinetz, S. B. (2002). 'Beyond the Catch-All Party: Approaches to the Study of Parties and Party Organisation in Contemporary Democracies' in Gunther, R., Montero, J. R. and J. J. Linz (eds.) *Political Parties: Old Concepts and New Challenges.* Oxford: Oxford University Press.

Index